THE RENEWED, THE DESTROYED, AND THE REMADE

The Three Thought Worlds of the Huron and the Iroquois, 1609–1650

ROGER M. CARPENTER

Michigan State University Press
East Lansing

The paper used in this publication meets the minimum requirements of ANSI/NISO Z39.48–1992 (R 1997) (Permanence of Paper).

Michigan State University Press
East Lansing, Michigan 48823–5245

Printed and bound in the United States of America.

10 09 08 07 06 05 04 1 2 3 4 5 6 7 8 9 10

Library of Congress Cataloging-in-Publication Data

Carpenter, Roger M., 1956–
The renewed, the destroyed, and the remade : the three thought worlds of the Iroquois and the Huron, 1609–1650 / Roger M. Carpenter.
p. cm.
Includes bibliographical references and index.
ISBN 0-87013-728-X (pbk. : alk. paper)
1. Iroquois Indians—History—17th century. 2. Iroquois philosophy—History—17th century. 3. Iroquois Indians—Colonization. 4. Wyandot Indians—History—17th century. 5. Wyandot philosophy—History—17th century. 6. Wyandot Indians—Colonization. 7. Europe—Colonies—America. I. Title.
E99.I7C37 2004
973.004'9755—dc22
2004012336

Cover design by Heather Truelove Aiston
Interior design by Bookcomp, Inc.
Cover art courtesy of the National Library and National Archives of Canada

Michigan State University Press is a member of the Green Press Initiative and is committed to developing and encouraging ecologically responsible publishing practices. For more information about the Green Press Initiative and the use of recycled paper in book publishing, please visit www.greenpressinitiative.org.

Visit Michigan State University Press on the World Wide Web at:
www.msupress.msu.edu

For Mom and Dad

CONTENTS

ILLUSTRATIONS

ACKNOWLEDGMENTS

THERE ARE MANY PEOPLE TO THANK FOR THE COMPLEtion of this endeavor. Rebecca "Monte" Kugel of the University of California, Riverside (UCR) history department provided guidance during the writing of this work and always offered encouragement. How Monte had the patience to listen to me drone on for hours about Iroquoian peoples, the thought world, and the technological imagination exceeds my comprehension. Clifford Trafzer, also a member of the UCR history department and the editor of Michigan State University Press's Native American series, is without a doubt one of the nicest people I have ever met. Cliff always provided encouragement, guidance, and advice. Sharon Salinger, like Monte and Cliff, read the early drafts of this work, and their comments and criticism have much to do with the book's final form.

Several other scholars deserve thanks for responding to my e-mails with suggestions and encouragement. James Axtell of the College of William and Mary was very helpful in guiding me to sources; Matthew Dennis of the University of Oregon also offered helpful suggestions, as did José António Brandão of Western Michigan University. I wish to thank Isabelle Contant of the Archives de la Compagnie de Jesus, province du Canada, français, at St. Jérôme, Quebec, for guiding me to the works of Lucien Campeau. Leo Hernandez, a colleague at the State University of New York at Oswego, offered insights. All of these individuals have, in varying degrees, affected the outcome of this work. The final product, however, is my responsibility alone.

There is one more thanks, and that is to my wife, Kim, for everything.

INTRODUCTION

ON A PLEASANT JULY AFTERNOON IN 1645, KIOTSEAEton, an Iroquois sachem, arrived at the French settlement of Three Rivers. Covered almost "completely with Porcelain beads," Kiotseaeton stood in the bow of the shallop carrying him and called out to the Hurons, Algonquins, and Frenchmen gathered on the shore that he brought with him an offer of peace.[1] A few days later, Onontio—the Indians' name for the governor of Canada—arrived at Three Rivers to begin negotiations.[2] Kiotseaeton began the meeting by planting two poles in the ground and suspending a cord between them. He then draped the cord with strings of wampum, which represented "the words that they wished to bring us,—that is to say, the presents they wished to make us, which consisted of seventeen collars of porcelain beads."[3] Kiotseaeton then proceeded to perform the first Iroquois condolence ceremony recorded by Europeans. Using the strings of wampum as mnemonic devices, Kiotseaeton detailed the seventeen words of his message. He acted out his journey to Three Rivers and recounted the recent history of French, Huron, and Iroquois relations. With one of the "words," Kiotseaeton figuratively and then literally restored a French captive to Onontio. Toward the end of his address, Kiotseaeton delivered the most important part of his message, the offer of peace that the Iroquois League commissioned him to present to the French and the Huron.[4]

But before this final act could take place, Iroquoian diplomatic theory required Kiotseaeton to place his listeners in a rational state of mind. To facilitate this, he took steps to focus his audience's attention on his words. Lacing his message with the symbolism of peace, Kiotseaeton told the assembly that his dead forefathers banished any thoughts he had of revenge by calling "out to me . . . my grandson . . . there is no means of withdrawing us from death. Think of the living . . . save those who still live from the sword and the fire." He told the Huron that peace meant that a clear road now existed between his country and theirs and that in the houses of the Iroquois, the Huron would find fires at which they could warm themselves.[5]

Later in the course of this same peace process, the French sent presents to the Iroquois, designed, in their words, "to console them and to wipe away their tears."[6] This action indicated that the French had some understanding of at least a few elements of the Iroquoian ritual of condolence. Like almost all other Europeans, the French could observe and copy the Iroquoian condolence ritual. However, the concept of renewal, the fundamental idea that undergirded not only the condolence ritual but also the entire Iroquoian worldview, escaped their notice.

"Nothing," wrote William N. Fenton, the dean of twentieth-century Iroquoianists, "has greater force in woodland society than the sanction of ritual and compulsion of renewal."[7] Iroquoian peoples saw human beings and the earth locked into an ongoing symbiotic relationship, one that required constant renewal. In order for humans and the earth to continue to exist, they deemed it necessary that renewal remain an ongoing and viable process. By using ritual and ceremony, and through the practical manipulation of the landscape about them, Iroquoian peoples ensured their own survival as well as that of the earth. The Frenchmen who viewed Kioseaeton's performance of the condolence ritual had no inkling that the act they witnessed dated from the founding of the Iroquois League itself. They did not—since it fell outside their cultural construct—recognize it as an act of renewal.

The date of the founding of the Iroquois League is a matter of dispute among scholars. Estimates ranging from a thousand years before contact to 1600 have been espoused by various researchers.[8] Recently, using astronomy and oral tradition, Barbara Mann and Jerry Fields have dated the founding of the league to August 31, 1142.[9] In nearly every estimate, scholars admit they are making a guess as to when the league came to be. However, the date of the founding is not important.[10] What is important is that at the time Iroquoian peoples began to have extensive contacts with Europeans the league was an ongoing concern, one that would shape the history of Iroquoian peoples, Europeans, and of North America as well.

By the mid-seventeenth century, both the Huron and the Iroquois League found themselves facing new, but very different, worlds. By 1650, external factors had wrought deep internal divisions among the Huron. Through extensive European interference and Iroquois aggression, their traditional, or renewable, world had begun to disintegrate. By contrast, because of the availability of European trade goods and technology, Five Nations peoples—consisting of the Mohawk, Oneida, Onondaga, Cayuga, and Seneca—saw the early seventeenth century as a period in which the possibility existed of remaking their world for the better. But to address these concepts of the Huron's destroyed world and the Iroquois' remade world, it is important to have an understanding of precontact Iroquoian peoples and the renewable and restorable thought world that they inhabited.

In the oral traditions of Iroquoian peoples, this renewable world began when a woman fell from the sky. One day in the sky world, above the earth, a tree fell down. Aataentsic, a woman living in the sky world, peered downward through the hole where the tree had been and saw an immense ocean that covered the entire earth. At this point, according to the several versions of the creation myth, she fell through the hole or, as some other versions have it, her husband gave her a good shove. As she plunged through the hole separating the two worlds, Aataentsic clawed frantically at the sky world's soil in an attempt to break her fall. Her efforts were futile, however, and Aataentsic had only seeds and grasses in her hands to show for her repeated efforts. The aquatic animals living in the ocean—the otter, the muskrat, and the beaver—saw Aataentsic falling from the sky and prevailed upon a large turtle to take her onto his back. But without land, Aataentsic could not survive. The beaver, muskrat, and otter all dived to the bottom of the sea in an attempt to find a bit of soil. Ultimately, the muskrat succeeded in bringing a bit of mud to the surface. Aataentsic took the mud and placed it on the back of the turtle, and the mud began to grow and became the lands of the earth. Planting the seeds and grasses that she had in her hand, Aataentsic watched as they grew, multiplied, and became the plants of the earth. It also turned out that Aataentsic had been pregnant when she fell from the sky world, and she soon gave birth to a daughter.

It is at this point that the cosmogonic myths of the Huron and Five Nations peoples diverge. In the version told among the Five Nations, Aataentsic's daughter dies while giving birth to male twins. One of the twins, named Sapling, created all that is good on the earth, while his brother, Flint, became the originator of evil. In being born, Flint killed his mother when he entered the world via her armpit and thus created death. Later, Flint sought to destroy all that his brother, Sapling, had created. Flint was not as powerful as his brother, and he could not destroy all that his stronger sibling had made. But he did have enough power to cause the imperfections of the world, such as thorns, thistles, and rivers in which the water ran only one way.[11]

The Huron creation story also claims that Aataentsic's daughter died in childbirth but that she bore only one son, Yoscaha, and that he took the role that Sapling played in the creation myth of the Five Nations. In the Huron versions, it is Aataentsic herself who develops a hatred for humankind, probably because of her daughter's death in childbirth. While most of the myths are not clear as to her motivations, she may have sought revenge against Yoscaha for killing her daughter in childbirth. In a quest for revenge, she sought to ruin the creation of her grandson. Like Flint, she could not destroy creation, but she could, by making the world imperfect, create difficulties for humans.[12] Nevertheless, despite her hatred of humanity, Aataentsic was the common ancestor and a mythic link of the two largest groups of Iroquoian peoples, the Huron and the Five Nations.[13]

The term "Iroquoian" refers to several different groups of people who spoke different dialects of the Iroquoian language. The Neutrals, Petun, Erie, and a few smaller groups spoke one variation or another of the Iroquoian language in northeastern America.[14] But in the early postcontact history of North America, the Huron and the Five Nations represented the two most important groups of Iroquoian-speaking peoples.

The Five Nations lived in what is now northern New York State. Iroquoia extended from the confluence of the Hudson and Mohawk rivers in the east to the Genesee River in western New York. The common dwelling of the Five Nations, the longhouse, served as a metaphor for their political league. The Mohawk guarded the eastern door, while the Onondaga, in the center, kept the council fire. The Seneca kept watch over the western door.

Located approximately two hundred miles north of the westernmost point of Iroquoia in what is now southeastern Ontario, Huronia, the home

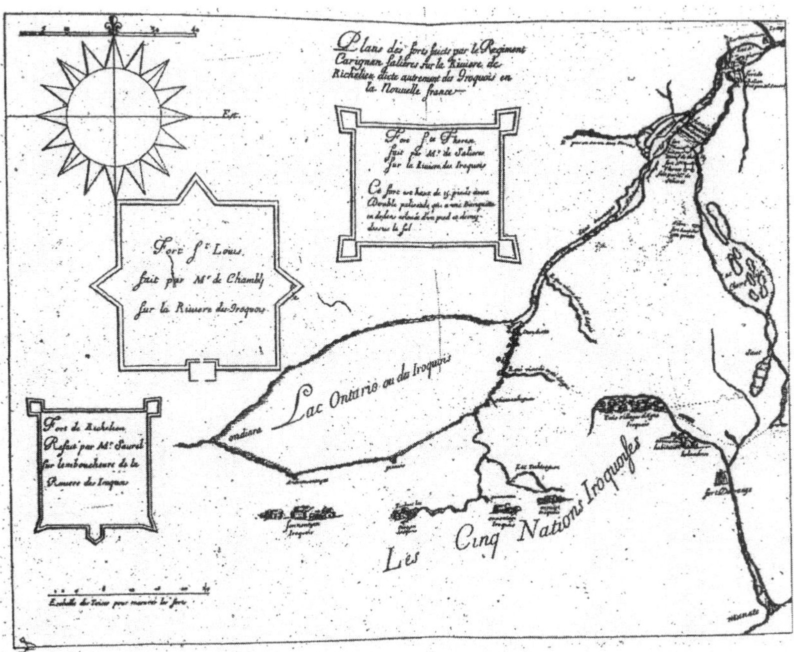

Map of Iroquoia. A map from the *Jesuit Relations* of 1664–1665, showing the location of the Five Nations. Courtesy of the National Library and National Archives of Canada.

of the Huron, extended from Georgian Bay in the north and to Lake Simcoe in the east. Like the Five Nations, the Huron confederacy also consisted of five tribes. The Arendaronnon, or Rock tribe, lived at the northwest tip of Lake Simcoe. West of the Rock tribe lived the Attingneenongnahac, or Barking Dog tribe. North and west of the Barking Dogs were the Ataronchronnon, or the Tribe Beyond the Silted Lake, who lived along the southernmost portion of Georgian Bay. To the south of them lived the smallest of the Huron tribes, the Tahontaenrat, or Deer tribe. The largest Huron group, the Attignaouantan, or Bear tribe, called the western- and northernmost points of Huronia home.[15]

Long after the creation of the world and before the Five Nations of the Iroquois formed their confederacy, legend claims that they lived in a state of perpetual warfare with one another. The extended kinship groups, known as *ohwachiras,* carried on continuous feuds with one another, and the resulting bloodletting meant that Iroquoia remained engulfed in a state of perpetual civil war. One man, an Onondaga named Hiawatha, sought to put an end to the internal strife by bringing peace-minded leaders together.[16] But Atotarho, one of his opponents, thwarted him by using magic and deceit to kill all of Hiawatha's daughters one by one. Driven mad by the deaths of his children, Hiawatha became a recluse, seeking refuge and solitude in the wilderness of Iroquoia. In his insanity, Hiawatha turned to cannibalism. He hunted humans, and when successful, he dragged their corpses to his lodge, where he cooked and devoured them.

At the same time that Hiawatha descended into cannibalism, another peace seeker, Deganawidah, left his home in Huronia and began the southward journey to Iroquoia. While he had a human form, Deganawidah sprang from the union of a young virgin and a supernatural being. Before his birth, his grandmother dreamed that the infant would set into motion a chain of events that would one day result in the destruction of the Huron nation.[17] After sharing her dream with her daughter, the two women made several attempts to kill Deganawidah during his infancy. On one occasion, they cast him under the ice of a frozen stream. In another attempt, they abandoned him naked in the snow. But after each attempt, they discovered the baby sleeping in their lodge the next morning, unharmed. Clearly, supernatural forces were at work on the infant's behalf, and since Iroquoian peoples knew better than to trifle with the supernatural, the two women decided that the fate of the Huron could not be avoided, and they raised the child to adulthood.[18]

One day, during his youth, Deganawidah had a vision in which he saw a large pine tree with five large white roots spreading in every direction carpeting the landscape. Deganawidah understood the tree to be "the law"—a Great Peace—and the roots to be the extension of that Great Peace, covering the earth and embracing all of its peoples. He understood this dream as a commission for him to go forth and to convince the Huron and other Iroquoian peoples to embrace the Great Peace of his vision. Unfortunately, Deganawidah had a serious speech impediment. In a culture that prized oratory, this represented a significant handicap.[19] Because of Deganawidah's speech defect and the unusual circumstances of his birth, many Huron shunned him. Since his own people refused to hear of his vision, he set out in a canoe of stone for the country of the Iroquois, where he searched for Hiawatha, whom he heard also sought peace. Arriving in Iroquoia, Deganawidah discovered that Hiawatha had gone mad and become a cannibal. Taking it upon himself to renew and restore Hiawatha,

A detail of Huronia from Franceso Bressani's *Novae Franciae Accurata Delineatio* (1657). Courtesy of the National Library and National Archives of Canada.

Deganawidah persuaded him to give up cannibalism, pointing out the inhumanity of the practice. Deganawidah performed the first condolence ceremony to clear Hiawatha's mind and to restore his sanity. He then enlisted Hiawatha's help in forming the league he envisioned. Deganawidah's performance of the condolence for Hiawatha—the restoring of the bereaved to clearmindedness—and the similarity of the Iroquois and Huron creation stories are the mythological bonds between the two peoples.[20]

Atotarho, the man who had killed Hiawatha's children, remained a major stumbling block to any peace plan. By this time, Atotarho's own evil had transformed him into a monstrous figure. Legend claims that Atotarho's hideous physical appearance—which in some versions included bear's feet, deformed hands, seven crooks in his body, and snakes entangled in his hair—reflected his twisted mental state. So hideous had Atotarho become that people feared to look upon him and birds that flew over his lodge fell dead to the ground. Upon encountering Atotarho, Hiawatha and Deganawidah began to sing the six songs of requiem. While Atotarho sat transfixed by the songs, Hiawatha and Deganawidah reconstructed his mind and began to remove the deformities of his body. The climatic scene of this encounter between madness and reason came when Hiawatha (which, roughly translated means "he, the comber") took a comb and raked the serpents from Atotarho's hair. As the serpents fell from Atotarho's scalp, the last vestiges of his insanity disappeared along with them. This founding myth of the Iroquois League concludes with Atotarho agreeing to become one of the leaders of the new confederacy.[21]

Even in terms of mythology, the founding of the Iroquois League seems to be unique, requiring the joint efforts of a human, Hiawatha, a product of the natural world, and of Deganawidah, a product of the supernatural. Moreover, Deganawidah, despite his partially supernatural origin, is flawed; his speech impediment made it necessary for him to seek out Hiawatha. Another unique aspect is the treatment of evil. Atotarho embodied evil, but rather than destroy him, Deganawidah and Hiawatha transformed him into a force for good.

Other versions of the Deganawidah epic identify his mother as the "Mother of Nations." In this role, she fed passing war parties, dissuaded them from warring on each other, and encouraged them to accept her son's message of peace. This part of the Deganawidah epic emphasized the important role of the matron in Iroquoian society.[22] Iroquoian women exercised their political power by caucusing behind the scenes and wielded considerable influence through their role in the selection of chiefs.[23] In the matrilineal kinship clans known as *ohwachiras,* the women often instigated wars by demanding that male clan members bring back captives to replace the *ohwachiras'* dead. However, women also played a role in maintaining peace. Because of their control of agricultural production, they could veto wars by simply refusing to provide foodstuffs to prospective war parties.

In large part, the story of the creation of the Iroquois Confederacy foreshadowed the future of Iroquoian peoples. The dream of Deganawidah's grandmother eventually came true, when large Iroquois armies devastated Huronia in the mid-seventeenth century. The White Roots of Peace, a central part of Deganawidah's vision, in Iroquoian theory should have embraced all peoples. But those peoples who refused the embrace of the league—and many did—could find themselves subject to the Iroquois paradox. While Deganawidah's vision called for people to join the league peacefully, those who refused would be incorporated by force, where they would replace the dead as a means of condoling the bereaved.

The first condolence ceremony performed by Hiawatha and Deganawidah reflected the Iroquoian belief that all humans are capable of either rational thought or madness. However, in general terms, Iroquoian peoples believed that rational thought exceeded the capabilities of those in mourning. As long as the bereaved remained in an irrational state, they could not think, act, or carry on day-to-day activities. As long as they were grieving, they represented a danger to society at large. This sort of irrationality precipitated the very blood feuds that Deganawidah and Hiawatha sought to extinguish.

Through the teachings of Deganawidah and Hiawatha, it became the obligation of those not in mourning—the clear-minded—to console those consumed by grief and to place them back into their right minds. They did this by figuratively removing the obstructions from the mourners' ears, clearing their throats, and drying their tears. Once the clear-minded had done this, the bereaved could hear, see, speak, and think clearly and with reason.[24] The restoration of the mourner to reason went far beyond the needs of the individual. Satisfying the mourners' grief, the Iroquois believed, restored society to normal. The death of *ohwachira* members could now be compensated either by presents, by a captive who replaced the deceased, or by blood, provided that the blood belonged to a person outside the Great Peace. The invention of the condolence, and the idea behind it, ended the blood feuds that wracked Iroquoia and imposed saneness on a society that teetered on the brink of madness.

The condolence and the league gave strength to a people who would soon face their greatest challenge: that of invasion. It is possible that Iroquoian peoples, but not necessarily Huron or Five Nations peoples, met French explorer Jacques Cartier along the St. Lawrence in 1534.[25] In the early seventeenth century, colonizers began to replace the explorers. The Iroquois and Huron experiences with Europeans differed. For the Huron, their relationship with the French in the seventeenth century—particularly the missionaries of the Jesuit order—undermined their culture. Their contacts with the Jesuits led to the creation of divisions so deep that clans separated along religious lines, and entire villages became either Christian or traditionalist. These divisions in turn contributed to the destruction of the Huron and Huronia by the Iroquois in the mid-seventeenth century.

By contrast, Iroquois contacts with Europeans included not only the French but the Dutch, English, and Swedes as well. And unlike the Huron experience, none of these encounters undermined Iroquois unity. Indeed, quite the opposite seems to be true; the position of the Iroquois in the early colonial period, due to external factors such as colonial rivalries and their geographic location, seems to have been strengthened. Despite occasional assertions to the contrary, the Dutch and other Protestant powers displayed little or no interest in converting the Iroquois or any other Native peoples for that matter. Part of their lack of effort seems to been the perceived difficulty of Iroquoian languages. One Dutch minister, baffled by American Indian languages, believed "they rather design to conceal their language from us than to properly communicate it."[26] Another minister, equally bewildered at the intricacies of Mohawk, asked a Dutch trader with twenty years experience for help. He received little assistance, however, since the trader "imagined they changed their language every two or three years."[27] French Jesuits expressed an ongoing interest in sending missions to the Five Nations, but the few Jesuits who ventured into Iroquoia made little headway. Indeed, the fortunate among them escaped with their lives.

Between 1609 and 1650, the Huron and the Five Nations Iroquois, like the other Native peoples of the continent, encountered, through contact with Europeans, a new world. While Europeans commonly used the term "New World" to refer to the Americas, contact and trade with Europeans and exposure to Christianity altered the Americas and their peoples. These encounters with Europeans transformed the old world of Iroquoian peoples into a new world for them as well. While Native societies, like societies everywhere, always experienced change, contact with European ideas and technologies greatly accelerated the rate of change.[28]

Yet despite the multitude of changes that occurred in the seventeenth century and beyond, Huron and Iroquois cultures retained a strong sense of continuity. Renewal, the fundamental concept that best expressed this sense of continuity, coexisted alongside powerful notions of change. While the world in the Iroquoian view retained the possibility—indeed, in their view the necessity—of renewal, this older idea had to share space with the two newer views of the world that began to permeate Iroquoian thought. One of these views, that of the destroyed world, became a reality for Huronia, if not for all of the Huron. The Five Nations, however, pursued a different goal and began the process of remaking their world.

1

THE RENEWAL OF THE EARTH

FOR IROQUOIAN PEOPLES, THE RELATIONSHIP BETWEEN human beings and the earth formed the most important component of the renewable world. Neither could supersede the other in importance, for in Iroquoian cosmology, humanity and the earth coexisted in a symbiotic relationship. Aataentsic's act of placing mud on the back of the turtle created land, brought the earth in its present form into being, and made it possible for humans to live upon it.[1] This original manipulation of the earth, this act of creation, could not, of course, be matched by any Iroquoian person who followed Aataentsic. Yet Iroquoian peoples manipulated the landscapes of Iroquoia and Huronia by burning, by planting, and, when the time was right, by letting the earth be. All of these were acts of renewal, the closest a mortal could come to creating the earth. Despite the polemics of some twentieth-century writers, the peoples of precontact North America did not live in an Eden.[2] Seventeenth-century Iroquoian peoples, or any other Native peoples of the past for that matter, cannot be ecological models for twenty-first-century Americans. Their world, thoughts, and technology were so different that they cannot be considered a feasible model for Euro-Americans of today. But if not Eden, the lands of Huronia and Iroquoia could, and did, provide a good life for the peoples who extracted a living from their forests, waterways, and soils.

The Iroquoian seasonal calendar reflected the belief that the world required constant renewal. Lewis Henry Morgan, the nineteenth-century ethnographer, identified six different Iroquois ceremonies, almost all of them linked to subsistence and invariably tied into the seasonal cycle.[3] These ceremonies, for the most part, demonstrated the dynamics of the reciprocal relationship between Iroquoian peoples and the earth. In these ceremonies, Iroquoian peoples attempted to "help" the earth regenerate itself and to thank the earth for helping them survive another year.

Beginning in the very early spring, as the days began to warm slightly while the nights remained freezing, maple sap began to flow. The maple ceremony itself lasted only one day. The Recollect missionary Chrestien Le Clerq observed that the Micmac Indians gathered sap by using an ax to make "a very small opening . . . ten to a dozen gallons may run out. A thing which has seemed to me very remarkable in the maple water is this, that if, by virtue of boiling, it is reduced to a third, it becomes a real syrup, which hardens to something like sugar, and takes on a reddish color."[4] Women boiled the maple sap down into sugar and stored it for use throughout the year. While people ate maple sugar as a treat in the spring, most of the stored sugar became flavoring for other foods.[5] Late winter represented the most perilous time of year for Iroquoian peoples. Food supplies often began to dwindle by this time. Stored corn was usually available, but much of it had to be set aside as seed for spring planting. Hunting in the late winter was difficult, and in all likelihood a hunter would not be successful. Even if a hunter did succeed, large game animals, such as deer, would have depleted their last fat reserves, and the scrawny animals would yield little meat. Like humans, the animals waited for spring. The running of the sap heralded the approach of spring and signaled that the time of shortages was nearing the end.[6] When the maple buds began to swell, the sap took on an unpleasant "buddy" flavor, and sugaring ended.[7]

Once the threat of frost diminished, Iroquoian peoples celebrated planting with another one-day festival.[8] Both the gathering of maple sap and the planting of maize had to be accomplished within a short period of time. For this reason, Iroquoian peoples limited these ceremonies to one day.

The ripening of the strawberries, and the attendant festival, signaled the arrival of summer. But the second festival of the summer, the green corn ceremony, was rivaled only by the midwinter ceremony in terms of importance to Iroquoian peoples. In its green state, maize is soft and edible and has a waxy appearance. When fully ripe, it assumes the dented appearance and grainlike hardness that permits easy long-term storage. The Iroquoian word for the ceremony (*ah-dake'-wä-o*) translates as feast. Corn, beans, and squash together were referred to as "our life" or as the "three sisters," which

Iroquois Women Making Maple Sugar and Planting Crops. From Joseph François Lafitau, *Moeurs des sauvages ameriquains comparées aux moeurs des premiers temps* (Paris, 1724). Courtesy of the National Library and National Archives of Canada.

emphasized the importance of the three plants in the Iroquoian diet. Because of its importance to the survival of Iroquoian peoples, the ripening of the corn must have been greeted with a sense of relief. The festival lasted for five days, during which the celebrants consumed large quantities of corn soup.[9]

Thanksgiving, the autumn counterpart of the green corn ceremony, took place in the fall after Iroquoian peoples harvested all of their crops. Doubtless, Iroquoian communities felt that the harvest assured their survival. Not only could they count on adequate foodstuffs for the winter, but there would also be enough seed for spring planting, so that the process of renewal could start again.[10]

The last in the seasonal cycle of important Iroquoian ceremonies took place in late January or early February. The midwinter ceremony encouraged people to look ahead to spring. Iroquoian peoples used the ceremony as a social event, playing games and holding dances. Dream guessing formed an important part of the midwinter ceremony. Parents named children during this time, and adults who so desired could change their names.[11] The ashes of old fires were stirred and swept away, and Iroquoian peoples kindled new fires with unburned logs.[12] On the fifth and climatic day of the ceremony, the men sacrificed and ate a white dog.[13]

The linkage of Iroquoian peoples to the earth was the common thread that ran through these ceremonies. In Iroquoian philosophy, human beings and the earth were engaged in a continuous reciprocal relationship in which each party ensured the other's survival. In their use of maize and other crops Iroquoian peoples, by collecting, storing, and planting the seed with care, helped ensure the propagation of the plant species. In turn, the cultivation, gathering, and consumption of the plant helped ensure Iroquoian peoples' survival.

Beyond ceremonies, however, Iroquoian peoples took practical steps to better the earth's chances of survival and their own as well. Both the Huron and the Five Nations Iroquois altered the physical environments of Huronia and Iroquoia to the limits of their available technology, but at the same time, these alterations of the landscape never strayed far from the ceremonial and seasonal round.

The Huronian and Iroquoian landscapes differed from each other in significant ways. Innumerable lakes and streams interlaced the fairly level landscape of Huronia. Streams also crisscrossed Iroquoia, but its topography consisted of numerous hills and valleys. While Europeans found northeastern America surprisingly cold, subtle ecological differences existed from one region to another.[14] Two important ecological factors, both of which affected their human inhabitants, differentiated Huronia and Iroquoia. Iroquoia had a longer growing season for maize and other crops than

Huronia. Huronia averaged about 120 frost-free days per year, while Iroquoia usually had 30 to 40 more.[15] Another environmental factor that affected the peoples living in these regions was the distribution of birch trees. The Huron used birch bark in making canoes, containers, and housing. But since birch did not grow to a useable girth south of the Adirondacks, the Iroquois had to use elm bark—sturdier than birch in some ways but much harder to work—for these same purposes.[16]

Finally, the human alteration of the landscape also differentiated Huronia from Iroquoia. The dense Huron population, estimated to be in the neighborhood of thirty thousand before 1630, required the clearing of much land in order to plant sufficient crops.[17] Samuel de Champlain stated that Huronia was "for the most part cleared" and "so very fine and fertile that it is a pleasure to travel about in." While the Iroquois also practiced agriculture, much of Iroquoia was "covered with forests, and not cleared."[18] This pleasant landscape that Champlain commented on resulted from Iroquoian peoples ongoing symbiotic relationship with the land and their efforts in renewing the earth.

The most effective technology that Iroquoian peoples had at their command in their efforts to mold the landscape to their liking was fire. Certainly Iroquoian peoples recognized and greatly respected fire's destructive potential. Champlain noted that the Huron kept their longhouses "separated from one another about three of four yards for fear of fire which they greatly dread."[19] But Iroquoian peoples considered fire to be constructive as well. They recognized that fire, used judiciously, could help them transform the environment to their advantage.[20] To twenty-first-century Americans, the idea of Native peoples who lived in the woods intentionally setting sections of the forest afire may seem like a form of madness. Woodlands, however, will at some point in their existence catch fire. In an undisturbed northeastern woodland, the accumulation of dead leaves and trees, fallen timber, and other organic matter creates what may be called a self-fertilizing effect. However, during dry periods, the organic matter coating the forest floor can easily be ignited.[21]

Realizing this, Iroquoian peoples used controlled burns, so that the forest would burn in such a way as to benefit them and to deprive fires started by lightning or other natural processes of fuel. Burning became a part of the seasonal round. In April and May, before the spring burning, the women spent a few days scouring the forest floor, collecting large quantities of firewood for the village.[22] Controlled burns of "the woods, plains, and meadows in the fall of the year," when the land was cool and moist, and again in the early spring, when rain and melting snow made the forest floor damp, allowed Native peoples to clear out much of the dead shrubs and undergrowth that could have otherwise fueled forest fires.[23] American Indians used "bush-burning" to "render hunting easier" and to "thin out and clear the woods of all dead substances and grass, which grow better the ensuing spring." These fires burned at low temperatures over the damp landscape of fall and spring, consuming the most flammable matter in the hardwood forests while "the green trees do not suffer. The outside bark is scorched three or four feet high, which does them no injury, for the trees are not killed." This did not hold true, however, if the fire found its way into stands of evergreens. There the accumulated bed of dead pine needles and "the resinous knots and leaves . . . promote the blaze."[24] Unlike summer wildfires fueled by the dry undergrowth, these burnings, because they took place while the land was damp, seldom reached the intense temperatures characteristic of full-blown forest fires. The resulting ashes of these controlled burnings recycled forest nutrients such as potash into the soil, creating favorable conditions for plant species that game animals preferred.[25] Champlain, in a sense, was more right than he knew when he wrote that the "meadows, swamps, and marshes . . . serve for pasture for the . . . animals."[26] Iroquoian peoples may have also viewed burning as a safety measure. By consuming much of the dry, dead matter on the forest floor, this technique minimized the danger of uncontrollable forest fires, an important consideration for peoples living in or among forests.

By removing the smaller, denser undergrowth, burning also made hunting and traveling easier. Europeans found the parklike openness of the northeastern American forests remarkable.[27] One observer wrote that "the country . . . is generally woody, but . . . [is] so clear that one may be seen above a mile and a half in the woods."[28] Another wrote of "beautiful groves of trees, not choked up with an undergrowth of brambles and bushes." Another writing of his experiences in traversing the American woods made the claim that "no shrub of underwood chokes your passage."[29] Yet another claimed, "The trees . . . stand more open and less confused. One could there chase a Moose on horseback."[30] One European observer came closer to the truth than he knew when he wrote that the forest seemed to have been "laid out by hand." It did not occur to Europeans that the openness of American forests resulted from human activity.[31] The probable answer as to why none of these writers recognized human agency in the appearance of American forests is precisely because they were forests.

In the European consciousness, large numbers of trees meant "wilderness." Improved land, although Europeans did not realize it, comprised much of the North American landscape at the time of contact. But since they did not see roads, fences, permanent structures, or anything else that their cultural construct recognized as "civilization," they regarded the Americas as a vast wilderness. Native peoples could not view the Americas as a "wilderness." They had already improved the landscape to the limits of their existing technology.

Fire also had the added benefit of killing off many insects and their eggs (but not all, of course) that otherwise could have ravaged Native peoples' crops.[32] Several species of insects, such as grasshoppers, white grubs, and corn earworms, lay their eggs too far beneath the surface to be affected by the burning of the fields; thus insect infestation, while somewhat alleviated, remained a problem.[33]

While Iroquoian peoples used controlled fires to clear the forest floor, burning in maize fields followed a different pattern. Cornfields radiated out from the palisades of Huron and Iroquois villages, bordered at the far end by the forest. Native peoples used smaller fires in clearing fields near the village or extending the existing maize fields. Usually the men cut down the smaller trees and piled them along with uprooted underbrush at the base of larger trees that they lacked the tools to fell. This meant that the people clearing the fields had several small fires going at once, and all had to be carefully tended. One could not simply set the field ablaze; a sudden shift of the wind in the direction of the village could spell disaster.[34]

Unlike the Five Nations, the Huron do not appear to have used burning to clear forests to any great extent. In large part, this may reflect the fact that much of Huronia had already been cleared, and many of the existing forests, located on lands that the Huron used as village sites over and over again, never reached maturity. Once the burning and clearing had been completed, Iroquoian peoples planted maize, the staple that made up approximately sixty-five percent of their diet.[35] The ecological differences between Iroquoia and Huronia meant that their approach to planting varied somewhat.

The folklore of Five Nations Iroquois dictated that the planting season, and the planting ceremony, begin when oak leaves reached the size of a red squirrel's foot.[36] But since maize formed the bulk of the Iroquoian diet, the planting of the crop was far too important to be determined by consulting only one strand of traditional knowledge. Using the cluster of stars known as the Pleiades—believed by the Iroquois to be a group of dancing children—as their guide, the Iroquois usually planted their crops in very late April or early May, when the threat of frost had greatly diminished.[37]

The Pleiades served as a fairly reliable harvest guide for the Iroquois. Their reappearance in the skies of Iroquoia in October, usually anywhere from 153 to 163 days after planting, signaled the beginning of harvest.[38] Since women did nearly all of the agricultural work, they probably paid much attention to astronomy. One Dutch observer noted that they were "the most experienced star gazers."[39] But men—"natural astronomers" in the Recollect friar Gabriel Sagard's words—also had an extensive knowledge of the stars, using them to navigate in the forests.[40]

Since they lived farther north than the Iroquois, the Huron could not use the Pleiades to reliably guide their planting or harvest. Huronia had a growing season of approximately 120 days, long enough for flint corn, but the shortness of the season provided little margin for error. Aware of this margin, and the dangers of a late frost or an insect infestation, the Huron hedged against famine by sowing "enough to provide food for two or three years, either for fear that some bad season will visit them or else in order to trade it to other nations for furs and other things they need."[41] Several hazards threatened the maize crop. The Jesuit Jean de Brébeuf noted that one spring "it was necessary to sow three times by reason of white frosts and worms."[42] Frost threatened the crop during both planting and harvest time. Huronia was known to have experienced frost as late as May and as early as September 10.[43]

In selecting seed corn, Iroquoian peoples sorted and picked the largest kernels, which they either soaked in water or placed on a piece of moist bark in a longhouse for a few days. The wetness and the warmth of the longhouse caused the seed to germinate, giving it a head start on growth.[44] Women then planted anywhere from six to ten seeds in hills one pace, or about two and a half feet, apart.[45]

It is very possible that, out of necessity, the Huron used a different strain of maize than the Iroquois. In his travels through British and French America, eighteenth-century Swedish scholar Peter Kalm noted the presence of several varieties of maize, including a "small" one that matured in as little as three months.[46] Gabriel Sagard claimed to have seen corn ripen in as little as "four months, or three in some places."[47] The Huron stored the surplus maize, using it either for seed in future plantings or for trade with Algonquin peoples farther north, such as the Ottawa, who lived in areas where maize could not be easily grown.[48] But the bulk of the Huron's surplus maize went into bark casks as insurance against famine.

Both the Huron and the Iroquois consumed most of their corn in the form of *migan,* or *sagamite,* a thin corn soup. The Huron made several variations of this dish, and Europeans found one, a form that included whole, uncleaned, ungutted fish as a primary ingredient, particularly repulsive. However, some Europeans found the corn powder used to prepare *migan,* when used as a travel ration, palatable. One could either eat the powder dry, add a bit of water and eat the *migan* as a paste, or bake it into a sort of bread.[49] Sagard noted the high nutritional value of maize, remarking that

> maize bread, with the *sagamite* made from it, is of very good substance, and I was surprised that it supplied such excellent nourishment . . . drinking only water . . . and eating this bread only very seldom, and meat even more rarely, and taking almost nothing but *sagamite* alone, with a very small quantity of fish, one keeps well and in good condition, provided that one has enough of it; and there is no scarcity of it while one lives in the country.[50]

However, Europeans found other Native ways of preparing maize revolting. The Huron buried green ears of corn "in water under the mud, leaving it two or three months in that state, until they judge that it is putrid."[51] Sagard claimed that the Huron "handle these stinking ears, just as if they were sugar-cane," but "the stink [is] worse even than sewers . . . nor did I willingly touch it . . . because of the bad smell it left on [my fingers] for several days."[52] Sagard, it seems, found life among the Huron to be one long gastronomical nightmare. During the summer, women and children prepared another dish that Sagard did not care for. They bit green corn off the cob, spat the kernels into large pots, and pounded them into a paste, which they then formed into loaves and baked in hot ashes. Sagard ate this "chewed bread" only out "of necessity and reluctantly."[53] But missionaries were not the only ones repelled by what they found on the culinary frontier. Native peoples often found European culinary foodways revolting. After using some native herbs that he likened to garlic or onions to flavor his *sagamite,* Sagard found that "the savages would not come near us nor bear the odour of our breath, declaring that it smelt too bad."[54]

The lands of Huronia and Iroquoia that produced the foods that Sagard found repulsive differed from each other somewhat. Most of Huronia's soils consisted of sandy loams. Champlain noted that "this soil seems . . . a little sandy, but it is none the less good for that kind of grain [maize]."[55] While adequate for growing corn, provided it rained enough, these soils lacked the fertility of the black soils of Iroquoia. After a few initial years of good crops, the sandy loam began to return decreasing yields. Ten to twelve years seems to have been the average length of time that a village site could be occupied before crop yields dipped to levels that could not support a Huron community.[56]

By contrast, the lands of the Iroquois needed little augmentation. Europeans observed that Iroquoia held some of the most fertile lands on the continent. Adrian Van der Donck noted that the Native peoples never manured their fields and that there seemed to be no need to do so.[57] One Dutch farmer "raised fine wheat on one and the same piece of land eleven years successively without ever breaking it up or allowing it to lie fallow."[58] Patroon Kiliaen Van Rensselaer wrote that the annual "overflow of high-water"—that is, flooding—helped his lands remain fertile for years without the application of animal waste.[59] Later European arrivals to the Mohawk River Valley found that its black sandy soils were "much richer . . . and exceed any soil . . . in any part of America."[60] Nor did the Iroquois (or any other group of Native Americans) use fertilizer. While colonists in New England did use fish as fertilizer, Native Americans apparently never did.[61]

Unlike European monocultural planting practices, Iroquoian peoples planted squash and beans in the same hills as the corn, using only hoes and wooden spades.[62] Hills were spaced apart to allow squash and pumpkin vines room to grow. To European observers, wedded to a form of agriculture that stressed neatness, order, and crops in rows, Iroquoian fields seemed to comprise a sort of human-made wilderness. Indeed, when writing about the resulting cornfields, interspersed with spreading squash vines and bean plants wrapping themselves around maize stalks, Europeans did not describe order but disorder. They did not describe a cultivated field but a form of wilderness. One missionary complained about the extent and unorganized appearance of Huron fields, claiming that he often lost "[his] way . . . in these corn-fields more than in the meadows and forests."[63] A Dutchman commented that Iroquois fields lacked a "neat and cleanly" appearance.[64] There was, however, a method to what Europeans regarded

יְהוָה

IHS

LE GRAND
VOYAGE DV PAYS
des Hurons, situé en l'Amerique vers la mer douce
ez dernieres confins de
la nouuelle France

Ou il est traicte de tout
ce qui est du pays & du
gouuernement des Sauuages

Auec un Dictionnaire
de la langue huronne

Par Fr. Gabriel Sagard
Recollect de St. Francois
de la prouince St. Denis

A. PARIS Chez Denys
Moreau rue St. Jacques à
La Salamandre 1632

Title Page from Gabriel Sagard's *Le Grand Voyage du Pays des Hurons* (Paris, 1632). Note the representations of Huron people at the top of the page, and the illustrations of a canoe and a longhouse at the bottom. Courtesy of the National Library and National Archives of Canada.

as the Native peoples' apparent madness. Corn stalks became ready-made beanpoles, while the beans, in turn, fixed nitrogen in the corn hill, providing essential nutrients. Squash, because of its sprawling growth pattern, made it difficult as it matured to hoe the weeds from the ground around the hills. But once the large leaves of the squash reached full growth, hoeing became largely unnecessary, as the squash leaves deprived weeds of sunlight and choked off their growth. At the same time, by blocking the sunlight, the leaves allowed the ground in the vicinity of the corn hill to retain moisture, thus helping the growth of all three plants. But these agricultural methods, while they maximized soil use, could not make up for the soil's innate deficiencies. Once the soil could not produce enough food, Iroquoian peoples usually moved their villages.

For Iroquoian peoples, village movement comprised a difficult but necessary task. On average, the Huron moved their villages after occupying a site anywhere between eight and thirty years.[65] Several factors compelled Iroquoian peoples to move their villages. The Jesuit Jean de Brébeuf wrote that the Huron moved their villages "when there is no longer sufficient wood for their fires, or when the land, long tilled, produces scanty crops."[66] James Fitting has argued that on average, the Huron moved their villages at about the same rate that a hardwood pole rotted in the sandy soil. He suggests that as the materials needed to rebuild or maintain the structures within a village became scarce, it became necessary to seek out a site with sufficient building materials.[67] Generally speaking, these moves, in normal circumstances, did not cover vast distances. Champlain observed that the Huron moved their villages "one, two, or three leagues from the former spot, if they are not forced by their enemies to decamp and move to a greater distance."[68]

Insect infestation could also cause Iroquoian peoples to move their villages. The Jesuits made numerous references to the destruction that pests "such as grasshoppers, worms, and insects" wrought upon Huron crops. The Jesuit Paul Le Jeune wrote of a Huron woman who caught a grasshopper and asked him "to teach some contrivance for killing these little creatures."[69]

Once firewood supplies grew short and crop yields dropped, Iroquoian peoples changed village sites. Huron women, when necessary, traveled great distances from the village to obtain firewood. Sagard noted that the Huron

> use only very good wood, preferring to go far in search of it rather than to take green wood or what makes smoke; . . . if they do not find trees that are

> quite dry they fell those that have dry branches . . . they do not . . . use the trunks of the biggest trees felled; they leave these to rot on the ground, because they have no saw for sawing them up, nor the means of breaking them into pieces unless they are dry or rotten.[70]

Both Champlain and Sagard claimed to have witnessed Huron women gathering a year's supply of firewood within a two-day period in March or April.[71] While possible, this feat could not have been accomplished on a regular basis. In all likelihood, Champlain and Sagard were speaking of recently occupied village sites. What does seem likely is that the women did go to the woods each March and April and tried to gather as much wood as they could before the annual "bush-burning." This not only provided the Huron with wood but also would have further reduced the danger of wildfires by removing potential fuel. It would have also rendered bush burning safer. Initially, firewood was plentiful at a new village site. Women did not have to walk very far into the surrounding forest to find it. But as time went on and nearby firewood supplies decreased, women had to venture farther and farther from the village. Usually women gathered branches that had broken off under the weight of the winter's snow or from trees toppled by high winds. The longer a village site was occupied meant that each spring there would have been less and less firewood in the immediate vicinity.

Despite the importance of firewood, the most important factor in determining the length of time that a village site could be occupied seems to be the fertility of the soil. Huronia's sandy loams could produce enough crops, provided there was sufficient rain. Black soil, however, retains much more moisture and fertility than sandy soils, and perhaps this explains why some precontact Iroquois village sites remained stable for periods of eighty to one hundred years.[72] Perhaps because of these soil conditions, lengthy occupations of village sites occurred in Iroquoia but not in Huronia. For the Huron, security concerns also increased when crop yields decreased. As the fields nearest the village lost their fertility, the Huron extended the fields outward, and the women who worked the fields farthest from the safety of the palisade became increasingly vulnerable to attack and kidnapping by enemy warriors lurking in the woods.

The constraints of the landscape and the needs of Iroquoian peoples for security, fuel, and cropland determined village locations. Sandy loam, the best available soil for maize, made up only 40 percent of Huronia's lands, and the Huron preferred to situate their villages on these sorts of soils, provided there was a nearby water source. Indeed, to the Huron, a reliable source of water and good soil appear to have been the two primary criteria for a village site. When possible, the Huron situated their villages on the banks of streams, where they could be more easily defended.[73]

Five Nations peoples often constructed their villages around the headwaters of streams and appear to have been far more concerned with the defensibility of village sites than were the Huron.[74] The Huron placed their villages adjacent to navigable waterways, while the Iroquois placed their villages "on the side of a steep high hill, near a steam or river which is difficult of access . . . and inaccessible from every side."[75] This difference in site selection could be attributed to how the different peoples viewed waterways. The Huron, living in a country interlaced with rivers and streams, saw them as highways. But to the Iroquois, waterways represented potential invasion routes that could be used by aggressors. To minimize the threat, "they withdraw from the rivers, as far as they can into the interior, in order to not be easily surprised."[76]

The lands of Huronia and Iroquoia and the people that lived on them existed in a reciprocal relationship. By clearing the land, by moving, and by choosing not to exhaust the soil too much, Iroquoian peoples saw themselves as fulfilling the implied relationship with the earth that Aataentsic had initiated. The seasonal cycle, and the ceremonies that went with it, helped them fulfill these obligations. Practices such as burning helped them to renew the earth and enabled them to manipulate the landscape for their benefit.

The other and equally important aspect of renewal, humans renewing humans, was not as old as Iroquoian peoples' relationship with the earth. But it was far more complex and originated with Deganawidah and Hiawatha. It was a process that saw enemy become friend and relative destroyed by kin.

2

THE RENEWAL OF HUMAN BEINGS

THE HURON SPEAKER TURNED TO HIS AUDIENCE AND intoned:

> Let every one remain quiet, open your ears, and close your mouths. What I have to tell you is important. We are here to resuscitate a dead man, and to bring a great Captain back to life. There he is, he who is clothed with that fine robe. It is no longer he whom you lately saw, and whose name was Nehap. He has given his name to another savage. His name is Etouait. Look upon him as the true Captain of this tribe. It is he whom you must obey; it is he to whom you must listen, and whom you must honor.[1]

The speaker then began to work his way through the assemblage and distributed presents to the guests. He told one guest that a present of a "collar of porcelain beads will tell your tribe that there is a Captain in Tadoussac, and that Etouait has come back to life." He then pointed to a pack of beaver pelts and told another guest that the gift would "proclaim in your country the fact that we have a Chief, and that death has not utterly destroyed the name of Etouait."[2]

In the ceremony that followed these remarks, the Huron, metaphorically and symbolically, raised the dead. This incident reveals some of the more important aspects of Iroquoian ideas concerning the renewal of human beings. Two motivations drove the Iroquoian practice of resuscitation, the restoration of the dead to life. One was to condole the bereaved by giving them presents and a person to replace the deceased. The other was the all-encompassing desire of renewal.[3]

By assuaging the grief of the bereaved and by restoring to a community or clan a lost member, the bereaved could revert to a normal state—that of clearmindedness—and everything would stay in balance, or at least be as it was before the loss of the deceased. Captives, however, could not replace all of the deceased. Many times this was a matter of numbers, but in some cases the families, for various reasons, refused to accept a replacement.

But nearly every death would be condoled. The Iroquois condolence ritual outlined by Deganawidah and Hiawatha consisted of five rites. Contained within these five rituals were sixteen events, all of which were designed to restore the bereaved to sanity.[4] The condolence ceremony began with "on the journey," the procession of the clear-minded to the house of the mourning family. The second ritual, "woods' edge," initiated contact between the clear-minded and the mourners. The clear-minded called out their welcome, and the mourners, following Iroquoian rules of hospitality, went to the woods' edge—perhaps the only nongendered space in Iroquois thought—to greet and build a fire to warm their visitors. The third step, the "requickening," took the form of the condolers using the "three bare words" to wipe the tears and clear the ears and the throat.[5] The mourners then took the clear-minded by the arm to the council place, where the clear-minded sang "the six songs":

> *Ha-i* (ten times)
> I come to greet my kindred . . .
> *Ha-i* (ten times)
> I come to greet the Great Law . . .
> Hear us, hear us, hear us
> My grandfathers, hear us.[6]

The ceremony ended "with over the forest," the departure of the clear-minded for their own homes.[7]

Many of the deaths that were condoled came about through warfare. While Iroquoian philosophy preached that all nations should be embraced by the White Roots of Peace, war formed a large part of the reality of Iroquoian peoples. For men, war, along with diplomacy, was their primary occupation; it defined who they were in Iroquoian thought and society, and it was their main pursuit when they went beyond the tree line—the place where the fields ended and the woods began—into the domain of men. For women, too, war was important. In the matrilineal society of Iroquoian peoples, women felt very much the death of a member of their clan. They encouraged men to go to war, usually for the purpose of bringing back captives to replace the dead. They took the lead in choosing which captives would live and which would die.[8]

Thus Iroquoian peoples linked warfare, in which lives were lost, to the practice of renewing human beings, in which they were reborn. While war did result in occasional fatalities, the acquisition of captives to replace the dead overrode all other objectives in Iroquoian warfare. Iroquoian warfare took lives, certainly, but not in the way the European mode of war did. Europeans sought victory on the battlefield by inflicting massive casualties on their foes and by taking large numbers of prisoners. Nearly all of these prisoners would be treated as neutrals and would be repatriated at the end of hostilities, provided the capturing power followed the "rules."

Iroquoian warriors certainly took lives on the battlefield—the notion of nonlethal warfare is an oxymoron—and they brought home prisoners. But unlike the prisoners of European wars, these captives, for the most part, would never see their homes again. In a sense, Iroquoian warriors stole captives from their former lives, clans, and communities. Many of these captives became the vessel in which a lost loved one was resuscitated. And yet while war captives represented, on one level, the embodiment of a dead loved one, they also could retain, to their detriment, the status of enemy.

The Jesuit Paul Le Jeune wrote that the Huron "never undertake them (wars) without reason." Le Jeune thought that the refusal of one tribe to give another gifts as required by a previous agreement was the most common reason for war. He also recognized the role of revenge, in retaliation for the killing of a tribal member, as another motivation for war.[9] Europeans did not regard revenge—"officially" at least—as a sufficient motive for war.[10] But Native notions of revenge went far beyond the simple killing of enemy peoples as retribution. The Iroquoian mode of war had a dual edge. On the one hand, it contained destructive characteristics, taking lives in the form of captives and robbing the enemy and its clans of tribal and clan members. But Iroquoian warfare also had a constructive aspect. War enabled the *ohwachiras* to replace their dead members. Revenge, then, in the context of Iroquoian thought, had a constructive corollary. Revenge meant captives, some of whom, after they underwent adoption rituals, replaced the dead within the community.[11] This sort of revenge strengthened Iroquoian clans while weakening those of the enemy.

While the acquisition of captives was the primary objective of Iroquoian war parties, the secondary goal of avoiding casualties nearly equaled this one in importance. Leaders of war parties tried to avoid sustaining excessive casualties or having their followers captured.[12] If a war party inflicted casualties on the enemy, that was all well and good, but it was only a secondary concern.[13] War parties that sustained many casualties, even those that brought home a significant number of prisoners, could only be considered failures.[14] Joseph Lafitau, writing in 1724, noted that

> they feel very much the loss of a single person because of their small number and any loss has such great consequences for the chief of a party that his reputation depends on it. The Indians expect a chief to be not only skilful but also lucky. They are so peculiar in this respect that, if he does not bring back all his people and if someone even dies a natural death, he is almost entirely discredited. This attitude, nevertheless, can result from good policy. It checks the chiefs and keeps them from exposing their people too boldly.[15]

Casualties also reignited the traditional cycle of Iroquoian warfare by requiring the taking of yet more captives to replace those killed in battle.[16]

So strong was the imperative to limit casualties that, at times, leaders of war parties opted to engage in single combat with one another rather than risk the lives of their followers. One Jesuit recorded a tale in the *Jesuit Relations* of a single combat between the leaders of opposing Montagnais and Iroquois war parties. As the two groups prepared for combat, their leaders discerned that their forces were evenly matched. Fearful of losing too many men, the Montagnais and Iroquois leaders parleyed and opted instead to decide the outcome of the battle through single combat, with the understanding that the followers of the loser would return home unmolested. The two men grappled for some time. The Montagnais finally threw the Iroquois leader to the ground and "triumphantly carried him on his shoulders," presumably to a slow death by torture.[17] Each of these two leaders thought it better to hazard their own lives in single combat rather than risk those of their followers and the condemnation of their communities.

Excessive casualties would have diminished their status as war leaders; indeed, if they lost too many men, they may have never have been allowed to lead another war party again.

While ambush and surprise were staples of Native warfare, opposing sides would sometimes parley before beginning a battle and agree on a set of "rules." This semiformal agreed-upon mode of warfare seems apparent in Samuel de Champlain's description of his first encounter with the Iroquois in 1609. After Champlain's allies finished constructing their barricade, the Iroquois

> sent two canoes . . . to learn from their enemies whether they wished to fight, and these replied that they had no other desire, but that for the moment nothing could be seen and that it was necessary to wait for daylight in order to distinguish one another. They said that as soon as the sun should rise, they would attack us, and to this our Indians agreed.[18]

The rest of the night passed with both the Huron and the Iroquois engaging in dances and hurling boasts and insults at each other.[19] At dawn the next morning, the Iroquois emerged from their barricade and, as agreed the night before, began their attack. The manner in which they advanced on Champlain and his allies suggests the formality of Native warfare: "They came slowly to meet us with a gravity and calm which I admired; and at their head were three chiefs. Our Indians . . . advanced in similar order, and told me that those who had the three big plumes were the chiefs."[20] Champlain's description of the measured pace and the sort of loose formation each side adopted demonstrates that the mode of precontact warfare had a formal, ritualized aspect; the two sides had agreed the night before on the time and place of battle. By design, this sort of warfare produced few casualties.[21] Without the presence of Champlain and his harquebus, this battle on the shores of Lake Champlain would have resulted in the shooting of arrows, the striking of clubs, and perhaps the taking of some captives by one side or the other. But there would have been few serious battlefield injuries, primarily because Iroquoian military technology emphasized the main objective of war, taking captives, by minimizing casualties.

Wood, stone, and animal or fish bone made up the business end of most Native weapons. Occasionally, projectiles would be tipped with copper, which more than likely came from the upper Great Lakes region. Resin or

Champlain Battles the Iroquois at Lake Champlain. Note that the artist, obviously unfamiliar with North America, included palm trees in the Illustration. From Samuel de Champlain, *Les voyages dv sievr de Champlain, Xaintongeois, capitaine ordinaire pour le Roy en la marine, divisez en devx livres, ou, Iovrnal très-fidèle des observations faites, és decouuertures de la Nouuelle France . . .* (Paris, 1613). Courtesy of the National Library and National Archives of Canada.

sinew usually secured the projectile to the shaft.[22] These missiles were designed to be lethal, but Native defensive capabilities, such as wooden armor and shields, largely neutralized them.

Personal armor, constructed of wood, bark, and reeds, provided a sufficient defense against Native-made offensive capabilities. Many observers described Huron shields as long, light, and large enough to cover the whole body. Usually made of hewn cedar and covered with animal skins, they were strong enough that "they may not be penetrated by spears and tomahawks." Father Paul Le Jeune described one of these shields as being "very long and wide. It easily covered my whole body, and reached from my feet to my chest." He also expressed some puzzlement as to how these shields were made: "I do not know how they can plane so large and wide a plank with their knives." In battle, these shields were carried "by a cord cast over the right shoulder, so that it protects the left side of the body; when they have cast their spears or fired their guns they slightly retire the right side and turn toward the enemy the left side, which is protected by the shield."[23]

In their 1609 confrontation with Champlain, the Iroquois fled, abandoning their wooden armor on the battlefield lest it weigh them down in their flight. Wooden armor remained in use for years, being employed mostly in war games between young men, but it also appeared in combat as late as the 1640s, long after European weaponry rendered it ineffective.[24] A Dutch observer visiting the Mohawk in December 1634 witnessed a mock battle that began when

> a man came shouting . . . through the houses. . . . I asked . . . what was meant by it . . . "we are going to play with one another" . . . there were 20 men under arms . . . they went at each other . . . some wore armor and helmets . . . made . . . from thin reeds and cord woven together so that no arrow or axe could penetrate to cause serious injury.[25]

Another aspect of Native warfare was their use of fortifications, not only the palisades that surrounded villages but also the ones they erected hastily while on campaign. On the warpath, the Huron set up their camps by felling

> big trees for a barricade on the bank of the river . . . they . . . do this so quickly that after less than two hours' work, five hundred of their enemies would have had difficulty in driving them out, without losing many men. They do not barricade the river bank where their boats are drawn up, in order to embark, in case of need.[26]

Attackers found these permanent forts difficult to reduce. In his second campaign against the Iroquois, Champlain noted the problems that he and his allies faced when they attempted to reduce the palisade that enclosed an Onondaga village. He told "the Indians that they must carry the place by storm . . . to do this, they must . . . fasten stout ropes to the posts that supported the barricades and pull them down by main strength."[27] Using their shields to protect themselves, the Algonquins, Montagnais, and Huron who made up Champlain's force were able to get close enough to the fort to carry out his plan.

Clearly, Iroquoian weapons, tactics, and stratagems were effective. Their offensive weaponry was capable of inflicting grievous wounds on an enemy, yet their defensive technology—armor and barricades—was more than equal to the task when up against Native weaponry. But despite these capabilities, killing the enemy was a secondary objective.

Despite the effectiveness of Iroquoian weapons, nearly all of the efforts of Iroquoian war parties remained directed to the securing of captives to replace the dead. Young men who became captives usually faced the prospect of death by torture.[28] However, Iroquoian warriors often spared "all the children from ten to twelve years old, and the women whom they take in war, unless the women are very old, and then they kill them too."[29] Captives, even if destined to be tortured to death, were given to individuals and clans who had lost relatives. The presentation of a captive was expected to "dry [the] tears and partly assuage [the] grief" of the bereaved.[30]

Captivity, because of its prevalence in the region, meant that there was a sort of interconnectedness in the Native Northeast. Captives, especially females who had been captured sometime after early childhood, since they were more likely to be spared, had to become peoples of two worlds. Female captives were a special element in the renewed world. They not only added to their new community themselves, but offspring of their union with their male captors added more people. While they apparently assimilated into their new communities, they also retained affection for their biological kin. When Champlain and a party of Algonquin allies assaulted and destroyed an Onondaga village, they discovered an Algonquin woman who, having lived among the Iroquois since her childhood, had married and raised a family. She saved her life by frantically attempting to explain to the assailants that she was one of them. She could only repeat over and over the single Algonquin word—*nir,* that is, "me"—that she recalled. While this action of speaking a nearly forgotten word saved her life, during the attack this woman witnessed the slayings of her husband and her children. The war party took her back to Canada with them, where she then had to change her life once again. Shortly after her arrival in Canada, the Jesuits converted her to Christianity.[31]

The mental landscape of Native peoples in northeastern America had to contain a sort of flexibility. One's life, as one knew it, could be easily disrupted, and one could find oneself—willingly or no—as part of a different family unit or community. The ability to adapt was critical.

How most captives felt about their new families and communities is hard to discern. Some did escape back to their former lives, but the penalty for failure, death by torture, was so high that many probably never made the attempt. In many cases, particularly those of children, they could recall no other life. Still others felt torn over their relations, wanting to be with both their biological and adoptive families. This desire could impose another sort of penalty for escape on adoptees. Fleeing meant permanent separation from friends and family in their adopted communities. One Algonquin woman decided to flee her Iroquois village and to return to Canada, hoping to find some of her biological family. She confided her plan only to her small son, telling him that "I am not of this country. . . . Thy father married me; but, my dear son, it would delight me to see once more my own country, I have resolved to leave thee." When the boy began to cry, she offered him comfort and an admonishment: "Remember that thou hast a mother in the land of the Algonquins, who loved thee with all her heart; but on no account betray me, for thou wouldst be the cause of my being burned."[32]

But not all Native people possessed this sense of duality, or flexibility, that allowed them to assimilate into one group or another. One Algonquin woman, finding herself a "prisoner [of] the Hyroquois," chose suicide, "destroying herself, together with a babe she carried . . . rather than be their servant or slave."[33]

Equally important was the mental landscape of those doing the adopting. In some respects, the act of resuscitation represented the grasping of a sort of immortality on behalf of the deceased. Jesuit Hierosme Lalemant noted that when a family member died, the survivors gathered and selected from their number a replacement and bestowed upon the individual the name of the deceased:

> He who takes a new name also assumes the Duties connected with it. . . . This done, they dry their tears, and cease to weep for the deceased. In this manner, they place him among the living, saying that he is resuscitated, and has come to life in the person of him who has received his name, and has rendered him immortal.[34]

There was the strong belief that the individual, who took on the identity of the deceased, actually became that individual. The Jesuit Barthelemy Vimont noted that the Huron resuscitated a name for several reasons, including recalling the memory of the deceased and facilitating revenge, "for he who takes on the name of a man killed in battle binds himself to avenge his death."

Practical concerns also guided the naming of a replacement for the dead. The man who took the name of the deceased "assumes all the duties of the deceased, feeding his children as if he were their own Father—in fact, they call him their Father, and he calls them his children." Among other relatives, there was a transferal of the affection they felt toward the dead clan member to the one who took his or her place.[35] In some instances, the transfer of affection, at least in the view of Christian missionaries, could go a little too far.

In one case, after a young man died, his wife, a Christian convert, took his replacement into the house as her husband, to the consternation of the Jesuits. When reprimanded by the fathers, she replied that she was still a Christian and that the replacement, to her mind, was her husband. Christian converts later blended Native ideas of resuscitation with Christian notions of resurrection. A converted Huron held a feast at which a young man took the name of his deceased nephew. He gave a speech in which he stated that he viewed "this resurrection of my nephew ... as a symbol of the true resurrection to which we look forward." The new nephew replied that the gathering should "rejoice, not in the image of the resurrection that we express by our ceremony, but in the true resurrection to which we look forward."[36]

Not all captives, however, were resuscitated; many, particularly young men, were subjected to torture and death. European observers—who came from a culture where torture was an instrument of the state—found the Iroquoian torture of captives horrific and its preliminaries puzzling. Whereas torture in the European view was entirely acceptable to use against those thought to pose a threat to society, the state, or the church, it was, by and large, not inflicted on prisoners of war. When an injured Iroquois prisoner was given to a Huron family, they cared for his wounds and prepared a feast for him.[37] In one case, a prisoner with badly injured hands was turned over to a family that had recently suffered a loss. However, the chief whose nephew he was to replace condemned him to die:

> My nephew ... when I first received news that thou wert at my disposal, I was wonderfully pleased, fancying that he whom I lost in war had been ... brought back to life.... I was ... preparing thee a place in my cabin, and thought that thou wouldst pass the rest of thy days pleasantly with me. But now I see thee in this condition, with thy fingers gone and thy hands half rotten, I change my mind, and I am sure that thou thyself wouldst regret to live any longer.[38]

This chief's comments revealed much about Iroquoian thought concerning captives. On the one hand, the powerful hope that the dead could be restored to life—the hope that "he whom I lost in war had been . . . brought back to life"—pervaded his remarks. But on the other, a duality is present. The chief had prepared a place for his newfound relation, yet upon realizing how badly injured the prisoner was, he had no qualms about consigning him to the flames. The captor was both cruel and kind. In the cruel vein, he tells the prisoner how close he came to being spared but then pulls the hope of life just out of reach. The chief decided that the prisoner should not be spared. Indeed, he believed the captive did not want to live. Perhaps this pulling away of the last slim hope of life was a sort of torture. But on the other hand, the prisoner could not, due to his injuries, become a productive member of the society. And he could die slowly and painfully from his injures. The chief offered him a way of death that, while horribly painful, would not cause him to linger long and, in Iroquoian thought, was considered an honorable way to die. One Jesuit noted that even though this prisoner was condemned to die, a sister of the dead man he would have replaced "brought him some food, showing a remarkable solicitude for him. You would almost have said that he was her own son, and I do not know that this creature did not represent to her him who she had lost."[39]

Male adult captives seemed to have played a dualistic, and sometimes contradictory, role. This dualism is one of the thorniest problems in attempting to decipher seventeenth-century Iroquoian thought. Rarely did an adult male captive escape torture. As the vessel for resuscitation of the deceased, his presence offered the bereaved some comfort. He represented the hope that their loved one had somehow overcome death. Yet at the same time his existence, and the knowledge that he was an enemy, may have helped the adoptive family recall the murder of their loved one or his death in battle. This may have made the thought of turning him over for torture easier for them.[40] Another practical reason for the torture and killing of male captives was the knowledge that they were far more likely to resist assimilation into a new community than women or children.

Adoption of male captives seems to have taken two forms. In one form, the captive was adopted, took the name of a deceased relation, and assumed his place in the clan. The other appears to have been adoption in name only. While the clan may fete and treat the captive kindly for a day or so and address him as "uncle" or "nephew," he was then given to the torturers. The solicitude of the adoptive family who had fed and treated him with kindness gave way to the cruelty and sarcasm of strangers. "Ah, it is not right . . .

that my uncle should be cold; I must warm thee," said a young Huron man to an Iroquois captive, while he passed a torch over his flesh. Another man taunted the captive, saying that he "must make him a present, I must give him a hatchet," and pressed an ax head, heated red hot, against the soles of the prisoner's feet. Yet another jokingly commented that the prisoner was a new canoe, which he must "calk and pitch."[41] These torments could continue for days, and the captive would sometimes be allowed to rest and be given food and drink so that he would endure his torments as long as possible.

Iroquoian torture seems to have followed a standard mode, with small variations from one case to another. In general, only men were tortured. Occasionally women and children were tortured, but this seems to have taken place only in special circumstances. As soon as a man was taken prisoner, his arms were pinioned behind him above the elbows with a set of ties that war parties carried for this purpose. His captors then either pulled some of his fingernails or broke and cut off some of his fingers. Or they would break one of his arms. These tortures were designed to make it impossible for the prisoner to wield a weapon. On the march back to the village of his captors, the prisoner would be continually beaten. When he arrived at the village, one of two things happened. He would either endure walking—not running—the gauntlet, or the matriarchs of one of the clans would pull him out of line of those prisoners awaiting torture. In most cases, warrior-age males, usually fifteen to fifty, were not spared. The prisoner would be given a feast, at which he would recite his war honors. The next day the young men gathered and used torches to torture him. Sometimes they would cut chunks out of his flesh, roast them, and force the prisoner to eat them. If there was more than one prisoner and the captors ascertained that two of them were related or very close to one another, they could be forced to torture one another or to eat of each other's flesh. The climax of a captive's agonies came when he was placed on a scaffold at sunrise. His tormenters would assault him with torches "which they thrust, all aflame, down his throat, even forcing them into his fundament." Hot hatchets were also applied to his body, and if a captive tried to sit "some one thrust a brand from under the scaffolding which soon caused him to arise."[42] The end came when the prisoner, nearly out of breath, collapsed motionless and could not be revived. Someone would then scalp him, and hot sand or

A Huron Prisoner Being Tortured by the Iroquois. Males of fighting age stood little chance of survival if captured. From Francesco Bressani, *Novae Francia accurata delineatio* (1657). Courtesy of the National Library and National Archives of Canada

melted pitch would be poured on the exposed skull. Then "one cut off a foot, another a hand, and at almost the same time a third severed the head from the shoulders, throwing it into the crowd.... As for the trunk ... a feast was made of it the same day."[43] In the case of a captive who displayed a great deal of courage during torture, his heart would be cut out and eaten by his torturers in the belief "that this renders them courageous." Other young men would mingle the prisoner's blood with their own in the belief that it made it impossible for the enemy to surprise them.[44] Daniel Richter has pointed out that the torture and execution of captives by the Iroquois contained a religious component, but European observers who witnessed the torments and deaths of captives were too shocked to fathom it.[45]

Perhaps much of the shock came from the notion of destruction; European observers would have been reporting what they witnessed. However, the renewal complex of Iroquoian peoples, contained in the practices of adoption, resuscitation, and taking of captives to replace the dead, was beyond the Europeans' understanding. These practices fell so far outside their cultural construct that they could not even recognize them.

The renewal of human beings represented an important part of the way that Iroquoian peoples viewed the world. This concept, and their notions of renewing the earth, would remain essentially unchanged during the early years of European contact. The Iroquoian practice of warfare would be modified by European contact and the objectives altered somewhat. Territory, pelts, and the infliction of casualties on an enemy would gain in importance. The quest for captives, the stealing of enemy peoples from their former lives, and their unique form of taking revenge, however, would remain a part of Iroquoian life. But an important part of their thought world, their relationship with the supernatural, would begin to change.

3

THE SUPERNATURAL

COLD, HUNGRY, AND TIRED, THE YOUNG HURON MAN "but fifteen or sixteen years of age" had fasted for sixteen days when a booming voice from the sky saying, "Take care of this man, and let him end his fast," startled him. With that, an old man "of rare beauty" descended from the sky and assured the young man that he would oversee the course of his life: "Have courage, I will take care of thy life. It is a fortunate thing for thee, to have taken me for thy Master. None of the Demons who haunt these countries, shall have the power to harm thee." The old man then described the young man's future wife and children and told him that "one day thou wilt see thy hair as white as mine." He then held out a piece of raw human flesh to the young man, who recoiled in horror. Seeing this, the spirit withdrew it and produced a piece of bear's fat and said, "Eat this." After the young man ate the fat, the old man disappeared back into the sky. Throughout the rest of this Huron man's life, his "Master" often appeared and "promised to assist him." His predictions about the young man's future family came true. As the years went on, the young man became a very successful hunter, taking many bears. "He attribute[d] this . . . to the piece of bear's fat that [he ate] . . . and he judges . . . that he would have had equal success in war, had he eaten the piece of human flesh that he refused."[1]

The spirit who appeared to this young man is one example of the Iroquoian conception of the supernatural. Iroquoian peoples believed that the personal visions young men experienced helped guide their lives.[2] Not all spiritual overseers appeared to their young charges in human form. They could present themselves as animals, such as "a dog, a bear, or a bird."[3] All of these spirits, regardless of the form they assumed, were believed to help the dreamer throughout the course of his life.[4]

In Iroquoian thought, these spiritual overseers, and the rest of the supernatural world, were as real as the natural world. Much like other prescientific populations, Iroquoian peoples viewed the world through a spiritual prism. In approaching Iroquoian notions of the supernatural, one must divest oneself of many of the notions of Western religions. Nor, in order to understand the Iroquoian conception of the supernatural, can one think in religious terms; one must attempt to think in *spiritual* terms. Iroquoian spiritual beliefs lacked the rigid dogma of Christianity. But complete agreement on spiritual matters was not important—indeed, it was not even desirable—to Iroquoian peoples. In a given Iroquoian community there could be general—but by no means unanimous—agreement on matters such as what happened to people when they died or the location of the Village of the Dead. One could say that Iroquoian peoples had a certain set of general beliefs, but each individual interpreted them as he or she saw fit. Christian missionaries encountered several variations on common, recurring themes concerning Iroquoian beliefs while working among them.[5]

To an Iroquoian person, the supernatural world contained all the reality and vastness of the natural world, and the boundaries between the two, while clear to most Iroquoians, frequently overlapped onto one another. This vastness and overlapping tendency make it nearly impossible for any discussion of the Iroquoian supernatural to be complete. But spiritual overseers, dreams, the linkage of the living to the dead, witchcraft, and the curing—and causing—of illness comprised the most important elements of the supernatural. Of these, overseers and the relationship between the dead and the living formed the nexus between the natural and supernatural worlds. In short, the Iroquoian conception of the supernatural mirrored the natural world but with important distinctions.

For a seventeenth-century Iroquoian person, the boundary between the supernatural and the natural worlds contained an element of ambiguity. While Iroquoian peoples saw the supernatural and natural worlds as divided and separate, an unclear merging of the two worlds took place in the Iroquoian mind. In large part, this could be attributed to the Iroquoian notion of connectedness; the unseen supernatural had definite links to the seen, natural world. Hence, the supernatural could not be ignored; it had the ability to intrude into the natural world, and it often did so.

Like all things in the Iroquoian thought world, the supernatural had a double edge; it contained elements of both good and evil. It offered Iroquoian peoples guidance and comfort, but it could also bring terror. The Iroquoian division of the world into the natural and supernatural spheres did not follow a neat, nonintertwined model, as seventeenth-century Christianity was apt to do. Indeed, there seemed to be a sort of blending; the events of the supernatural, to a degree, had to be satisfied on the natural plane as well.

Spirituality pervaded nearly every facet of an Iroquoian person's life. Spirits, or "Other Than Human Persons," could be found nearly anywhere. A man who succeeded on the hunt took care to handle his kill properly and thank the Other Than Human Person of the animal for giving up its life.[6] Some rocks, especially those believed to have once been human, also possessed a great deal of power and had to be treated with respect. In 1624, the Recollect Gabriel Sagard witnessed the Huron offering tobacco to a large rock that they claimed had once been a man and asking that it grant them a safe journey on their travels. A dozen years later, the Jesuit Jean de Brébeuf observed the same practices (and possibly the same rock).[7] Nor did one trifle with these spirits. A Dutchman mocked his Mohawk companions when they offered tobacco to a rock on Lake George. The Other Than Human Person of the rock, as the Mohawk told it, capsized the Dutchman's canoe, drowning the blasphemer.[8]

Contact with the supernatural, or with a being that became one's spiritual overseer, had long been an important part of Iroquoian life. Usually only young men actively sought the spiritual guidance of a vision. The rigors of a vision quest—self-induced hunger, exposure to the elements, and sleep deprivation—precluded the elderly and the weak.

Nor as a rule did women seek visions; Iroquoian societies imposed a sort of sexual division on the natural world. As a consequence, if this gender division did not entirely limit women's contact with the supernatural, it largely closed off the active mode of supernatural contact—the seeking of a vision—to them. With few exceptions, the domain of Iroquoian women extended from the center of the village to the edges of the cornfields. In this sphere, agriculture and village chores were accomplished all of which, with few exceptions, were women's tasks. But the tree line delimited the worlds of men and women. When one crossed the tree line and stepped into the woods, one entered the domain of men, where men carried out the tasks of war and hunting. In a way, it may be said that Iroquoian women centered their lives around the physical village or community, while men centered theirs around tasks external yet essential to the community. Whereas Europeans tended to view the world in a hierarchical or vertical framework, the Iroquoian conception of the world was more like a horizontal plane. Women occupied the village, the center of this world, while their menfolk pushed themselves toward its margins, the forests.

Young men seeking a vision went into the woods, seeking a margin of another sort, and isolated themselves from their communities. During this time, they fasted and remained awake until a vision appeared to them. The lack of food, together with sleep deprivation and the lack of human contact, helped induce a vision, or what twenty-first-century Americans would term a hallucination.

To some degree, the relationship between humans and the supernatural had to be negotiated. By embarking on a vision quest, a young man actively sought out supernatural intervention in his life. And when his "Master," that is, his supernatural overseer, approached him, a vision seeker exercised some degree of control over the encounter. In the case of the young Huron whose story opened the chapter, his selection of bear's fat over human flesh helped determine the path that his life would take. And his choosing to eat the bear's fat signaled his acceptance of the spiritual overseer, with whom he entered into a sort of partnership that served him throughout the rest of his life.

Whereas the vision quest was the active mode of seeking contact with the supernatural, contact could also come about—though not often—through serendipity. Not all Iroquoian peoples had to go on an active quest to obtain a vision. In one case, a Huron woman left her cabin one night and saw "the Moon stoop down . . . appearing to her as a beautiful tall woman, holding . . . a little girl like her own." The vision told the woman she was the "seignior general of these countries," and she listed presents—tobacco, deerskins, and robes—that she wanted given to her. The apparition also told the woman, "I love thee, and . . . wish that thou . . . be like me. . . . I am wholly of fire, I desire that thou be . . . the color of fire." With that, the vision commanded the woman to acquire a completely red outfit.[9] These unbidden, unsought visions that occurred during waking hours were unlikely avenues to the supernatural, and they seem to have been rare occurrences. For most Iroquoian peoples, however, the simple act of falling asleep would initiate most of their supernatural encounters.

The most common supernatural experience that most Iroquoian peoples would have in their lifetimes would be the dream. They regarded the events of dreams to be as real as those that occurred during one's waking hours. Brébeuf noted that "the dream . . . is in truth, the principal God of the Hurons. . . . If a Captain speaks one way and a dream another, the Captain might shout his head off in vain,—the dream is first obeyed."[10] Native peoples went hunting and fishing at the behest of dreams. Feasts that could consume a year's worth of provisions might be given to fulfill a dream. Dreams also predicted success in war. Iroquoian peoples believed it imperative that dreams be satisfied, because they expressed either the desires of the dreamer's soul or those of supernatural beings who appeared in the dream.[11]

Dreams provided the Huron with much of what they knew about the Village of the Dead. When Father Brébeuf debated theology with Hurons, he questioned them as to how they could be familiar with the Village of the Dead, since only the dead could go there. They replied that the dead often appeared to them in their dreams and spoke to them of the Village of the Dead. And many of the living had dreams in which they visited their dead relations.[12]

Dreams, Iroquoian peoples believed, also helped form the intellect of the individual, since they were the most common source of a priori knowledge. One's soul would travel far away during a dream and "give us knowledge of things far distant and quite beyond the reach of the body."[13] Iroquoian peoples further believed that dreams also said something about the dreamer. They believed that every person had "desires, which are . . . inborn and concealed. These, they say, come from the depths of the soul," which made "these desires known by means of dreams, which are its language."[14]

This knowledge provides some clues as to how Native peoples saw themselves as human beings. They considered humans to be comprised of physical and mental parts, but they realized that some parts of the human psyche were so complex that one could remain a mystery to oneself. Using this theory, they saw that there was a sense of elusive "wholeness" in human beings, that the physical and mental were intermixed. The dream, then, was a psychoanalytic tool. It unraveled, to some degree, the complexities of the human psyche, revealing innermost desires to the individual, who otherwise remained ignorant of that which he or she truly desired.

Upon awaking, the dreamer attempted to make the events of the dream become fact in the waking world. Many Iroquoian peoples believed that satisfying a dream could cure illness. The soul may have expressed a desire for material objects such as "a canoe ... a new robe, [or] a porcelain collar." It may want social events given by or in the dreamer's honor, such as "a fire-feast [or] a dance."[15] At times, the soul's desires bordered on the extreme. A sick Huron once dreamed that he would be cured if he slew a Frenchman and set out (unsuccessfully) to do so.[16]

Dreams could also help the dreamer avoid illness. By showing the physical self the soul's desires—or, in the language of twentieth-century Freudian psychoanalysis, showing the conscious half of the individual the desires of the subconscious—Iroquoian peoples believed that the "whole person" was helped. Recognizing the division of human begins into mental and physical spheres, it was not a big leap for Iroquoian peoples to suppose that unmet desires—even if not articulated during waking hours—could lead to psychosomatic illness.[17]

It was believed that if the dream remained unsatisfied, the soul would become "angry, and ... not give its body the ... happiness that it wished to procure ... but ... it ... revolts against the body, causing various diseases, and even death."[18] Indeed, it was thought that the details of the dream had to be adhered to.

Sometimes the soul's desires might be beyond the means of the individual or his or her community to satisfy. One woman dreamed that for her sick child to get well, she must give him "a hundred cakes of Tobacco, and four Beavers, with which she would make a feast." She could only obtain ten cakes of tobacco, however, and "the Beavers which were out of season were changed to four large fish." The soul's desires remained unsatisfied, and the child died.[19]

Dreams could also tell one how to avoid fate by acting out, to a degree, the events of the dream. A Huron man dreamed he saw himself captured, tortured, and devoured by the Iroquois. He consulted several chiefs, who decided that in order to avert this fate, the dreamer must act out his dream. Building "twelve or thirteen fires," each chief took a firebrand and burned the dreamer while he ran by, shrieking "like a madman." The chiefs encouraged him, saying, "Courage, my Brother, it is thus that we have pity on thee." At the end of the tortures, the dreamer "seized a dog . . . and placed it at once on his shoulders, and carried it among the Cabins as a consecrated victim, which he publicly offered to the Demon of war, begging him to accept this semblance instead of the reality of his dream." The torturers and the tortured man then killed and ate the dog "at a public feast, in the same manner as they usually eat their Captives."[20] The man underwent the tortures of his dream, and at the last minute the dog stood in for him and was killed and devoured in his stead. By acting out the dream in reality, the events that the dream foretold were considered to have actually occurred, and the dreamer would be spared having to suffer the events that his dream foretold.

Dreams also affected the conduct of warfare. In his first campaign against the Iroquois, Samuel de Champlain's Huron allies asked him each morning if he had dreamed the night before. Champlain claimed that "I dreamed that I saw . . . our enemies the Iroquois drowning before our eyes. . . . I therefore told them [the Huron] what I had dreamed. This gave them such confidence that they no longer had any doubt that what was coming to them would be to their advantage."[21] In all likelihood, Champlain had quickly learned that a dream predicting success, whether he actually had one or not, would encourage his allies. But he also learned that he could not control what the Native peoples dreamed. One year Champlain's campaign against the Iroquois almost floundered because his Native allies "dreamt that if he went there he would die, and all the rest as well." In the aftermath of Champlain's first—and from his point of view—successful battle against the Iroquois, his Native allies deserted him, after one of them dreamed "that the enemy were in pursuit, they set off in an instant, though it was a very bad night with rain and heavy wind."[22]

Another Frenchman, the Jesuit missionary Paul Le Jeune, also learned to appreciate the value of dreams. When the band of Montagnais that Le Jeune wintered with in 1634 ran short of food, his main adversary, a medicine man, took advantage of the situation and claimed he dreamed that he saw the entire band perish of starvation. To avert this fate, his dream told him that they must abandon Le Jeune in the woods, where he would die alone of starvation and exposure. Le Jeune responded that he had a dream of his own in which he saw the Montagnais kill a moose. Fortunately for Le Jeune, the Montagnais hunters did take a moose that day, and they considered Le Jeune's presence a good omen.[23]

Despite being outsiders, both Champlain and Le Jeune quickly realized that the dream, because it must be obeyed and because it predicted success or failure, could be a route to gaining credibility with Native peoples. Obviously, this strategy entailed some risk. Credibility could only be gained and sustained if the events of the dream came true. Because he had his harquebus and other armed Frenchmen with him, Champlain may have been fairly confident of his ability to make his dream of leading the Huron to victory over the Iroquois a reality. Le Jeune presumably had to rely on the power of prayer for his dream to become actuality.

A less benevolent sort of power among Iroquoian peoples that could transform desires into reality was witchcraft. Perhaps the reason that witchcraft held such credence among Iroquoian peoples was the belief that events could not occur on their own. Everything had to have a cause. Witchcraft came in two primary forms, beneficial and harmful.

If one died or became ill for no apparent reason, a displeased soul was one probable cause. But if a person had been healthy and seemingly happy, witches and witchcraft were suspected. The presence of witchcraft could be detected either by a medicine man or by an individual who may have dreamed that he or she had been bewitched.[24]

The practitioners of witchcraft came in two distinct types. One of these was the people the Huron called *oky ontatechiata,* literally, "those who kill by spells." The Jesuits called these people "sorcerers" or "witches" and noted they were "greatly feared, and . . . one . . . dare not offend them, because they can, the people believe, kill men by their arts."[25]

There was another class of persons who, while not *oky ontatechiata,* were thought to possess similar magic powers. The Huron called them *arenidioouanne.* Unlike the *oky ontatechiata,* the *arenidioouanne* practiced their magic in public. Iroquoian peoples thought these persons could find the meaning of the most confusing dreams. Like that of nearly all persons who had powers, however, Iroquoian peoples believed that their magic could be dual edged. They had both the power to kill or to heal. *Arenidioouannes* helped others by "thrust[ing] themselves forward as Prophets . . . or . . . they discover hidden things."[26]

Individuals who practiced witchcraft in secret, such as an *oky ontatechiata,* were considered malevolent. An accusation of witchcraft rendered a person very vulnerable in Iroquoian society. Unlike other killings that could be avenged or compensated, witches "even when they are only suspected . . . are slain with impunity." Brébeuf wrote that "when such people are caught, they are put to death on the spot . . . and there is no disturbance about it. As to other murders, they are avenged upon the whole Nation of the murderer; so that is the only class I know about that they put to death with impunity." No one avenged the death of an *oky ontatechiata,* and the killing of them was "authorized by the consent of the whole Country . . . whoever takes them in the act has full right to cleave their skulls and rid the world of them, without fear of being called to account, or obliged to give any satisfaction for it."[27]

Since the deaths of these malevolent practitioners of magic benefited the community, no one attempted to take revenge when one was slain. The Jesuit François Joseph Le Mercier wrote of a Huron woman who was invited to a feast by a person who thought she had bewitched him. When she arrived, her host accused her of witchcraft and sentenced her to death. She was killed with an ax, dragged outside, and her body burned in the center of the village.[28]

Another Jesuit noted how easily one could come under the suspicion of being an *oky ontatechiata*: "The fancy of a sick man, who will say that . . . one is causing his death by a spell; or the malice of an enemy . . . or the too suspicious imagination of some one who, because he has seen him in the woods or in some out-of-the-way part of the country, will say that he was preparing spells there."[29] Either the Jesuits did not realize—or chose to ignore, as the *Jesuit Relations* emphasized the savagery of Native peoples—that Iroquoian society imposed checks on witch hunts. While it is true that those who slew an *oky ontatechiata* often did not have to fear reprisals, it seems likely that this was a function of carefully choosing whom to accuse of witchcraft. One probably chose a person who was widely disliked and whose clan, for whatever reason, either would not or could not retaliate. By broadcasting the allegation of witchcraft, the accusers tried to obtain the tacit consent of the majority of the community. Even so, it also appears that there may have been disagreements over the killing of witches. After Le Mercier witnessed the killing of a female "witch," he overheard one of the Huron captains argue that killing her promptly was the correct course of action because "the old men were too lenient, and that, if she were kept till morning, her life would probably be spared."[30]

But such disagreements, animosities, hatreds, and individual desires for revenge were usually suppressed within Iroquoian communities. However, a celebration known as *Ononhouaroia,* or "turning the brain upside down," allowed all the participants—men, women, and children—to "run about as if they are mad," and many of them acted on long suppressed desires. During this time, the revelers entered lodges, and "if they find kettles over the fire, they upset them; they break earthen pots, knock down the dogs, throw fire and ashes everywhere, so thoroughly that often the cabins and entire villages burn down." The revelers would shout, "We have dreamed." The occupants of the lodge they invaded would then try to guess which objects the dreamers had dreamed of and had to give them goods they named until the revelers declared they had guessed correctly. Laden with goods, the revelers then would leave the lodge and go into the woods, where they would cast out their madness.[31]

In all likelihood, the *Ononhouaroia* may have been considered healthy since it allowed people in Iroquoian communities to act out their animosities and frustrations without having to accept blame for their actions. The actions taken during the "upsetting of the brain" represented the perfect opportunity for revenge. Despite the assumption on the part of the Jesuits that "a public madness" was present during the *Ononhouaroia,* it appears that many Iroquois used the ceremony as an opportunity to settle personal scores. In several cases, Christians were attacked during the *Ononhouaroia.* During one such celebration, some converts were "rudely struck, and the hatchet of the infidels almost gave this Church a martyr; but it only half dealt its blow, having drawn only the blood, and not the whole life of a good Christian."[32]

It is probable that the lucky Christian had offended the sensibilities of other Hurons by following religious practices alien to their culture. The Christian requirement that one forsake one's former beliefs would have created friction. Christianity also diminished the "personhood" and spirituality of nonhumans.

While elements of the relationship between the living and the dead touched, as all aspects of Iroquoian life did, on the supernatural, the interactions between the living and the dead were also considered a part of the natural world. Iroquoian peoples conceived of the living and the dead, in both a physical and spiritual sense, as being part of a single, shared, yet segregated community. This could be seen in the physical layout of Huron and Five Nations villages. Near every Iroquoian community—"a harquebus-shot distant" in the words of one early missionary—was the village cemetery.[33] The cemeteries, temporary abodes for the *atiskens*—the sensitive portion of the soul that remained among the living—were deemed so important that "if fire should break out in their village and in their cemetery," the living "would first run to extinguish the fire in the cemetery and then the fire in the village."[34]

Most Iroquoian peoples agreed that nearly everyone went to the Village of the Dead after death.[35] In general, they had a vague notion that the Village of the Dead lay somewhere far west of their earthly homes in Huronia and Iroquoia.[36] Unlike Christians, who believed the destination of the soul after death was connected to salvation or good works, Iroquoian peoples believed the destination of the soul was determined not by how one lived but by how one died. Those who died violently or by suicide had their own Village of the Dead and could not associate with the souls of people who died by other means. Nor did the souls of infants go to the Village of the Dead. Parents interred them near paths, so that their souls could enter the wombs of pregnant women as they walked by and animate the fetus.[37]

Like nearly all things in the Iroquoian thought world, souls were considered to be dualistic. The Huron attributed several characteristics to the soul. They believed souls possessed a certain dualism and that this duality took one form during life and another after death. In addition, the Huron believed that most living people had at least two souls—one sensitive soul and one or more souls that were "endowed with reason or intelligence."[38] The Huron called the sensitive soul the *atisken* and the reasonable soul the *esken*. There were exceptions to this; some people claimed to have more than two souls, and some claimed to have no souls at all. Hurons who dreamed of a faraway place believed that their reasonable soul—which did not operate the physical body—traveled to the place they saw in their dream. Hurons who stopped having dreams believed that the reasonable soul had departed their body forever. The sensitive soul controlled the physical body and its functions and remained with it throughout life. After death, its relationship to the body and its ability to move away from it changed. Upon death, the two parts of the soul separated from one another.[39] One portion of the soul, the *atisken,* stayed with the physical remains, while the *esken* traveled to the Village of the Dead.

The *atisken* that remained with the body, which was interred in the cemetery adjacent to nearly every Huron village, became part of the community. The *atisken* would occasionally—often unbidden and unwanted—

interact with the living.[40] Upon death, the body of a Huron did not leave his or her home through the door. Instead, the mourners rolled up or removed the bark wall nearest the body and carried the corpse out that way. The *esken*—the transformed reasonable soul—departed for the Village of the Dead. But the *atisken*—the former sensitive soul, now separate from but always near the physical remains—preceded the body on its way to the cemetery.[41]

The living believed the souls of the dead to be a physical presence. The physical dimension of the *atisken* allowed it to pierce the thin, permeable line that demarcated the worlds of the living and the dead. Immortal and corporeal, the *atiskens* walked through the Village of the Living at night, helping themselves to some nourishment if someone left food in a kettle.[42] Iroquoian peoples believed that the dead differed very little from the living; they experienced sensations such as hunger, heat, and cold, for example. Since the dead could not always satisfy their hunger or provide for their own comfort, their living relatives assumed this responsibility. Two Jesuits witnessed

> a band of Savages . . . having a feast near the graves of their . . . relatives; they gave them the best part of the banquet, which they threw into the fire; and, when they were about to go away, a woman broke some twigs and branches . . . [and] covered the graves. . . . [She said] she was sheltering the souls . . . from the heat of the Sun.[43]

Many Huron regarded the responsibilities of the living to the dead as so important that they could transcend death itself. A Jesuit interviewed an elderly Huron woman, who he believed was dying. The woman later recovered and told him:

> I was dead, and passed . . . the cemetery to go . . . to the village of souls. . . . I came upon one of my dead relatives, who asked where I was going and what I intended to do,—saying that if I did not change my mind . . . there would be no more relatives to prepare food for the souls thereafter; and that is what made me return and resolve to live.[44]

While the living acknowledged the presence and fulfilled the needs of the *atisken,* this relationship, on the part of the living, contained an element of fear. If the living believed an *atisken* had entered their house, they rushed outside and beat the exterior with sticks and clubs in order to drive it away. In a lodge where there had been a recent death, fishing nets were stretched over the door to keep the soul of the deceased from returning. If an *atisken* remained undetected in a dwelling, he or she could develop an affection for one of the occupants. The living feared that if this happened, when the *atisken* finally departed for the Village of the Dead, the *atisken* could carry this person off with him.[45]

While the inhabitants of the Villages of the Living and the Dead occasionally interacted, both tried to limit their contact with one another. Just as the living endeavored to keep the dead out of their world, the dead sought to keep the living out of their domain. In one Iroquoian myth, the favorite sister of a young man died. Determined to bring her back to life, he set out toward the west and walked for more than three months until he reached the Village of the Dead. He encountered Oscotarach ("pierce-head")—the spirit who removed the brains of the dead—who immediately shut himself up in his cabin, astonished at the sight of a living person. The young man proceeded to the lodge of Aataentsic, where he found the *eskens* dancing. As soon as he entered, the souls, shocked to see a living person in the Village of the Dead, vanished. Eventually, they returned and began to dance again, but they remained wary of the intruder. Among the dancers, the young man spied the *esken* of his sister. He seized her and struggled with her all night before securing her in a pumpkin. Oscotarach instructed him on how to resuscitate his sister's corpse, emphasizing that the participants in the ceremony must keep their eyes closed. But during the rite, a curious person opened his eyes before the unification of the *atisken* near the corpse and the *esken* in the pumpkin could be completed. The *esken* escaped and fled back to the Village of the Dead, leaving the young man with no choice but to carry his sister's decaying remains back to the graveyard.[46]

The reaction of the dead in this tale, their flight from the young man and the struggle of his sister's soul to escape him and being returned to the Village of the Living, emphasizes the boundary that existed between the living and the dead. It also indicates that, like the living, the dead regarded the vague, permeable line between them and the living as important, despite the close physical proximity of the living and the dead to one another.

Some forms of communication between the living and the dead were permissible; but in this case, the young man in the story seems to have broken an unspoken protocol by physically going to the Village of the Dead. Acceptable methods of communication included feeding and shading the dead and caring for their graves. Perhaps the most frequent way the living and the dead made contact with one another was the dream.

The living prepared the dead for their journey to the Village of the Dead by wrapping them in mats or beaver skin robes. The living interred the dead with those things they would need for their trip to the Village of the Dead: hatchets, kettles, food, and wampum. Asked why they did this, a Huron replied that the items belonged to the dead, and the souls of the items would accompany them to the other world, so that they could use them.[47] Brébeuf noted that since "the Village of souls is in no respect unlike the Village of the living,—they go hunting, fishing, and to the woods; axes, robes, and collars are as much esteemed as among the living."[48] Food would be thrown into a fire so that the dead might consume the soul of the food. In the case of very small children, mothers pressed milk from their breasts and burned it next to the grave.[49]

Nearly all of the goods that went into the grave were made by humans and hence possessed spiritual power. The materials that made up these goods—such as wood, stone, or in the case of European goods, metal—had a sort of power in their raw, unaltered state. But when manipulated by humans, a sort of transference took place in which the artifact gained a bit of the human's soul. The resulting artifacts, whether they be cooking vessels, cutting tools, snowshoes, or weapons, now had, like the human who molded them, a soul and could thus accompany their owners to the Village of the Dead.[50]

After a period of five to fifteen years, or when the fertility of the fields around a village declined, the living and the dead said good-bye to one another in the form of the Feast of the Dead, the most important ceremony among the Huron.[51] While the relatives of the dead looked on, designated individuals disinterred the bodies in the village cemetery. The relatives then took the remains of their loved ones and removed the remnants of their burial mats and robes. They stripped the bones of any remaining flesh and wrapped them in new beaver skin robes. The community dug a large ossuary and lined it with beaver skin robes. Participants from other villages arrived, bearing their dead, who would join the dead of the host village in the ossuary. Presents for the dead were placed in the ossuary. At the close of the ceremonies, all of the host community's dead, and those of invited communities, were interred in the ossuary.[52] The living of the host and visiting communities attached great significance to the mingling of their dead in the ossuary. It had the effect of strengthening ties among the living. Gabriel Sagard noted that

> by means of these ceremonies and gatherings they contract new friendships and unions amongst themselves, saying that, just as the bones of their deceased relatives and friends are gathered together and united . . . they themselves ought during their lives to live all together in the same unity and harmony, like good kinsmen and friends.[53]

Like many Iroquoian ceremonies, this one had elements of renewal; the Village of the Living would relocate to a new site, and the mingling of their dead renewed and restrengthened the ties between Huron clans and villages. For the dead, the ceremony had an additional element of renewal. The *atiskens,* now freed from their linkage with the physical remains, could begin their journey to the Village of the Dead.

Christian missionaries who observed these practices commented on the tenderness with which the Huron treated their dead and contrasted their devotion to the dead with what they considered to be European Christians' relative indifference toward theirs. After observing the grief the Huron displayed, even for those long dead, Sagard wrote:

> Christians, let us . . . see if our zeal for the souls of our relations . . . is as great as that of the poor savages for the souls of their dead in like circumstances . . . we shall find that . . . they have more love for one another . . . than we who call ourselves better. If it comes to giving alms on behalf of the living or the dead, we . . . do it with . . . grief and reluctance . . . as though it were tearing [our] bowels out.[54]

Brébeuf witnessed the Huron treatment of their dead a decade later. After observing relatives cleaning corpses "swarming with worms," without apparent revulsion, he compared the Huron to Europeans who refused to tend to the sick in the horrific hospitals of the time. "Is not that a noble example to inspire Christians, who ought to have thoughts much more elevated to acts of charity and works of mercy toward their neighbor? After that, who will be afraid of the stench of a Hospital?"[55] The Huron, in Brébeuf's view, treated their dead, even if corrupted and rotting, far better than Europeans treated their sick.

The Huron believed that when the Feast of the Dead concluded, the *atisken* began its journey to the Village of the Dead, where it rejoined the

A European Artist's Fanciful Depiction, Complete with Articulated Skeletons, of the Huron Feast of the Dead. From Joseph François Lafitau, *Moeurs des sauvages ameriquains comparées aux moeurs des premiers temps* (Paris, 1724). Courtesy of the National Library and National Archives of Canada.

esken. Here the soul would reunite and become whole again. Not all *atiskens* made the trip. Much like their earthly bodies, the *atiskens* of the very elderly and of very young children were thought to be physically incapable of making the journey. These souls would establish a village of their own on the site of the former Village of the Living.[56] Nor did all of the *atisken* who began the trip west reach the Village of the Dead. Oscotarach waylaid many of them and removed their brains; these unfortunate souls wandered about, brainless and heedless. Many Hurons believed that Oscotarach removed the brains of the dead so that the dead would not think about returning to the living; in effect, he served as a barrier between the worlds of the living and the dead and safeguarded the two worlds from each other.[57] Other souls failed in their efforts to cross the rivers on their way to the Village of the Dead. They fell in the water and drowned.[58]

In many respects, the afterlife in the Village of the Dead resembled life among the living. There, souls participated in many of the same activities as they did in life. Souls slept during the day and at night hunted "the souls of Beavers, Porcupines, Moose, and other animals using the soul of the snowshoes to walk upon the soul of the snow."[59]

The supernatural and the points at which it merged with the natural world formed the parameters of precontact Iroquoian spiritual thought. To a large degree, it would continue to shape the way that the Huron and the Iroquois thought during their initial contacts with Europeans. Both peoples would see their thought worlds altered, but in ways that would have differing consequences for both of them. Christianity would take hold among many Huron and would create friction within Huron villages—indeed, villages would, in time, become wholly Christian or wholly traditionalist—and it would cause divisions within clans as well. But among the Iroquois, Christianity made no headway. The Dutch were not serious about converting them, and those Jesuits who did go among the Iroquois before 1650 were fortunate to escape with their lives.[60] Yet while the Five Nations did not accept Christianity, they did become enamored of many facets of European technology. They began to see many of these forms of technology—especially firearms—as the tools that they would use to remake their world and, even though they did not know it, that of the Huron as well.

4

THE JESUIT ASSAULT OF THE HURON THOUGHT WORLD

ONE DAY IN FEBRUARY 1636, IN A CHAPEL IN THE FRENCH colony of Quebec, a Jesuit priest overheard a conversation between a woman and her spouse. The woman expressed concern for their son: "I do not know what ails our little François Olivier; when he is dressed in the French way he laughs all the time, when he is dressed in our way he cries and grieves; when I hold him he is sad and mournful, and when a French woman holds him he acts as if he wants to jump all the time."[1] Despite his French name, little François Olivier was of Huron parentage. Doubtless, the Jesuit who overheard and recorded this exchange found it to be music to his ears, for in a small way it signified a victory in the contest between Huron and European cultures. To the Jesuit who eavesdropped on the Huron couple, it appeared that European culture had won out.

This report of one small battle between French and Huron cultures appeared in *The Jesuit Relations.* The *Relations* had a dual purpose. In one sense, it served as propaganda, informing Catholic France of the successes of the Jesuit fathers among the "savages" of the New World. In another, the Society of Jesus—which had been organized along military lines—viewed the *Relations* as a collection of intelligence that would assist future missionaries in New France.[2] Collecting this intelligence, however, was not as easy as it seemed. While the Jesuits reported on what they saw and heard, their cultural constructs constrained—as perhaps they did in the case of little François Olivier—their understanding of what they witnessed. Another obstacle, albeit frequently unrecognized, was that the Huron sometimes told the Jesuits what they believed the fathers wanted to hear. The Jesuits, more than any other entity, launched the assault on the Iroquoian thought world during the first half of the seventeenth century.[3]

"Thought world" is a term that, to my knowledge, originated with Calvin Martin. While Martin did not provide a definition, the concept encompasses a culture's logic, ontology, epistemology, and values. However, it can be defined as a culturally adapted mode of thought. To a large degree, all of us are the products of the culture into which we are born and which surrounds and shapes the way we view and construct the world as we mature. As a result, our mode of thought is very much a cultural construct. Seventeenth-century Puritan clergy and many, if not most, of the members of their congregations conceived the world about them in spiritual terms.[4] Eighteenth-century Virginia planters viewed the world primarily in secular terms, and—though they periodically seemed to feel a sort of self-loathing over this—in a materialistic vein.[5] As twenty-first-century Americans, we think primarily—albeit often unconsciously—in secular and technological terms because our culture has conditioned us to do so. The thought world, and its junction to the external physical world, often manifests itself through the manipulation of the surrounding environment and the ways that other humans are dealt with. Technology, in contemporary American culture, is an extraordinarily important conduit to the thought world as well as the means that enables the thought world to be expressed externally. One can, for example, imagine the transformation of a forest into a field. But one thinks of the process of that transformation much differently if one lives in a culture where the creation of the field is accomplished by chopping down each individual tree with a stone ax, rather than knocking them all down at once with a bulldozer.

Cultural conditioning influenced the thought worlds of both seventeenth-century Iroquoian peoples and the missionaries whom they encountered. Both groups perceived the world in spiritual, rather than secular, terms. However, each group's mode of spirituality differed greatly from that of the other. The thought worlds of both groups, however, were in a state of flux. For Iroquoian peoples, European technology and religion contributed to a process that created new, altered thought worlds. The missionaries, especially the Jesuits, because of their scholarly interest in science, represented a European thought world that also began to change. In Europe, the Enlightenment began a process in which the secular overtook the spiritual as the primary mode in which the European thought world operated.[6]

In their attempts to convert the Native peoples of North America, the Recollects and the Jesuits adopted opposing strategies. Believing the Catholic faith to be beyond the comprehension of "savages," the Recollects favored a process of first "civilizing" the Huron and other peoples and converting them later. The Jesuits, by contrast, focused their efforts on conversion of the Huron and other Native peoples, believing that the process of "civilizing" would inevitably follow.[7] Limited by their small numbers and their philosophy of "civilization first," the Recollects converted few Native peoples. In 1632, Louis XIII's chief minister, Cardinal Richelieu, and the Royal Council expelled the Recollects from New France because of their lack of progress. The Jesuits, with their more realistic approach to Native conversion and their prior experience in attempting to convert non-European peoples in Asia, had a free hand in Canada for the next four decades.[8] By 1650—less than two decades after the Recollects left—the success of the Jesuits had grave consequences for the Huron. Christianity and the resulting alteration of the Huron thought world split their nation from within and contributed greatly to their destruction and dispersal from without by the Iroquois.[9]

The Jesuits adopted several tactics that they hoped would facilitate conversion. One way to maximize the effect of their efforts was to separate newly won converts from their "pagan" tribe members. Jesuits encouraged converts to move to other villages with large Christian populations.[10] Obviously, the missionaries had great difficulty in convincing many Huron to take this route to conversion, but it served to make their successes, albeit modest, more complete and helped plant seeds of doubt into the Iroquoian ethos. It also separated converts or soon-to-be converts from those who would challenge their new faith.

Jesuits often linked Christianity to European technologies and introduced the notion that a superior culture postulated a greater and more accurate truth concerning the afterlife. Christian missionaries—and it is obvious which culture they considered superior—caused many Huron, once they accepted the idea of a superior culture, to begin questioning their own culture.

While in the mind of Jesuit missionaries there existed a set criteria that they equated with "complete" conversion, in the mind of the Huron convert these criteria, while taking their cue from Jesuit expectations, were wholly different. For the Huron, to convert completely—in Jesuit terms—meant to forsake all that they knew and to deny a cosmology that provided order to their understanding of the world. Indeed, cosmology was the foundation of the Iroquoian thought world; it provided the explanation for their existence.[11] While aspects of Jesuit teaching may have been impressive to Hurons, the expectation that converts must accept a faith that was in many ways alien to their existing thought world raises questions as to the quality of many conversions.[12]

In order to effectively convert Iroquoian peoples, the Jesuits realized that they needed to attack their religious beliefs, which formed the central element of their thought world. The Jesuits decided not to attack Huron culture, but they failed to recognize, at least at first, that Iroquoian culture and spiritual beliefs were so inexorably linked that an attack on one constituted an attack on the other. This made the adoption by Iroquoian peoples of what the Jesuits regarded as acceptable religious mores more difficult.

Iroquoian languages presented a major obstacle for the Jesuits. French missionaries had to invent Native equivalents for "Glory, Trinity, Holy Spirit, Angels, Resurrection, Paradise, Hell, Church, Faith, Hope and Charity, and a multitude of others."[13] Missionaries also learned that the terms "father" and "mother"—so important to the transmission of Catholic ideas—could not be said in the presence of a Huron whose parents had passed away. Father François Le Mercer wrote that "the mere word 'father' or 'mother' puts them into a passion."[14] Gabriel Sagard noted that if the terms "father" and "mother" were spoken in the presence of a Huron, "they easily get exasperated and lose patience out of irritation and anger caused by the recollection being brought to them, and in fact they could handle roughly whoever approached them with it."[15] Jean de Brébeuf reported that one woman "almost lost her desire to be baptized because the command, *Thou shalt honor thy Father and thy Mother,* had been inadvertently quoted to her."[16]

The idea of sin also defied translation. The nearest Iroquoian equivalent was the word *peche,* which meant "mistaking one matter for another." This fell far short of the idea that the Jesuits wished to communicate, that sins were offenses against God.[17] In Iroquoian thought, standards of right and wrong existed. Offenses could be committed against another person or even against an *atisken*; but the Christian notion of sin, the idea one could commit a wrong against a supposedly omnipotent being, defied Native peoples' logic. An omnipotent being, they reasoned, could prevent wrongs from occurring in the first place.

Perhaps the most significant impact Christianity had on Iroquoian thought concerned the ideas of the relationship between the living and the dead. Whereas Christians drew a sharp distinction between the two, Iroquoian peoples conceived of the living and the dead, in both a physical and spiritual sense, as being part of a single, shared, yet segregated community. In the process of bringing Christianity to the Huron, the Jesuits not only divided this shared community, they also split families apart and indeed fractured the Huron confederacy along religious lines.

Unlike Europeans, who drew clear divisions that delimited the secular and the sacred in everyday life, all things and all activities in the world of a Huron had some sort of spiritual significance.[18] In a sense, this made the task of Christian missionaries more difficult, since conversion meant that a Huron would have to change nearly every aspect of his or her life. In cultures where clear boundaries exist between the temporal and the divine, the act of conversion can be limited to altering one aspect of the life of the converted. But the Huron had a more holistic view of the world; everything, in some way, had a connection to all other things. Therefore, conversion to Christianity meant that all facets of a Huron person's life changed.

Or perhaps not. Hurons seemed to have adopted several strategies in response to Jesuit efforts to convert them. One option that some Hurons chose was to ignore the Black Robes and their efforts to convert them. Many Huron seem to have opted for a sort of halfway approach. One converted but did not give up all of his or her Native beliefs, regardless of what the fathers said. This approach, which seems to have been the most common, led to the creation of a syncretic form of Christianity.

One example of how the Huron could easily sway back and forth between Native and Christian beliefs occurred when a Huron captain fell ill. Near death, he received instruction and baptism from the Jesuits. The man quickly regained his health and "never wearied recounting what had occurred, and that he owed his life entirely to the baptism he had received." But the captain then forsook his new-found faith when he saw that "as a result of his profession of Christianity, he would have to leave certain diabolical fraternities, of which he was the chief, and also the function and duties of the ministry of Satan."[19]

The Jesuits' presence also encouraged the development of traditionalist factions in Huron villages. Using alcohol or the Ononhouaroia (the turning over of the brain) as camouflage, traditionalists often attacked Huron converts.[20] They also disseminated anti-Christian rumors and accused the Jesuits of spreading disease among them. In addition, they attacked writing, which many Native peoples regarded as a powerful form of magic. Traditionalists argued that writing was the primary means by which the Jesuits spread disease and killed Native peoples.

Another response was to convert to Christianity completely and to forsake all of one's former beliefs. Those who chose the route of conversion heeded Jesuit demands that they throw away all of their good luck charms and not attend traditionalist ceremonies or "eat all feasts." This presented great difficulties to the individual who converted. Not participating in feasts and ceremonies cut off the convert from many in his or her society. A Huron male who converted may have had to forsake all but his first wife, and unhappy spouses could no longer separate. Huron warriors who converted could not contemplate revenge killings without a great deal of soul searching.

When the Jesuits arrived in Huronia, a large part of their attempts to convert the Huron included destroying Huron religious beliefs.[21] Perhaps the most effective missionaries in the New World, Jesuits received training in rhetoric, logic, and linguistics. A Native person who verbally defended his or her spiritual beliefs found a Jesuit to be formidable adversary.[22] Lacking the organized theological basis of Christianity, American Indians often had difficulty responding to the Jesuits' arguments. By the same token, the Jesuits' familiarity with the Christian philosophers made it possible for them, usually, to respond quickly to questions from Native peoples. When asked questions such as the whereabouts of God before the creation of the world, Jesuits had ready answers—at least according to their *Relations*—derived from their study of Augustinian and Thomistic philosophy.[23]

The Jesuits' training in logic seems to have given them little help in Canada, primarily because like most Europeans (and most people for that matter), they wore a set of cultural blinders. They, like the Iroquois, were mentally locked in to their own thought world, and this made it difficult for them to fully understand the peoples that they ministered to in North America. They tended to ignore the framework of Iroquoian cognition. Just as the Iroquois and the Huron were the products of a thought world that framed a particular mode of thinking, so, too, were the Jesuits. Given the ethnocentrism of both the Jesuits and the Iroquoians, differences in spiritual beliefs were not easily resolved.

Iroquoians also had great difficulty with Christian ideas about the nature of the physical universe. Most Iroquoians believed that souls and the afterlife obeyed the same physical laws as living beings. The Jesuits, who regarded themselves as the representatives of a rational culture, preached to native peoples about an unseen supernatural world where the physical laws of the seen world did not apply. The idea of an unseen supernatural world presented no difficulty for the Huron, but they regarded the unseen and supernatural world to be much like the visible world and thought that it followed the same physical laws. Because of this difference in beliefs, Jesuits fielded questions and concerns from converts and potential converts such as, how could people get to heaven if their legs were too weak to make the journey? And, once there, what is to keep them from falling? In much the same way that the Jesuits' questioned the Huron's knowledge of the Village of the Dead, the Huron asked the Jesuits how they knew of heaven or hell. The Jesuits, the Huron pointed out, had never been to either place, nor they did they know anyone who had been and returned to tell them of it.[24]

In bringing the Christian message to Iroquoian peoples, the Jesuits found that they could use the apparent magic of European technologies such as magnets, compasses, and magnifying glasses could awe their native audience. It could also make the Jesuits appear to be the most powerful sorcerers. Using almanacs, they predicted eclipses of the sun and the moon, making it seem as if they had power over celestial phenomena.[25] When Montagnais hunters poked fun at his inability to speak their language properly, Father Paul le Jeune shocked them into silence when he produced a compass and told them that it enabled him to know the shape of the earth and where the sun went at night.[26] A Huron made the analogy that a predicted eclipse of the moon by a Jesuit confirmed "what we [the Jesuits] taught . . . the future resurrection will one day prove just as true as what we had predicted to them of this eclipse."[27] Demonstrations of this sort of power by the Jesuits gave native converts a potent weapon in their arguments with traditionalists. Converts pointed to the Jesuits' celestial knowledge and European metal technology as evidence of a superior religion. One convert pointed out to other Huron that

> the matters of your salvation that the French propose to you are new things, and customs of their own which will overthrow ours. You tell them that every country has its own ways of doing things; that, as you do not urge them to adopt ours, so you are surprised at their urging us to adopt theirs in this matter, and to acknowledge with them the same Creator of Heaven and Earth and the universal Lord of all things. I ask you, when at first you saw their hatchets and kettles, after having discovered that they were incomparably better and more convenient than our stone hatchets and our wooden and earthen vessels, did you reject their hatchets and kettles, because they were new things in your country?[28]

Using the superiority of European technology and trade goods as the basis of his argument, this convert made the analogy that the religion of the French, while new, must also be superior to their own. European metal goods were vastly superior—they were sharper, more durable, and more portable—to the clay, stone, and wood goods made by Native peoples. It seemed reasonable to assume that European religion and magic would be superior as well.

Writing, which Iroquoian peoples regarded as a form of extremely powerful magic, undermined the Iroquoian thought world far more than any other form of European technology. While guns could injure their bodies and axes and kettles would enable them to more fully exploit their environment, writing attacked the notions of truth based on the memory of oral traditions that undergirded Iroquoian societies.

But Iroquoians also regarded writing as an astonishing form of witchcraft that permitted one to read the thoughts of others over vast distances. Disturbed by the ability of the French to read each other's minds at a distance, some Huron believed them to be "devils, not men."[29] French lawyer and historian Marc Lescarbot noted that "the savages most wondered at, to see by a piece of paper I make known my will from one end of the world to the other; and they thought there was enchantment in the paper."[30] Gabriel Sagard stated that native peoples "filled with wonder at writing, by means of which one can be understood though absent." Perhaps hoping that they could learn or somehow acquire this power for themselves, "they liked to hold our books . . . and admired the pictures and letters . . . [and counted] the pages."[31] Indeed, Sagard noted that Native peoples liked to handle the books, particularly the Bible, so much that the books "were reduced to tatters."[32] Especially disconcerting to Iroquoian peoples was the ability of the missionaries to read the thoughts of individuals who were long dead.[33]

The Abenaki received an early demonstration of the power of writing. An early Jesuit recorded a tale, told to him by an Abenaki, of a Basque who, offended by the Abenaki's smell, told them to go away. When they refused, he threatened them by saying that he would write their names on a piece of paper and that they would all die. Shortly afterward, an epidemic broke out among the Abenaki, causing them to give credence to this story.[34] Such events were stunning proof to Native peoples that writing gave the French powers far beyond their own. In the interconnected Northeast, such accounts were passed from tribe to tribe in the course of trade and warfare. It is likely that the Huron heard this Abenaki tale.

Like many oral cultures, Iroquoian peoples valued the spoken word. They frequently exercised a "great prudence and moderation of speech."[35] In a society that relied on oral communication, a Huron had to consider his or her words carefully; once spoken, they could not be retrieved.[36] Iroquoian peoples also observed certain protocols regarding speaking and listening. One did not interrupt a speaker and did not ask a second question until the first one had been answered.[37] Nor did one speak hurriedly. If a person brought news from a trip, other people, "knowing that he brings news . . . sit down near him; yet no one says a word to him,—for, as he came for the purpose of talking, it is for him to begin."[38] Nor did the Huron speak unnecessarily. Paul Le Jeune noted that when a man returned from the hunt, he left his kill outside and would eat and warm himself before informing the other occupants of the lodge that he had left beavers or porcupines outside. "This indifference astonished me . . . but they told me rightly that one ought not to weary a man who has more need of rest than words."[39] Native peoples also stressed listening, the other essential skill in an oral culture. Before a meeting with Christian converts, a Huron captain instructed Le Jeune on how to listen: "Be wise, Father Le Jeune, keep quiet; let not thy mind wander, that thou mayest not lose a word of what I am about to say."[40]

Ironically, the Jesuits' oral skills and training in rhetoric helped them undermine the Huron's faith in the spoken word. Native cultures, since they were also oral cultures, held those who excelled at public speaking in high regard. Many Huron admired the Jesuits' public-speaking ability and their grasp of the native peoples' use of metaphor. Ironically, the Jesuits often used their oratory to impress upon the Huron the superiority of the written word.[41]

The most telling blow that writing inflicted on the traditional Huron thought world was its challenging of existing notions of truth. The Jesuits frequently pointed out to native peoples that the spoken word was never said the same way twice. They contrasted this to a word on the printed page that could never be changed and could be copied numerous times so that the words on the page would never be lost. Equally important, the Jesuits argued that if that which is printed could never be altered, then it must be more "true" than that which is spoken. As the Jesuits frequently pointed out, the devil could easily change what one remembered as being spoken.[42] "The art of inscribing upon paper matters that are beyond sight," the expression of thoughts and ideas in writing, also impressed Native peoples. The Huron found the consistency of the written message equally impressive. "They are astonished that the same things are told them at Kebec as we preach here."[43] Writing, in the eyes of Native peoples, also gave the Jesuits a measure of credibility. "[It causes] . . . them to see through this means that those who have preceded us . . . have been able to impart to us a knowledge and assurance of what we have been preaching to them, while they can have no proof that what their fathers have taught them was not invented by them."[44]

As early as 1637, writing began to break down Native peoples' faith in their oral traditions. A Jesuit overheard one man question the veracity of oral traditions: "If our ancestors had known how to write, they would have left us great books filled with fables and falsehoods."[45] As early as the mid-1640s, some Hurons began to equate writing with truth. A Christian convert interrupted—that in itself being a breech of Huron rules of civility—a recitation of the Huron creation myth:

> Thou tellest only fables, which have no foundation but lies. . . . Where are the writings which give us faith in what thou sayest? If each one is permitted to invent what he will, is it strange that we know nothing true, since we must acknowledge that the Hurons have been liars from all time? . . . the French . . . preserve from all antiquity the Sacred books, wherein the word of God himself is written, without permission to any one to alter it the least.[46]

Clearly, the introduction of writing challenged existing notions of truth and caused some Hurons to question the value of the spoken word. The man who interrupted the telling of the creation myth made it clear that he no longer could accept the veracity of the spoken word.

Writing introduced another element that altered the Iroquoian thought world. Whereas the dream had been the primary source of a priori knowledge in precontact times, the book, and its apparent magic, now rivaled the dream as a source of knowledge. Traditionalists regarded the book as an imperfect source of a priori knowledge because, unlike the dream, the individual—unless he or she learned to read, which very few Iroquoians did—could not experience it directly. Knowledge derived from writing had to pass through the Jesuits, who in the minds of traditionalists were, at best, suspect.

While writing was a formidable weapon in the Jesuits' arsenal, Iroquoian peoples found the Jesuits' use of formal logic less impressive. The Jesuits' education did not always give them the upper hand in theological disputations with Native peoples. Often, Native peoples simply terminated these arguments by questioning the Jesuits' intelligence, saying, "thou hast no sense." In most Native societies, confrontations and insults were avoided when possible. One may debate, and disagree, but once consensus had been reached, debate ended. The tenacity of Jesuits in their arguments and their use of face-to-face confrontation, something avoided in close-knit Native societies, was unexpected and often had unintended consequences.[47]

One consequence was that while the Jesuits saw themselves as men of God, Native peoples, perhaps because of what they regarded as the Jesuits' rudeness in debate, often perceived them in other ways. When visiting one of the more distant Huron villages, Father Jerome Lalemant noted that "the name of Echon (which the Savages have given at all times to Father de Brebeuf) resounded on all sides, as that of one of the most famous sorcerers or demons that had ever been imagined." Indeed, the Huron held Brébeuf's name "in such abhorrence that it was used for terrifying the children."[48] Epidemics of European diseases, which the Jesuits survived but which carried off American Indians in droves, also led the Huron to accuse the Jesuits of witchcraft.[49]

Nor did Native peoples accept the Christian concept that the souls of the dead went to a place that rewarded or punished them for their conduct in life. While Native peoples feared death, they saw the next life as similar to this one. The idea that good and bad places existed for the dead, totally unlike earth, did not fit Iroquoian notions of the universe. Iroquoian peoples derived their conceptions of the afterlife from what they observed in everyday life; the notion of heaven or hell made no sense. Hell, they reasoned, could not exist, "because . . . there could be no fire where there was no wood; . . . what forests could sustain so many fires through such a long space of time?" One Jesuit refuted this "absurd reasoning" by producing a piece of sulfur and asserting that it was "a piece of this land of Avernus . . . that it burned by itself." After several Indians examined the sulfur and concluded that it was of the earth, the priest placed some of it on some live coals. Amazed to see it burn, the Native peoples, according to the Jesuit who recorded the scene, "believed in the word of God that there is a lower world."[50]

The exposure of the Huron to Jesuit teachings did lead to many conversions, but many times the results were not what the Jesuits had in mind. The Jesuits expected to make the Huron, if not into Frenchmen, at least into good Christians. But instead, many Huron blended their own religious beliefs with Christianity. The result was a syncretic form of worship, one that used the language of Christianity while keeping many traditional forms. Just as the Huron had believed that the dead appeared to them in their dreams and described the afterlife to them, they now believed the dead came to them to provide information about heaven. A dying woman had a dream in which she went to heaven and saw many "wonderfully beautiful" Frenchmen and her sister and uncle. Her uncle told her to go back and ask Father Brébeuf for a bracelet. The woman related the dream upon waking, then "lost consciousness and died."[51] Huron reports of heaven, however, did not always agree with Jesuit teachings. One man said he saw nothing that the fathers had described, but he met many of his relations there, and they wished to celebrate his arrival with very un-Christian-like dances and feasts.[52] In a way, this man may have presented the Jesuits with an example of religious syncretism taken to its farthest extreme. He visited the place that is the ultimate goal of every Christian, yet he saw nothing there that could be considered Christian. Instead, his relatives offered to fete him with the very practices that the Jesuits railed against.

Some Native peoples began incorporating elements of Christianity into their efforts to cover all of the possibilities concerning the eventual destination of their soul. Some Huron "did not hesitate to tell us that they were the best Christians in the world . . ." yet the Jesuits often saw these same people as "complete turncoats, addressing their vows and making their offerings to all the sorcerers of the country. . . . They . . . have recourse to demons."[53] Other Hurons, while they may not have truly desired to become Christians, went through the motions of conversion anyway in the belief that baptism would give them long life and protect their children from disease.[54]

The Jesuits had trouble combating the Native peoples' belief that the soul could decide, after death, where it wanted to spend eternity. For the Huron, both the *esken* and the *atisken,* once they could venture far from their physical remains, could go anywhere they wanted within the context of the afterlife. To Christians and Muslims, the primary importance of life on earth is that one must do those things that are necessary to get to heaven or paradise. Iroquoian peoples regarded life as important; but this life was no more important than the next one. They assumed that salvation—of the Christian sort—could be done retroactively after death. Brébeuf told of an old man who fell sick. When Brébeuf pressed him to convert, the old man dismissed him, saying that he would go where his ancestors were. Some days afterward, the old man recovered from his sickness and approached Brébeuf, saying, "Rejoice . . . for I have returned from the country of souls, and I have found none there any longer; they have all gone to heaven."[55]

When another Jesuit pressed a dying women to consent to baptism, her sister intervened and confronted him: "My brother . . . thou hast no sense; it is not yet time—she will decide upon that when she is dead."[56] This woman argued, in effect, for the Huron belief that the destination of the soul could only be determined by the soul, since it was a free agent, and not by the living.

Many Huron objected to the idea of going to heaven because their friends and relatives would not be there, and they feared that it would be filled with Frenchmen. One Huron on his deathbed told the Jesuits that "I have no desire to go to heaven; I have no acquaintances there, and the French that are there would not care to give me anything to eat." Another Huron refused to hear talk of either heaven or hell; he resolved to go wherever his relatives were.[57]

Over time, as Jesuits made inroads into Iroquoian society, Christian beliefs began to undermine traditional Iroquoian ones. One prominent example was the practice of Christians asking God for success in the hunt.

A Huron young man lost in the woods prayed for a moose to kill. When he successfully bagged a moose, "he knelt . . . [and] thanked his benefactor." One Native person made a present of a bear he killed to the Jesuits, explaining that "this animal does not belong to me, for God made me kill it, not through my own merits, but in virtue of the prayers made by the French; so it is to them it belongs, and not to me."[58] Attributing success in the hunt to the Christian God irritated traditional Hurons. Christians ceased the precontact practice of thanking the *oki,* or soul of a slain animal. Instead, they gave thanks to God for giving them the animal to slay. Traditionalists believed that success in the hunt should be attributed to the animal for allowing itself to be taken. To ensure continued success in the hunt, traditionalists burned the bones of the animal and never gave them to dogs. If they did, the Huron believed that the soul of the animal would report this mistreatment to living animals, who would then make themselves difficult to catch.[59] Christian converts began ignoring these practices, much to the dismay of traditionalists.[60]

Another significant change among Hurons who accepted some Christian beliefs was that Oscotarach, the spirit who extracted the brains from the *atiskens* as they walked to the Village of the Dead, now assumed something of a quasi-Christian identity. Traditionally, the Huron did not believe Oscotarach to be either good or evil. They simply regarded his presence along the path that the dead walked as a fact. They also realized that he was necessary, for if he did not remove the brains of the dead, they could remember their lives and try to return to them. In a way, Oscotarach safeguarded the worlds of the dead and the living by keeping them away from each other. After the introduction of Christianity, however, many Iroquoian peoples identified him as the personification of the devil, who now not only robbed the dead of their brains but also ate them.[61]

The adoption of Christianity by Huron converts also affected the traditional conception of a shared community of the living and the dead. Christian converts began to demand that they be buried only in consecrated ground, in cemeteries separate from their traditionalist tribe members. Splits along religious lines carried over from the world of the living to the world of the dead. Yet just as some traditional beliefs faded, other sincerity beliefs flourished. They required some negotiation with the Jesuits. A man whose niece died asked that she be buried in the French way. "Make a big grave, for my brother . . . wishes to place with her little belongings." The native peoples wanted to include two of the girl's favorite dogs among her grave goods. The Jesuits refused to bury the dogs in the French cemetery, but they did permit the girl's family to inter the animals near the graveyard.[62] When the Jesuits buried a young boy, they told his relatives that they would inter the grave bundles with him but that the soul had no use for the items contained therein. The relatives replied that "we believe so, too; but we remove them from our sight what would cause our grief, recalling to us the dead."[63] It is likely that these families, like many other Huron, practiced a mix of traditional and Christian beliefs. They wanted Christian burials for their children, but harking to older Huron traditions, they wanted to ensure that their children had all the material goods they would need in the afterlife.

Syncretic beliefs developed regarding beliefs other than burials. A new convert surprised one of the fathers when he refused to confess his sins; he claimed that he had never committed any. Another Huron dumbfounded the Jesuits with the observation that "it seems . . . that God does not love us; he gives us commandments that we cannot keep."[64] Some Hurons, like this man, saw the Ten Commandments as a catch. Many Huron viewed them as so difficult to keep that one would invariably fail and be sent to hell. In the mind of Iroquoian peoples, believing in the Christian God opened the gates of hell as well as heaven. But if individuals did not accept Christianity, then hell, and heaven for that matter, did not apply to them. They could simply choose to go to the Village of the Dead instead. Other Huron converts had trouble with the idea of eternal punishment. One convert told the Jesuits: "I can see very well that there is a GOD, but I cannot endure that he should punish us for our crimes."[65]

Traditionalists mounted numerous efforts to undermine the Jesuits. Several rumors circulated in Huronia that shook the faith of many native converts and interfered with the Jesuits' efforts to convert others. Some Huron claimed they met a convert who had died and returned to life. She warned them not to believe the Jesuits and that the souls of the French amused themselves by torturing the souls of the Huron. Upon reaching heaven, she said, "the French . . . welcomed [her soul] . . . with firebrands and burning torches, with cruelties inconceivable . . . the French . . . cross the seas, and come into these regions . . . in the hope of bringing back some captive." Another man claimed to have died and met two Englishwomen who told him that the Jesuits had come to Canada to kill all the Native peoples. Yet another man claimed that Yoscaha, the son of Aataentsic, appeared to him while he was fishing and told him that "I am the one the French wrongly call Jesus, but they do not know me . . . the strangers [Jesuits] travel throughout the country . . . spreading the disease everywhere. . . . You can prevent this misfortune; drive out from your village the . . . black gowns."[66]

Traditionalists also attacked the Jesuits' most impressive form of magic, writing, by linking it to disease. After Huron traditionalists claimed that the missionaries "made them perish by . . . spells, which are shut up in . . . inkstands, [and] in . . . books," one Jesuit reported "we dared not, without hiding ourselves, open a book or write anything." Other traditionalists claimed "that they had seen the black gowns in a dream . . . unfolding certain books, whence issued sparks of fire everywhere, and no doubt caused this pestilential disease."[67]

By using the baffling eruption of previously unknown diseases to attack the Jesuits, traditionalists appealed to the evidence of Iroquoian peoples' own experiences. Like nearly every group of Native Americans, Iroquoian peoples sustained a substantial loss in population because of European diseases. The correlation between mortality and the presence of Europeans did not escape their notice. At nearly every opportunity, Native peoples used the increased mortality in their arguments against the Jesuits. When one of the Jesuits' Native foes learned that more Hospital Sisters and Ursulines would soon arrive in Canada, he commented bitterly that the Jesuits taught "that the first woman . . . brought death into the world; what they say is true,—the women of their land are capable of such wickedness, and that is why they bring them into these countries—to make us all lose our lives. If the few they have already brought here have killed so many, those whom they expect will destroy all that remain."[68]

Many Huron traditionalists argued that accepting the missionaries' teachings equaled certain death, "believing [in Christianity] and dying were one and the same thing for them." One mother, after her eldest son died following baptism, berated the Jesuits when they attempted to baptize her remaining children.[69]

While traditionalists still interred their dead in cemeteries that adjoined their villages, Christian cemeteries tended to be placed next to Jesuit missions. Frequently, however, Jesuits located their missions within Iroquoian villages. This created uneasiness among traditionalists, who felt that having a cemetery in the midst of the living made it easier for the dead to walk among them at night and to remain undiscovered in their houses. The placement of cemeteries reveals a conflict in European and American Indian constructs of secular and sacred space. Traditionalist Hurons deemed it important that the shared community remain segregated, that the living and the dead coexist yet remain apart. The Christian construct of sacred and secular space, through the act of consecration, allowed the placement of the dead within the midst of the living. Christians believed, unlike traditionalist Hurons, that the dead were in either heaven or hell and could not walk among them.

The placement of cemeteries sometimes led to conflict within Native communities. When the Jesuits in the village of St. Joseph erected a large cross in the Christian burial ground, most of the inhabitants of the village "threw stones at the cross and covered it with filth." They stopped when a convert rebuked them by reminding them of their traditional honoring of the dead. "Dead bodies are sacred things; and even among you infidels they are shown respect, and one commits a crime if he touch a paddle suspended to a sepulchre."[70]

Christian converts further dismantled the linkage between the living and the dead when they began refusing to allow the remains of their dead to be disinterred and mingled with those of other Hurons during the Feast of the Dead. As early as 1636, entire villages of Christian converts refused to participate in the feast. In a 1642 meeting, Native Christians made several resolutions articulating their position, telling the Jesuits that they would "inform our Relatives who are not of the same Faith as we, even if they be our fathers and our children, that we do not wish our bones to be mingled together after our death, since our Souls will be eternally separated, and our affection will not continue beyond this life."[71]

In effect, these Huron contemplated more than the splitting of the communities of the living and the dead. Relatives would no longer provide for or feed the dead. Nor would the dead be mingled together in an ossuary. They would now go into single, lonely graves, cut off from their fellow Hurons for all time. The Village of the Dead would also be less populated. One could go there after death, but until deceased people arrived, they would not know if they would find their loved ones there. These Huron were, in a larger sense, contemplating the separation of the natural and supernatural worlds.

Within the natural world, the impact of Christianity was obvious. Christian influences tore at Huron communities from within. Traditionalist spouses separated from their partners who converted to Christianity. One neophyte told his spouse that if she did not convert, "he would banish her from his side, and would marry a Christian." The spurned wife demonstrated her thoughts concerning divorce by attacking her husband with a knife. Fortunately for him, his robe suffered the brunt of her assault. In another instance, a woman who converted to Christianity, upon hearing that her traditionalist former husband planned to visit her, "took refuge in a corner of her cabin and armed herself with a knife, being resolved to kill him if he approached her." Another Huron convert found himself "abandoned by his wife and children."[72]

Traditionalist warriors refused to fight alongside Christians. Traditionalist and Christian Hurons began going to war separately, with the result that they sometimes did not have sufficient numbers during battle.[73] Many traditionalist Huron claimed that Christianity made men into women, by making them timid and cowardly, and that they used prayer in the place of courage.[74] When traditionalist Huron consulted a conjurer before a battle, the Christians among the group refused to participate in the fight.[75] Many Christians, because of their newfound faith, refused to take up arms anymore at all.

Jesuits witnessed how the faith they brought to Native communities split them apart and altered the thought world of Native peoples. Some Jesuits rationalized it as the will of God. Hierosme Lalemant, in the 1642 *Relations,* noted that "faith is a sword that severs the Soul from the body, and children from their fathers."[76] Indeed, the new faith had severed traditional Huron notions of community. Many of the living no longer attended to the needs of the *atiskens.* Christianity dissolved the shared community of the living and the dead, and many Huron rejected the notion that truth could be contained within an oral tradition. A Huron Christian, returning presents to a traditionalist perhaps because he thought Satan inspired the giving of them, said it best: "There is no bond of friendship that Faith will not sever, rather than see us separated from GOD."[77]

5

ALCOHOL AND THE SUPERNATURAL

ONE DAY IN THE LATE AUTUMN OF 1636, FRANÇOIS Gand, one of the Hundred Associates, the fur-trading company licensed by the French Crown to conduct business in Canada, pondered the problem of intemperance among the company's Native trading partners. In the eyes of the Hundred Associates, the Native peoples' excessive consumption of alcohol, and the violence that often accompanied it, hindered the expansion of the fur trade. While the company did sell alcohol to Native peoples, it restricted the amounts and types of spirits that their trading posts exchanged for animal pelts. Gand and his partners knew that other fur traders—individuals not affiliated with the company—often traded alcohol illegally to Native peoples. Gand took it upon himself to lecture a group of Hurons on the benefits of temperance and to announce a new ordinance that, with their help, would hopefully restrict the liquor trade. Using the supposed lethality of alcohol as the main thrust of his argument, Gand told his audience that liquor was killing them in great numbers. Telling them "death was so common among them they must ascribe it to these drinks, which they not know how to use in moderation," Gand encouraged the Huron to turn in Frenchmen who gave them alcohol.[1]

A few Hurons in Monsieur Gand's audience brushed aside his warnings concerning alcohol, retorting that "it is not these drinks that take away our lives, but your writings; for since you have described our country, our rivers, our lands, and our woods, we are all dying, which did not happen until you came here." The Jesuit Paul Le Jeune quickly attempted to remove the onus from writing and to place it back on alcohol by responding that "we described the whole world . . . our own country, that of the Hurons, of the Hiroquois, in short, the whole earth; and yet they did not die elsewhere as they did in their country. It must be, then, that their deaths arose from other causes."[2] Many Huron believed that alcohol had supernatural qualities, and it was not necessarily considered bad. Writing, however, because of its similarities to witchcraft, had the possibility of being used for evil.[3]

But other Hurons thought Gand had a point, and they asked him, "Why dost thou not write to thy great King . . . to have him forbid [the] . . . bringing over [of] these drinks that kill us?" Gand responded that Frenchmen needed alcohol at sea and in the cold of Canada. The Huron accepted this but told him to "[a]rrange it . . . so that they alone drink them."[4]

While some Hurons opposed the new regulations, Gand's speech received a mixed but generally positive reaction. Some Huron expressed skepticism, questioning if the French would really enforce these new regulations. They asked Gand "three times if [he] . . . spoke in earnest, or if he were only indulging in words." Gand responded each time that both Native peoples and Frenchmen would be punished if they violated the new ordinance. When told that he wanted their help in enforcing the prohibition against the trading of alcohol, many expressed their approval, "saying that, if the French did not give them either wine or brandy, their wives and children would have something to eat, inasmuch as they could make a good living from their Peltries." Others expressed satisfaction with the plan, claiming that if the French gave them "bread instead of a drink of brandy, we shall be far better satisfied." Le Jeune, who observed and recorded the proceedings, expressed pessimism about the Native peoples' comments. Familiar with the problems that alcohol caused in native communities, even as early as 1636 Le Jeune knew of the wide gulf that separated Native peoples' intent and action concerning alcohol. Le Jeune wrote that this was "[v]ery well spoken, according to the voice of reason . . . but not according to the senses, they are only too eager for our drinks,—both men and women expressing a singular pleasure, not in drinking, but in becoming drunk, glorying in this and in making others so."[5]

Le Jeune's commentary on the proceedings encapsulates much of the Huron attitude and reaction toward alcohol. Iroquoian peoples came to recognize the destructive effects of alcohol, seeing for themselves the damage that it wrought in their communities. Yet at the same time, many of them had difficulty resisting the temptation of alcohol when it was in their presence. And as Le Jeune pointed out, they enjoyed getting drunk, if not the actual drinking itself. Iroquoian peoples, like many other Native Americans, were of two minds concerning liquor. On the one hand, many of them found intoxication to be a pleasurable and, in some cases, a spiritual experience. But at the other extreme, throughout the historical record are found members of Native communities, both leaders and ordinary people, who clearly recognized the damage that the consumption of alcohol inflicted on their societies. In the late seventeenth century, the Recollect Chrestien Le Clercq wrote of the terrible effects that alcohol had on the Native peoples of Nova Scotia. "Lewdness, adulteries, incests, . . . are committed through the trade in brandy." Le Clercq also noted that violence escalated within Native communities because of drunkenness.[6]

Alcohol, when first introduced to Native peoples, was a new and strange substance. Hendrick Hudson, in 1609, brought Native leaders aboard his ship and "gave them so much Wine and *Aqua vitæ,* that they were all merrie. . . . In the end one of them was drunke . . . and that was strange to them; for they could not tell how to take it."[7] Native leaders complained to the Dutch at Fort Orange in 1642 that alcohol made "the young Indians . . . crazy, as they were unaccustomed to drink."[8] The strangeness of the sensation of being inebriated seemed to many Native people to be an experience that placed one in a supernatural state. A Jesuit, in 1668, heard a Cayuga exclaim, "I am going to lose my head; I am going to drink the water that takes one's wits away."[9]

Drinking, however, did not cause problems only on the Native peoples' side of the frontier. In 1642, Kiliaen van Rensselaer complained bitterly to New Netherlands governor Willem Kieft when the Dutch West India Company billed him for wine consumed by his employees. "Can it be," wrote the annoyed patroon, "that Fort Orange is a wine cellar to debauch my people, exhausting them as long as they can find something to pay and after that charging it to my account?"[10] Fifteen-year-old Pierre Radisson, despite the terror of his first night of captivity among the Iroquois, dreamed of "drinking beer." Radisson comforted himself that night by recalling that "[the Iroquois] lived among Dutch people in a place called . . . Fort Orange, where without doubt I could drink beer." In fact, some months later, when Radisson visited Fort Orange in the company of his adoptive Iroquois relatives, Dutch traders feted him with alcohol once they realized he was a Frenchman.[11] It is also possible that the traders were attempting to get Radisson's Iroquois companions intoxicated so that he would have a chance to get away.

European difficulties with alcohol consumption did not go unnoticed by Native peoples. A party of Native peoples visiting Fort Amsterdam in 1642 told the commander that "they had even seen our people [the Dutch], who were habituated to strong drink, frequently intoxicated, and fight with knives."[12] Two drunken Frenchmen disturbed a New Year's Eve mass at Quebec as the year 1646 came in. They caused "much scandal to some frenchmen and savages who saw them." When the Native peoples complained that "they make us take the discipline when we get drunk, and they say nothing to the french." Hearing this, the French made an example of the two drunkards, placing them "on the chevalet, exposed to a frightful Northeast wind."[13] In any case, it is clear that Europeans brought their taste for alcoholic beverages and a heavy style of drinking with them to the Americas, as illustrated in Van Rensselaer's difficulties with his employees and the case of the two unfortunate Frenchmen who disturbed mass.[14] Alcohol, Native Americans and Europeans agreed, caused problems for both peoples.

But the difficulties that alcohol caused Europeans were by no means new to them; they had experienced them in the Old World as well as the New. Nor did Native peoples and Europeans drink in the same way. Europeans, while they did drink to intoxication at times, often used alcohol to complement a meal or to ward off the winter's chill.[15] Indeed, one Jesuit, commenting on the coldness of the North American climate, thought the coldness of Europe was comparable but easier to bear "because of the many palliatives of cold, such as wines, brandy."[16] Native peoples, for the most part, drank for none of these reasons. They drank to get drunk.[17] Native peoples told the Jesuit missionary Barthelemy Vimont "that they did not buy our liquors on account of any pleasant taste that they found in them, or because they had any need of them, but simply to become intoxicated."[18]

While alcohol, as these Native peoples told Vimont, was not a necessity, it could facilitate, as far as many Native peoples were concerned, contact with the supernatural. Contact with the supernatural, or with an Other Than Human Person who became one's spiritual overseer, had long been an important part of Iroquoian life.[19] In precontact (and prealcohol) times, an Iroquoian person could have a supernatural experience through the passive mode of the dream or through the active mode of seeking a vision. Persons seeking a vision did so to obtain spiritual guidance. These individuals isolated themselves from their communities, went without sleep, and fasted until they had a vision that they believed gave them direction. The lack of food, together with the isolation and sleep deprivation, helped induce the vision, or what twenty-first-century science would call a hallucination.

Using twentieth-century studies of the effects of alcohol, historian Peter Mancall has argued that since alcohol does not cause hallucinations, we should assume that Native peoples did not drink to induce visions. This argument contains two flaws. First, a twentieth-century study, regardless of its results, does not tell us why people drank three hundred years ago. Second, it assumes that a modern study, carried out by Western researchers using Western subjects, can tell us about the motivations of peoples of a different culture, living in another time. True, such a study tells us that alcohol does not induce hallucinations or dreams. But a Native person who drank in the seventeenth century could have *believed* that alcohol would cause him or her to have a supernatural experience, including a vision or a dream. Alcohol, to peoples not familiar with its consumption, creates an altered form of reality. The physical and psychological effects that it had on the bodies and minds of seventeenth-century Iroquoian peoples were important to them but not, obviously, in a clinical sense. The fact that a modern study says that alcohol does not cause dreams, in this context, means little. In all likelihood, seventeenth-century Iroquoian peoples valued the feeling of unreality that alcohol induced, as much as they valued dreams or visions that they thought alcohol could cause.[20] Indeed, a state of drunkenness may have been regarded as a vision itself. Because of its ability to induce an altered state, alcohol was regarded as supernatural; hence, in the thought world of Iroquoian peoples, it had to have a connection to the other aspects of the supernatural.

Iroquoian peoples regarded alcohol as a peculiar form of European technology; as such, it represented another jump in the technological imagination. While the Jesuits preached a new form of spirituality, alcohol delivered a new spiritual encounter to Iroquoian peoples. While previous supernatural encounters fell into the realm of either the dream or the vision, alcohol was something different. It was intoxication. It did not require that one fall asleep or that one deprive oneself of food, water, and rest. It was a new technology that allowed an Iroquoian person to seek the supernatural by the simple act of ingesting alcohol.

Alcohol, for seventeenth-century Iroquoian peoples, became a new means to seek the guidance or advice of a spirit person or to induce a vision. For Native peoples, alcohol made connecting with the supernatural a far simpler matter.[21] Seeking a vision through the traditional process of self-deprivation could be arduous, painful, debilitating, and, on occasion, fatal.[22] Elderly or sickly people could not very well search for a vision, because depriving themselves of food, water, or sleep endangered their own well-being. But they could drink. Alcohol provided a painless and far less risky route to a supernatural experience. Drunkenness also opened the portals of the supernatural to those who in precontact times usually did not, or could not, engage in the active search for the supernatural by means of seeking a vision. And alcohol, in some ways, made seeking a vision a safer experience.

Alcohol probably opened up a new avenue that brought women closer to the supernatural. In the world of Iroquoian peoples, with its gendered boundaries, it was normally only men who could go into the woods—their domain—and actively seek a supernatural experience. Women, because of the constraints of the gendered Iroquoian landscape, rarely engaged in the active search for the supernatural. Alcohol, because it erased the need to physically cross the tree line, made it easier for people other than hunters and warriors to have access to the supernatural. Paul Le Jeune, lamenting the effects of brandy on Native peoples, wrote, "there is scarcely a Savage, small or great, even among the girls and women, who does not enjoy this intoxication."[23]

It is possible that Native peoples viewed those under the influence of alcohol in much the same way as they saw a person seeking a vision in the traditional way. In both instances, the vision seekers deprived themselves of food—Native persons tended not to eat when they consumed alcohol—and saw things that remained invisible to others.[24]

The use of alcohol for spiritual purposes escaped the notice of European observers, primarily because such a use fit neither into European concepts of spirituality nor into European patterns of alcohol consumption. Unable to discern a religious motivation, most Europeans simply saw Native peoples getting drunk as fast as they possibly could. Le Jeune observed that the Huron drank "brandy and wine, which they love with an utterly unrestrained passion, not for the relish they experience in drinking them, but for the pleasure they find in becoming drunk." Indeed, they took "pride in getting drunk and making others drunk." Le Jeune noted that the overconsumption of alcohol gave Native peoples an inflated sense of self-esteem in that they "imagine in their drunkenness that they are listened to with attention, that they are great orators, that they are valiant and formidable, that they are looked up to as Chiefs." The Native peoples' drinking habits, Le Jeune believed, caused the illnesses that killed them in droves.[25]

The manner in which Native peoples consumed alcohol—Le Jeune claimed that if one gave "two savages two or three bottles of brandy, they will sit down and, without eating, will drink one after the other until they have emptied them"—may have been derived from the traditional "eat all feast."[26] The "eat all" probably had its origins in times or circumstances when food could not be preserved, so it all had to be eaten at once lest it go to waste—an important consideration among peoples who entertained doubts as to where their next meal was coming from. The "eat all" tradition, coupled with the desire for intoxicants, led to the creation of the "drink all party."[27]

But another, perhaps more likely explanation for the mode in which Iroquoian peoples consumed alcohol is that drinking to excess was the route to the supernatural. They did not drink for nourishment, nor did they drink because they liked it. They drank to get drunk and for the feeling of unreality that it induced.

Alcohol was considered an entity with a will independent of the individual who consumed it. Native peoples considered alcohol to be a spirit; hence, the spirit, not the intoxicated individual, bore responsibility for the actions committed while one was under its influence. In 1632, when the French returned to Quebec after a brief English seizure of the territory, Le Jeune recorded the story of an "English Clergyman" who related how a proposed peace between Quebec and the Iroquois had been shattered by two drunken Montagnais brothers who killed an Iroquois prisoner. When the clergyman reproached one of the culprits, he denied responsibility and shifted blame to the English, by replying, "It is thou and thine, who killed him; for if thou hadst not given us brandy or wine, we would not have done it."[28] When a Native person murdered a Dutchman in 1642, chiefs visited Fort Amsterdam and "laid the blame upon our people, saying that it was because we sold the young Indians brandy or wine."[29] Le Jeune also noted the extent of the Native peoples' intoxication at this time, writing that "they are heard shouting and raving day and night; they fight and wound each other." Once sober, however, they told the French, much like they told the English, "It is not we who did that, but thou who gavest us this drink." They also suggested to French officials that they "[p]ut thy wine and thy brandy in prison" because they "do all the evil, and not we." They approached those they attacked while drunk not to express remorse but to make it known that the alcohol, not they, bore the blame for the assault. One man, apologizing to a person he assailed while drunk, said, "Thou art my brother, I love thee; it is not I who wounded thee, but the drink which used my arm."[30] Another Jesuit writing in the latter part of the seventeenth century noted "excesses of drinking and insobriety furnish them, by custom, a valid excuse for any evil."[31]

Many Native people sought to excuse the violence, but to European observers, these disorders were the most disconcerting effect alcohol had on Native communities. In the small, close-knit societies of eastern North American peoples, animosities and rivalries were often suppressed, lest the village or community be wracked by dissension. Alcohol use released inhibitions and led to a lessening of these social restrictions. Those who drank often imagined that they became "persons of importance, taking pleasure in seeing themselves dreaded by those who do not taste the poison."[32] "Brandy," noted François Vachon de Belmont, "causes them [Native peoples] to undertake with vigor and bravado almost any evil action such as anger, vengeance, or impurity." Some individuals, perhaps enjoying the alcohol-fueled notion of power, brawled with other Native people, biting "each other's noses and ears so that there are few whole, entire visages remaining." Nor did the inebriated stop there. "They run about with knives in their hands; they delight in seeing their women and children run before them."[33] Drunken individuals released their inhibitions and acted out their hostilities, comfortable in the knowledge that since alcohol was a spirit, it, and not they, was responsible for any action they took while under its influence. Le Jeune wrote that they would be "entirely excused from the crimes they commit, when they say that they are drunk."[34]

Le Jeune noted that many of the Native peoples after a night of drinking had "badly bruised faces; even the women get drunk, and shriek like furies." Nor did the Native peoples confine the violence only to themselves. Le Jeune commented that "it is not safe to go and see them without arms, if they have any wine."[35] Violence, and its connection to the consumption of alcohol, greatly concerned many Huron leaders, who obviously recognized what it did to their people. When the Jesuit André Richard visited the village of Saint Joseph in 1642, Huron leaders asked him to "[w]rite to France, and tell the Captains to send ships here, and not to send anymore of the poisons [alcohol] that destroy us, that take away our senses, and cause us untimely death." In the middle of this meeting, Father Richard received an unplanned demonstration of some of the problems alcohol caused. "A young man, strong and robust, bereft of his senses through drink, entered, entirely naked, the cabin where the Assembly was being held, defied the Captain, and challenged him to bind or have him bound with an iron chain that he himself carried on his shoulders, threatening to kill the first one who approached." In another incident, a Jesuit described a drunken Huron who began to behave "like an unchained Demon . . . [he] strikes all whom he meets, and overthrows the cabins. . . . He takes an arquebus . . . and fires three or four shots into the face of [a] boy." The victim, as well as the assailant, was drunk—the boy so much so that he did not even realize that he had been shot.[36] A Jesuit observer echoed the fur-trader Gand's concern that alcohol, when used in trade, sometimes led to violence. Native traders "will murder some Frenchman in their drunkenness; and the Frenchmen, in defending themselves will kill some Savages, and behold the ruin of the trade for a time."[37]

Many of the individuals in these Iroquoian communities became so desperate that they resorted to doing what the young man who interrupted the assembly at Saint Joseph challenged them to do: they resorted to tying up intoxicated persons, fearing that if they did not, they would harm others. Le Jeune noted that among the Native peoples at Quebec, "When one of them is very drunk, the others tie him by his feet and arms, if they can catch him." An Iroquois visiting Montreal told the fathers through an interpreter that he had drunk brandy in a Dutch settlement and that he "became so tipsy that it was necessary to bind my feet and hands, for fear lest I should injure some one."[38]

The seizing and binding of dangerous individuals reveals a subtle difference in the way that Iroquoian peoples viewed the supernatural states of the dream and of intoxication. One did not interfere with one who attempted to fulfill a dream; indeed, others encouraged a dreamer to act out his or her dream, even if it involved murder or great harm to himself or herself, because if they interfered and the dream went unfulfilled, the entire community *might* suffer. Iroquoian peoples took steps to keep drunken individuals from carrying out acts of violence. Seeing a drunken, violent person in front of them, they realized that they must act, otherwise, the community *would* suffer.

Intoxicated persons may have also used their drunken state to carry out directed acts of mayhem, but unlike a dreamer, other members of the community apparently viewed drunken individuals as a threat to others and took steps to restrain them. This implies that in some ways, Iroquoian peoples did not view the influence of alcohol as being the same as a dream. While they probably regarded drunkenness as a supernatural state, they recognized that drunkenness differed from a dream. While Native peoples probably granted that the drunkard was in a supernatural state, it was a state that was detrimental to others. Whereas dreamers were encouraged to act out their dreams, Native peoples tried to keep intoxicated individuals from carrying out their more violent intentions, as a form of preserving a community's well-being.

Another factor in the differing ways that Iroquoian peoples treated drunkards and dreamers involved their understanding that the former may not have been truly intoxicated. Pseudo-drunks may have used the consumption of alcohol as a "cover" for carrying out acts of violence against their personal enemies. Le Jeune suspected that Native peoples were not always as intoxicated as they acted. Drinking Native peoples, Le Jeune observed, could "feign madness very well when they wish to hide their malice."[39] In the 1660s, two missionaries of the Sulpitian order noted, "It is a somewhat common custom amongst them when they have enemies, to get drunk and afterwards go and break their heads or stab them to death, so as to be able to say afterward that they committed the wicked act when they were not in their senses."[40]

European observers often associated alcohol with violence in Native communities, but periodic violence, particularly in times of festivity, seems to have been a feature of Iroquoian life prior to the introduction of alcohol. Before European contact, gambling could often incite violence within Iroquoian communities. While some observers thought that most Hurons did not mind losing at gambling, others noted that they often attempted to avenge their losses.[41] At times, the stakes could be quite high. One could lose a spouse, children, or even a finger in these wagers. Some Huron told the

Jesuits that "gambling . . . is almost the sole cause of assaults and murders." One young man, after losing a beaver robe and a large quantity of wampum, committed suicide rather than face his family. Another man who lost at gambling, a "yroquois," went to the winner's "cabin . . . in order to run him through with his javelin."[42]

While animosities and hatreds were usually suppressed in Iroquoian communities, a celebration called Ononhouaroia, or the "upsetting of brain," allowed all the participants—men, women, and children—to "run about as if they are mad." In the course of the "upsetting of brain," brawls, similar to those that occurred while people were intoxicated, took place. During this time, the revelers entered lodges and upset kettles and broke pots.[43] In all likelihood, the *ononhouaroia* was considered healthy; it allowed people in Iroquoian communities to act out their animosities and frustrations without being blamed for their actions. It represents a "time out of mind," in which the actions taken during the "upsetting of brain," like those undertaken while drunk, represented a chance to blow off steam. It also represented, like drunkenness did, the perfect opportunity for revenge. Despite the assumption that "a public madness" was present during the *ononhouaroia,* it appears that many used the ceremony as an opportunity to settle scores with their enemies. In particular, traditionalists used this time as an opportunity to attack Christian converts with impunity.[44] Indeed, it is possible that the *ononhouaroia* was viewed as the time to punish those who violated community norms. By attacking Christians during the *ononhouaroia,* traditionalists made themselves immune to reprisal.

The *ononhouaroia* represented a socially sanctioned period of time set aside by the society as a whole in which people could, with impunity, engage in behavior that was not normal for them. Indeed, they behaved in ways that would normally lead society to condemn them. Alcohol changed this. Drunkenness meant that aberrant, socially unsanctioned behavior, rather than being set aside for a particular time, could now appear at any time, and the individuals who acted out in socially unacceptable ways were as impervious to punishment as one was who participated in the *ononhouaroia.*

The use of alcohol also brought death to Iroquoian peoples. While not on the scale that European pathogens did, alcohol brought death nonetheless. Le Jeune, who believed alcohol, more than any other factor, increased Native peoples' mortality, lectured Native peoples about their drinking.

He once admonished a Huron, explaining to him how alcohol adversely affected his health. "Dost thou not feel thyself burn when thou hast drunk brandy? That consumes thy liver and dries it up . . . and causes sickness." The Huron admitted that Le Jeune was probably right. Le Jeune also noted that the large number of deaths meant that "there are many orphans among these people,—for they die in great numbers since they are addicted to drinking wine and brandy,—these poor children are scattered among the Cabins of their uncles, aunts or other relatives"[45]

Both French and Dutch trading concerns made efforts to restrict the selling of liquor to Iroquoian peoples. The amount of vigor they put into these efforts is open to question. By and large, in spite of the several ordinances that both colonial governments made to halt the traffic in brandy, rum, and other spirits, the trade flourished. One reason, of course, can be found in the greed of individual European traders and in the lax—indeed, sometimes nonexistent—enforcement of the ordinances that forbade the sale of liquor to Native peoples. But the chief factor that fueled the trade was the Native peoples' demand for intoxicants. "They are," in the words of one missionary, "to the last degree passionately fond of drink, and are easily intoxicated, when they can trade for any; thence follow the indecent sins, especially in the youth."[46]

The primary reason for lax enforcement was the possibility of high profits, which were almost too tempting to be ignored by many colonists. Dutch patroon Kiliaen van Rensselaer, who had lamented the affects of alcohol on his own employees, considering profiting from the liquor trade. "If I had a supply of brandy and . . . a sloop [I could sell] it . . . to . . . the savages and others . . . for furs [such as] as beavers, otters, etc."[47]

The Dutch West India Company passed several laws in 1645 that forbade "all Tapsters and Inhabitants" from selling or giving "Wine, Beer, or other Strong liquors to the Indians."[48] Penalties included fines of 500 and 1,000 guilders; for a third offense, one could be banished from the colony. Apparently, this law, or rather its enforcement, was somewhat lax, because in 1648 another law, rendered necessary because colonists suffered "serious annoyance from drunken Indians," reiterated the previous fiscal penalties, and added "arbitrary corporal punishment."[49]

The problem with the Dutch laws seems to be a lack of enforcement.[50] When "strong liquor was sold to the Indians by Aert Jacobsz by wooden bowlfuls," it appears that while Jacobsz ended up in court, the tribunal took no steps to punish him.[51] In one rare case, a tapster was caught selling alcohol to Native peoples and was banished from the colony. Overall, however, few Dutch traders who appeared before a magistrate received meaningful punishment.[52]

Native leaders often pleaded with the French and Dutch to do something to curtail the liquor trade. In 1642, Father Richard noted that the Huron at Saint Joseph "begged that the Bark that goes to trade with them should not bring any such liquors."[53] That same year, Native peoples informed the commander of Fort Amsterdam that they "desired that no liquor be sold to the Indians."[54] A year later, Barthelemy Vimont reported that "the Christians have begged our Fathers to do all that they can, in order to prevent the French from trading either wine or brandy to their people." But as Le Jeune sadly commented nearly a decade earlier, "there is always some one . . . who will sell them a bottle now and then in secret."[55]

In 1648, Christian Native peoples became alarmed enough at the violence in their communities that they were willing to impose European punishments on those who disturbed the peace. They proposed "drunkenness . . . be banished, and driven from their cabins; and that, should any fall into this crime, he shall be placed in prison, and made to fast for several days,—not on bread and water, but on water only, without other nourishment." In another incident, leaders of Christian Hurons proclaimed that those whose "lips had touched the wounds of Jesus Christ on his image should be severely chastised if, in the future, they profaned their lips by drunkenness." This proclamation had a remarkable response. Native peoples who had hidden casks of brandy underground brought them to the Jesuit priest, telling him "as long as he kept their familiar Demon in prison, he could not injure them."[56] While the term "familiar demon" is perhaps a French version of "spirit helper," it is significant that Iroquoian peoples now began to personalize alcohol, in this case as a malevolent spirit that could do them harm.

Christian converts seemed to have two minds concerning alcohol. While they lamented its use, many could seemingly not resist its appeal. Some, after recovering their wits, wished to pay a sort of penance. At the end of a mass, one man drew "forth a great whip; he has himself severely flogged by another." Mothers use this as a lesson for their children, as they viewed the whipping, they said to their offspring, "[W]ill you be naughty? Will you ever lie? See how they treat the disobedient."[57]

Alcohol, to Iroquoian peoples, seemed to be a supernatural being that was attacking them. It assaulted their thought world in two ways. First, it had the mostly beneficial effect of widening access to the supernatural. But at the same time, it introduced a sort of violence—which was by no means new to Iroquoian peoples, but this new violence was randomly timed. This violence brought mayhem and death, and it was neither controllable nor predictable. One inebriated Iroquoian person with a weapon could kill or injure another with impunity. The socially approved "time out of mind," when people could step outside of their normal character, had been replaced. A new "time out of mind" in which alcohol, and not the society, determined when a drunken individual could step out of his or her normal character now took over.

6

THE CHANGED RELATIONSHIP WITH THE BEAVER AND OTHER NONHUMANS

IN THE FIRST FIFTY YEARS OF THE SEVENTEENTH CENTURY, the views and attitudes of the Huron and the Five Nations Iroquois toward the nonhumans that populated the landscapes of Huronia and Iroquoia underwent a marked change. In a span of only four decades, these two culturally similar groups of peoples found it necessary to alter their relationship with the beaver, the animal whose pelt became the basis of the fur trade. Beaver pelts provided Iroquoian peoples with the technologies that changed, destroyed, and, in the case of the Five Nations, remade their thought world. But in order for this change to take place in this short period of forty years, Iroquoian peoples had to transform the beaver from a creature they accorded a measure of respect into a commodity.

Considering the role the beaver played in Iroquoian cosmology, such a transformation was a dramatic development. Indeed, Iroquoian mythology pointed out that the beaver was present and had a small hand (or paw) in the creation of this world. When the beaver and the other animals that inhabited the sea that covered the earth saw Aataentsic plunging down through the sky, they quickly took steps to rescue her and, by extension, all future Iroquoian peoples. The aquatic animals dived to the bottom of the vast ocean, seeking soil to make land so that the woman might live. In many versions of the creation story, several or all of the animals die, or nearly die, in their attempts to retrieve a bit of mud from the ocean floor. Nearly every version of the Iroquoian creation story mentions that the beaver was present at the beginning of this world and affirms that it predates Iroquoian peoples.[1] The creation story also presents the beaver as a Being Other Than Human, willing to give of itself for the benefit of human beings.

Iroquoian peoples thought of the beaver, like all things living and nonliving, as an Other Than Human Person or as a Being Other Than Human. An Other Than Human Person could take the form of an animal, a tree, or natural phenomena such as rain, wind, or lightning. The spirits of these Other Than Human Persons could aid, cure, or assist humans if treated with the proper respect and ritual. However, if humans neglected their duties to the Other Than Human Person, disaster, in the form of illness, starvation, or death, could result.[2]

Iroquoian peoples believed that the beaver and other animals had the capacity to reason.[3] Yet in Iroquoian beliefs, the beaver's status as an Other Than Human Person and its possession of reason did not anthropomorphize it—or any other animal for that matter.

The notion of an animal that is a "person" and at the same time does not posses human characteristics requires explanation for Euro-Americans living in the twenty-first century. They live in a culture that anthropomorphizes wildlife or segregates it from humans to such a degree that when humans do interact—if they interact—with wildlife, it is usually in an artificial or vicarious manner. There is also a tendency to focus on the word "person" and translate it as "human." This is due, in large part, to the increasing control that humans have been able to exert over their environment. The logical extension of this is to control the behavior of the animal populations. Even in national parks, where one can supposedly experience "wilderness," animals that step out of their role as benign entertainment are tranquilized and shipped off to another remote location. If the offending animal has committed a serious enough transgression, it is hunted down and killed. Americans have become accustomed to watching numerous wildlife shows, such as *Nature* and *Wild America*. Animals on these shows are shown in their natural habitat. But those habitats are so alien from what most Americans are accustomed to that they seem almost otherworldly. While the animals on these shows go about their lives, they are regarded not as beings but as another form of entertainment.

There is also what could be called the "Disney effect" on people's conception of nature; otherwise intelligent people anthropomorphize wildlife to such a degree that they begin to regard animals in human terms. While they do not expect an animal to talk, they do see the animal as possessing human intelligence. They also, depending on how the species was presented to them, assign different characteristics to animals. A person who has seen *The Lion King,* for example, may regard lions as noble and possibly as cute and cuddly. On the other hand, hyenas are presented in a less favorable light, as ugly and stupid yet conniving. Indeed, the "Disney effect" has enabled Americans to regard particular animals in human terms. At the same time, the "Disney effect" has made it possible for those who anthropomorphize animals to denigrate the humanity of another Homo sapiens, particularly if that human is a hunter.[4] These factors—the artificiality in which nature and wildlife is presented to and accepted by most present-day Americans—make it difficult for them to grasp the concept of the Other Than Human Person. Ironically, the hunter, seeing animals as they really are, is probably more appreciative of the concept of the Other Than Human Person than is a person who anthropomorphizes wildlife.

The Other Than Human Person in Iroquoian thought is not, then, in human terms, a person. Rather, animals regarded in this way were seen as individuals and were thought of in terms of their somatic makeup. A beaver in Iroquoian thought might be a person, but it did not lose its tail or teeth. Nor did a bird lose its beak or feathers. The conception of the Other Than Human Person meant that the animal, in Iroquoian thought, assumed an individual identity. It became a *person*—an individual who warranted respect, who had needs, and, most important to Iroquoian peoples, who had special powers. But it remained its own person and assumed none of the characteristics of humans.

As an Other Than Human Person, the beaver served Native peoples' needs in a variety of ways, both tangible and intangible. Beaver flesh and hide became food, clothing, and wealth. Native peoples used beaver pelts for their beds, blankets, wall hangings, and robes. Robes also served as ritualistic clothing for prisoners about to be tortured and as diplomatic gifts. Five Nations peoples considered pelts a form of wealth and a medium of exchange in precontact times. The beaver also served the dead, not only in the physical sense as burial robes but also as food for the departed. Just as the living hunted beavers and other animals, the souls of the dead stalked those of dead beavers while wearing the soles of snowshoes.[5]

The opening of the fur trade began a process that changed the Iroquoian view of the beaver. Europeans, who had depleted their continent of furbearing animals, sought to acquire pelts in the Americas. Scarcity had made furs very valuable in western Europe by the sixteenth century. Furs had become a luxury in Europe, and great profits could be realized. While furrier guilds still existed and laws specifying who could wear fur remained in force in most European societies, most of the fur-bearing animals native to western Europe were either extinct by the sixteenth century or protected by law. Hats made from beaver hair became fashionable in the sixteenth century, but hatters found themselves forced to pay high prices for furs from Russia or Scandinavia.[6] New World furs represented a relatively cheaper and more reliable source of animal pelts.

While many Europeans valued the beaver's fur, others prized the animal's supposed medicinal properties. Adriaen van der Donck, a Dutch businessman who "handled and exchanged many thousand [beaver] skins," sounded like a latter-day snake oil salesman when he described the curative powers of the mammal. Indeed, Van der Donck seemed to believe that products derived from the beaver could fill a pharmacopoeia by themselves. "Beaver testicles," according to Van der Donck, "were infallible remedies." Smelling them would cure insomnia; if one felt drowsy rubbing a beaver testicle on one's head could provide a quick pick-me-up. And, said Van der Donck, it could cure more than the ills of the body: "Taken in water, it removes idiocy." Beaver urine, if kept stored in the castor's bladder, "is an antidote for all poisons." Among the other maladies that Van der Donck claimed beaver extracts of one kind or another could cure were dizziness, trembling, rheumatism, lameness, stomachaches, earaches, toothaches, apoplexy, gout, and "stoppages in the body." Nor was that all. Consuming "two quarts of the [beaver] oil . . . will restore the menses to women, and remove the second birth."[7]

In exchange for beaver pelts, and possibly other parts of the animal, Europeans offered Native peoples a multitude of trade goods. In terms of European money, Native peoples at the beginning of the seventeenth century received the equivalent of 10 livres per pelt.[8] As early as 1610, Marc Lescarbot noted that there had already been a significant rise in fur prices. "Eight years ago," Lescarbot wrote, "for two biscuits or two knives, one had a beaver, while to-day one must give fifteen or twenty."[9] As the trade developed, prices at Montreal and Fort Orange began to stabilize. The French, however, could not match the prices that the Dutch, and later the English, paid for beaver pelts. A good gauge in terms of price is to look at the sort of goods a Native person received in exchange for a given number of pelts.

In 1689, which is a little outside the time frame of this work, a Native person trading for a blanket needed one pelt in Albany and two in Montreal to make the trade. Likewise, if a Native person desired four shirts or six pairs of stockings, the same ratio of one pelt in Albany and two in Montreal held. If a Native person wanted firearms and ammunition, these ratios deviated even more. A musket cost two beavers in Albany and five in Montreal. Forty pounds of lead, from which shot would be molded, could be had for one beaver in Albany but cost three in Montreal. And for eight pounds of powder, without which the musket and lead were useless, a Native person paid one beaver to the English and four to the French. In all, it cost a Native person twelve beaver pelts for a weapon and ammunition in Montreal, but he or she could obtain the same items in the same quantity—and often of superior quality—for only four pelts in Albany.[10] Besides clothing and firearms, Iroquoians and other Iroquoians received European foodstuffs such as beans, peas, and flour and metal versions of stone tools they already possessed, such as hoes, axes, and kettles.[11]

But to acquire these goods on the large scale that the fur trade and Iroquoian peoples' own appetite for European items demanded, they could no longer think of the beaver as an Other Than Human Person. One of the precepts of the renewable, or traditional, Iroquoian thought world was that the beaver, like all other animals, possessed reason. Indians, wrote one Frenchman, believed that beavers "have so much Wit, Capacity and Judgement, that they cannot believe their Souls die with their Bodies. . . . That if they were permitted to reason about things invisible, and which fall not under their Senses, they durst maintain, that they are immortal like Ours."[12]

In return for giving of itself for the benefit of Iroquoian peoples, the beaver wanted its remains treated with respect. But in order for the Iroquoian thought world to accommodate the demands of the fur trade, the beaver had to be divested of its personhood and transformed into a commodity that made the acquisition of trade goods possible.

In the first half of the seventeenth century, several different factors, including Christianity, economic concerns, and a process of intellectual rationalization, began to change the status of the beaver in the minds of Iroquoian peoples. Whereas Iroquoian beliefs held that the earth had to be renewed through the ritualistic activity of human beings, Christian thought, to which the Huron were exposed by the Jesuits and the Recollects in the early seventeenth century, maintained that the earth and the creatures on it were given to humans by God. Humans, in Christian thought, bore no responsibility for maintaining the earth. This was reflected in the words of a Christian convert who, after traditionalist Huron berated him for giving beaver bones to dogs, retorted, "These animals are made for us ... it is a deception of the Devil to remain in these superstitions; you are dwelling in falsehoods, and you shut your eyes to the truth."[13]

The Christian worldview, derived from Scripture, that humans are to have "dominion . . . over every living thing that moves upon the earth," began to supplant traditional beliefs among the Huron but not the Five Nations, who had little contact with the Jesuits or any other missionaries for that matter.[14] Christianity worked very well with the need of the Huron to rationalize their altered behavior toward animals.

Traditionalist Iroquois, however, could not use Christian doctrine to justify their altered behavior toward the beaver. They used a form of intellectual rationalization that began to appear in new, postcontact myths. The precontact beaver that appeared in the Iroquoian creation myth, the being who gave so much of itself for Iroquoian peoples and who received a large measure of respect in return, now became a malevolent figure instead. In a myth containing postcontact elements such as the horse, the beaver, alarmed that humans now valued its pelt, planned to destroy the houses of humans in the midst of winter so that they and their children would freeze to death. It is found out and is fittingly punished by having its hide become a source of warmth for those it would have exposed to the cold.[15] By making the beaver into a being capable of evil, Iroquoian peoples now had an appropriate rationale for their behavior toward it in the postcontact era.

Before contact, Iroquoian peoples understood that the beaver, as a being possessed of reason, should be treated with respect. Knowing this, Iroquoian peoples extended certain courtesies to Other Than Human Persons, including the beaver. Beaver hunts, for example, took place only during certain parts of the year, and the Native peoples left the animal in peace the rest of the time. Indeed, one French observer claimed that Native peoples viewed the beaver as what twentieth-first-century ecologists would call a sustainable resource. This was accomplished by sparing "a dozen of Females and half a dozen of Males" of each beaver community during a hunt.[16] In 1616, Father Pierre Biard noted that the Native peoples had two different beaver-hunting seasons each year. The first, "in the month of February and the middle of March, is the great hunt for beavers."

The second season occurred in October and November.[17] Gabriel Sagard observed that "beavers are hunted usually in winter, chiefly because they stay in their lodges then and their fur holds at that season, while in summer it is of very little value."[18] Hunting seasons served to strike a balance between Native peoples' need for beaver pelts and meat and the need to preserve the animal's population. The influx of trade goods, and the perceived need for them, led to the chase encompassing all seasons.

Unlike Huronia, Iroquoia still abounded with beaver during the first half of the seventeenth century. The animals thrived because Native hunters did not pursue them with the same tenacity as they did their cousins of the upper Great Lakes, who had the misfortune of having thicker, more desirable pelts. While some scholars, most notably George T. Hunt, have asserted that the Iroquois had depleted their country of beaver by 1640, there is a wealth of evidence that suggests that beavers were plentiful in Iroquoia at that time.[19] A Dutch observer, writing in 1650, noted that there were wolves that preyed on beavers, implying that the castor was still extant in that area.[20] The Reverend Johannes Megapolensis, writing in 1644, noted that the Mohawk had enough beaver to make clothing for themselves.[21] Other Dutchmen wrote that there were large numbers of beaver in Iroquoia. David deVries, writing in 1642, said there were "beavers in great numbers."[22] And Adriaen van der Donck, writing in the 1650s, claimed, "beavers are numerous in the New Netherlands."[23] The Iroquois supplemented the number of pelts they trapped themselves by raiding Huron fur-trading fleets for the more valuable northern Great Lakes pelts. This enabled the Iroquois to maintain economic relations with their Dutch trading partners. It also meant that the thought world of Five Nations peoples, regarding animals, did not undergo the same sort of shift that the Huron's thought world did: they did not have to regard the beaver in a different light. Pillaging the furs of the Huron meant that they did not have to change their direct relationship with the animal. Whereas the Huron now had to regard the beaver strictly as a commodity, Five Nations peoples could take a more dualistic approach, regarding it as both an Other Than Human Person and as an article of trade.

While the Iroquois still had, according to Van der Donck and De Vries, many beavers in the first half of the seventeenth century, the Huron, it appears, had almost none. To compensate for the shortfall, the Huron traded French goods to peoples farther west in exchange for beaver pelts and took care to conceal their routes from the French in order to keep this trade for themselves.[24] Iroquois war parties lying in wait along these routes made the trade uncertain.

Throughout the seventeenth century and well into the eighteenth, Iroquoian peoples continued to employ traditional hunting methods in their quest to catch the beaver. In the precontact period, Native peoples took beavers with harpoons, deadfall traps, and nets.[25] But as European trade grew in importance, mass hunts, in which large numbers of animals were taken, became more common. This type of hunt had its roots in precontact practice but followed the practice of deer hunts, rather than beaver hunts. Samuel de Champlain witnessed one such mass deer hunt. The Native peoples "in less than ten days" constructed an enclosure with "stakes eight or nine feet in height." When all was prepared, the Native peoples conducted a deer drive that netted them "one hundred and twenty deer, with which they made good cheer ... keeping the fat for the winter as we do butter, and a little of the meat which they carry home for their feasts."[26] Mass hunts enabled Native peoples to obtain large quantities of meat or hides in a short period of time. Since the Huron had experienced times when they had to acquire quickly a large quantity of beaver pelts, such as the approach of the periodic Feast of the Dead, it is reasonable to assume that mass beaver hunts occurred in the precontact period.

Mass beaver hunts in the postcontact period, however, relied on one particular form of European technology, the steel ax. While beavers were sometimes taken in deadfall traps, this method did not kill enough beavers to satisfy the demands of the fur trade.[27] Beaver lodges were "wonderfully made ... no musket ball can pierce [them]." To overcome this, Native peoples with steel axes broke "with blows from the hatchet the Cabin or house of the Beaver." Even this apparently was not an easy task. One Jesuit observed: "The materials of which it is composed ... [are] so well joined and bound together that I have seen our Savages in Midwinter sweat in trying to make an opening into it with their hatchets." Once the security of their lodge was compromised, the beavers abandoned the lodge and fled into their pond, seeking thin spaces in the ice where they could get air to breathe. Native hunters waited at these spaces and clubbed their prey to death.[28] There were some variations on this technique. One was to break the beaver's dam the night before so that the water would run out, and when the hunters attacked the next morning, the beavers would find themselves on dry land

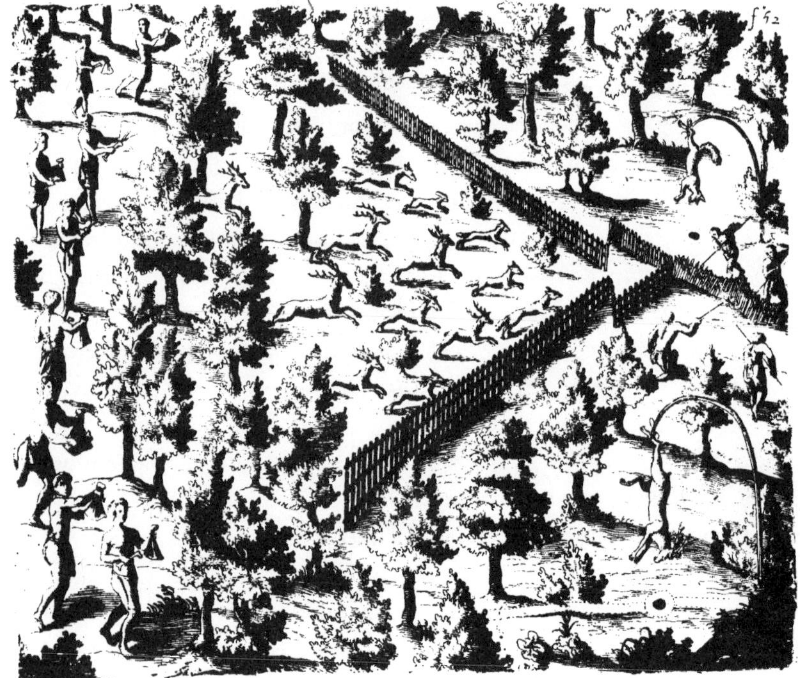

A Huron Deer Hunt. From Samuel de Champlain, *Voyages et descouvertures faites en la Nouvelle France, depuis l'année 1615, jusques à la fin de l'année 1618* (Paris, 1619). Courtesy of the National Library and National Archives of Canada.

as they tried to flee. Being literally out of water, the beavers were then easy prey for the hunters and their dogs.[29]

In Huronia, the periodic Feast of the Dead provided a major impetus for occasional mass beaver hunts. These feasts occurred every ten to fifteen years or when a large village moved to a different location. A cemetery adjoined almost every Huron village site. In this way, deceased members of the community remained close to their loved ones. In Huron beliefs, the dead did not go away completely, as the physical portion of their soul, the *atisken,* remained. When a large village moved, the living and the dead could not move together. The feast could be considered a way that the living and the dead said farewell to each another. The feast also released the *atisken* so that it could travel west to the Village of the Dead, where it could reunite with the *esken* and become whole again.[30]

In preparing for the Feast of the Dead, designated individuals disinterred the dead, and the relatives of the dead stripped any remaining flesh from the bones of the dead and burned it along with their burial mats and robes. The relatives then encased the bones of the dead in new beaver skin robes, each of which required five to six pelts, and bore them to their new burial site, a large pit lined with beaver pelts. The living then placed the dead in the common grave and reburied them.[31]

The European diseases that increased Huron mortality also placed a strain on the beaver population. At each phase of death—burial and reinterment in an ossuary—an individual required a beaver skin robe. The Feast of the Dead, plus the demands of the fur trade, greatly depleted the beaver population of Huronia. French observers noted that by the mid-1630s the Huron "have not a single beaver, going elsewhere to buy . . . skins."[32] It seems likely that these two factors—the Feast of the Dead and the fur trade—worked together to deplete the beaver population of Huronia, which, if anything, at one time may have been better beaver country than Iroquoia.[33]

Another indication of the altered relationship with the beaver involved the abandonment of traditional hunting seasons. Like most tribes in the eastern woodlands by the early seventeenth century, both the Iroquois and the Huron abandoned defined hunting seasons and began hunting beavers year-round. Some French observers commented on the number of beaver in Canada. "You cannot go four or five Leagues in the Woods of *Canada,* but that you meet with a little Beaver-Lake: So that one may say, that all this vast Continent is a Country for *Beaver hunting*."[34] Yet as early as the 1620s, Gabriel Sagard wrote that the Huron took "such a quantity of them [beavers] . . . that I cannot think but that the end is in sight."[35] A decade later, the Jesuit Paul Le Jeune wrote that "when the Savages find a lodge of [beavers], they kill all, great and small, male and female."[36] This indiscriminate killing of beavers resulted in the Huron having to trade their corn with nations farther west to obtain pelts to trade in turn to the French and for their own use.[37] Indeed, Le Jeune became so alarmed by the carnage that he proposed setting aside parks so that the beavers could survive yet still be harvested for their pelts. Writing about the beaver-hunting habits of the Montagnais in 1635, Le Jeune thought that "there is a danger that they will finally exterminate the species in this Region, as has happened among the *Hurons*."[38]

Native Peoples Hunting Beaver. From Abbé Prevost, *Histoire généraledes voyages, ou, Nouvelle collection de toutes les relations de voyages par mer et par terre* (Amsterdam, 1747). Courtesy of the National Library and National Archives of Canada.

European diseases also increased the need of the Huron for beaver pelts, since when of the Feast of the Dead arrived, there were more dead. This in turn meant larger burial pits, which meant more pelts to line the burial pit, and each of the deceased required a new beaver skin robe. In the winter of 1635, an epidemic of either smallpox or measles ravaged the Huron, which, besides killing a number of people, left the survivors too debilitated to fish or harvest crops and, presumably, to trade.[39]

Perhaps nothing revealed the immense changes wrought in the traditional Huron relationship with the beaver than the observance of the Feast of the Dead. During the 1636 feast, which Jesuit observers recorded in great detail, the living kept the robes after placing the bones of the dead into the burial pit. Beaver pelts had become too valuable to inter with the dead. This practice stands in stark contrast to the Feast of the Dead witnessed a decade earlier by Recollect Gabriel Sagard. Keeping the robes in no way reflected a lack of affection for the dead. Father Jean de Brébeuf noted the extent of the mourning and the tenderness with which the living handled the bones of their loved ones. He noted also the abundance of gifts, such as beads and wampum, that the living bestowed upon the deceased. But Brébeuf also observed that the robes of the dead were "thrown . . . into the midst of the crowd, for any one who could get hold of them . . . when two or three got hold of a Beaver skin, since, as none of them would give way, it had to be cut . . . and thus they found themselves almost empty-handed."[40]

One Huron man saw the opportunity to profit from the melee over the beaver robes. Knowing that there "had been nothing so valuable in this Country, this year, as Tobacco, he kept some . . . in his hands which he . . . offered to those who were disputing over a skin, and thus settled the matter to his advantage."[41]

It took an estimated 480 pelts to line the grave for the 1636 feast.[42] Removing the robes of the dead in the 1636 feast demonstrated how much the values of the Huron had been transformed. Before contact, beaver pelts were viewed in terms of their utilitarian value and as a gift from the beaver. The behavior of many Huron at the 1636 feast demonstrated that the commercial value of beaver pelts now began to take precedence over the practice of properly caring for the dead.

The shift of the beaver from Other Than Human Person to commodity, in a span of only forty years, is but one example of the alteration of the Iroquoian thought world in the years after contact. Other examples of changes in Iroquoian practices and values occurred in war and diplomacy, but in some way all of these changes had links to the fur trade. What should be clear is that contact with Europeans altered the thought world of Iroquoian peoples in permanent and significant ways. The complete and comprehended precontact world did not exist anymore; the alteration of the relationship with the beaver represents but one break with the traditional past, which irrevocably slipped away from the Iroquois and the Huron.

7

EUROPEAN TECHNOLOGY AND THE SEPARATION OF IROQUOIAN PEOPLES FROM THE EARTH

> The matters of your salvation that the French propose to you are new things, and customs of their own which will overthrow ours. You tell them that every country has its own ways of doing things; that, as you do not urge them to adopt ours, so you are surprised at their urging us to adopt theirs in this matter, and to acknowledge with them the same Creator of Heaven and Earth and the universal Lord of all things. I ask you, when at first you saw their hatchets and kettles, after having discovered that they were incomparably better and more convenient than our stone hatchets and our wooden and earthen vessels, did you reject their hatchets and kettles, because they were new things in your country?[1]

Thus did a Huron convert end a harangue that he directed against non-converts. The convert pointed out to his listeners a fact that many of them already acknowledged: the superiority of European technology to their own.

To Iroquoian peoples, and other Native Americans for that matter, the knowledge that Europeans could fabricate material items of iron and cloth that Native peoples could not did not imply that Europeans were superior to them. But clearly, Native Americans recognized that European-made goods, such as the cloth that replaced animal skins or metal versions of their own stone tools, such as axes or knives, represented a tremendous leap over their existing technologies. European technology caused Native peoples to approach their physical world—and hence their spiritual world—in different ways.

All groups of human beings create and utilize technology of varying degrees of complexity. However, the aim involved in the creation of technology is generally the same. All humans seek to exert a measure of control over the world about them, and in their attempts to control the environment around them, humans create tools with which they can acquire food and build shelter. Food and shelter represent the basic goal of all human technology: security. Security is further defined as security from hunger and from the elements. But from there, the creation of technology flows outward, as does the need for security. To protect their shelters and food supplies, humans create walls or palisades to prevent other humans or animals from taking what they have made. The weapons they created for food acquisition are used to defend themselves from other humans. The making of these technologies begins at home, in the environment where one lives. For the Native peoples of North America, most of the tools with which they manipulated the landscape, with the exception of those they obtained in trade with other Native peoples, were derived from the landscape about them.

The influx of European tools and their superiority in terms of durability, convenience, and reliability compared to those manufactured by Native peoples represented a tremendous shift in what I term the "technological imagination" of Iroquoian peoples.[2] The technological imagination can best be described as the junction of the unimagined and nonexistent technologies that people might subtlety wish for and the extent to which their existing technology allows them to create new technologies. This junction is usually completed when the desire for the unimagined technology and an existing technology allows people to create a new form of technology.

Understanding the concept of the technological imagination might require the use of examples. Prior to the introduction of European trade goods, it was entirely possible that an Iroquoian person could spend a cold drizzly day wrapped in a robe of animal skin wishing that his or her garments were warmer and that they could be quickly dried. The individual would not have been thinking in terms of European woolens, which were warmer and dried faster; the person would only have thought in terms of the improvements—warmth and the ability to dry quickly—that he or she wished for.[3] Likewise, in gathering firewood, women often passed standing timber as they made their way far into the woods to pick brush or fallen limbs off the ground. They might have wished they had the means to knock down the trees that were so much closer to the village. They would not, however, have been imagining a steel ax. They were thinking in terms of what they wished they could do, not so much in terms of the specific tool or technology that could give them the ability to do what they wished, in this case, to easily fell these trees. As it was, the ability of Iroquoians to create new technologies was limited. Iroquoian peoples fashioned their homes, weapons, tools, and ornaments from bone, stone, wood, and perhaps the odd piece of copper acquired in trade with peoples from the upper Great Lakes.

The technological imagination of Iroquoian peoples, then, had reached its limit. The subtly wished for unimagined technologies remained beyond the grasp of Iroquoians because their existing technology could not create them. Technological development, in most cultures, has been the result of a series of small steps. In most societies, new technologies are built on the subtle desires of the people within it, combined with the capabilities of their existing technology to fabricate a new technology. But by not having a new material, such as iron, or the knowledge of how to make substantial tools of it, Iroquoian peoples could not make a steel ax, though they could imagine its capabilities. Nor, in the case of woolens, did they have sheep from which to harvest wool or the knowledge of how to make it into cloth. Thus, while they could imagine a desired capability, they could not imagine the object that would give them this capability.[4]

European technology and its ideological implications brought about a major shift in the Iroquoian thought world. Human beings seek a measure of control to exert over the physical world around them. The level of control, however, is tied in large part to the technology that specific human groups have at hand or are able to fabricate. People also, primarily through shelters and clothing, seek to create technological barriers between themselves and the natural world. In essence, human beings manufacture environments they can control that are within, yet separate from, the ecosystem in which they live. This effort to control the environment—to establish a level of security and comfort—extends to their dwellings, their food production, and nearly every aspect of their lives. Thus, when Iroquoian peoples—and other Native peoples for that matter—found themselves able to procure woolen garments and blankets that kept them drier and warmer than animal skins, they leaped at the chance. Likewise, they eagerly sought to acquire metal tools that were lighter, more durable, and sharper than their stone ones. Other, more mundane items such as iron door hinges enabled them to better control their environments, making it possible for them to build doors that shut out the weather far better than a blanket or a fur robe could.[5]

The desire to better exploit their environment spurred Iroquoian peoples' acquisition of metal goods. The Five Nations Iroquois and the Huron, as well as other Native peoples of the Northeast, have been described as having a Stone Age culture at the time of contact.[6] While stone was the material that often became the cutting edges of the knives and axes that permitted precontact Iroquoian peoples to exploit the environment around them, Iroquoian culture also relied heavily on wood. Nearly all of their artifacts—lodges, cooking vessels, tools—had a wood component. Metal tools, particularly cutting tools such as axes and knives, allowed Iroquoian peoples to mold wood more easily and quickly into useable form. The Huron and Iroquois quickly saw the advantages of steel axes and knives over stone ones. Steel knives and axes did not break easily, held an edge, and sharpened more easily than stone implements and tools. Metal axes made the felling of trees easier by eliminating the time-consuming task of burning and girding. Trade axes also helped alter Native peoples' settlement patterns to some degree. For peoples who frequently shifted village sites, metal axes made the process easier by allowing them to clear a new village location of trees more quickly. For more settled peoples, such as the Iroquois and the Huron, axes increased the length of time that a village site could be occupied by allowing them to augment the firewood supply with previously unexploitable supplies of wood. Steel axes allowed Native peoples to harvest live trees for fuel, whereas earlier they would have had to let them stand or else fell them through the laborious process of burning and girding.[7] Steel knives also made the skinning and butchering of game a simpler matter.

Metal cutting tools made it easier for Iroquoian peoples to strip bark from trees. Just as wood formed the basic material of Iroquoian culture, bark provided covering for houses and was the primary material from which watercraft were made. Twine, usually made from the inner bark of trees, helped hold Iroquoian houses, canoes, and cooking vessels together. Other tools, such as steel hoes and mattocks, made it easier for women to break ground for planting.[8]

Metal kettles quickly replaced ones made by Native peoples.[9] Metal kettles seem to have been the item that Iroquoian peoples modified the most, often cutting them up to make tools and jewelry. But increasingly, in about the 1620s, they began to use them in their intended roles as cooking vessels. Prior to the introduction of metal kettles and pots, Iroquoian peoples constructed cooking vessels of wood, bark, and clay.[10] Cooking with these vessels was laborious and time consuming. A cook would fill the container with water and then heat "a quantity of stones and gravel red-hot in a good fire" and place "them into a kettle filled with water in which the meat or fish was to be cooked." This required that the stones be constantly removed and other red-hot stones placed in the pot until "the water was heated and the meat cooked to some extent." The Huron and Iroquois did make earthenware pots, but they became "soft and break at the least blow given them."[11] Metal kettles, then, made cooking easier and probably resulted in food being more thoroughly cooked.

Very quickly, Iroquoian peoples realized that they could obtain much of this desirable technology, such as metal kettles and axes, for what they regarded as old, smelly beaver robes and for the fresh pelts of the plentiful animal. The Jesuit Paul Le Jeune wrote of a Montagnais who jokingly told him, "The Beaver does everything perfectly well, It makes kettles, hatchets, swords, knives, bread; and, in short, it makes everything." On another occasion, this same man showed Le Jeune a "very beautiful knife" and proclaimed that "the English have no sense; they give us twenty knives for one Beaver skin."[12]

While beaver pelts became the primary means by which Native peoples of the Northeast obtained European trade goods, the potential value of furs was not foremost in the minds of Europeans who colonized the continent in the early seventeenth century. Samuel de Champlain, in about 1615, enumerated the products of the Americas that could be turned into a profit and listed animal skins after fish, whale oil, lumber, potash, naval stores, dyes, and mining and only before precious stones and agricultural products.[13]

But of all these goods, beaver pelts, because of their desirability in Europe and the readiness of Native peoples to hunt them in exchange for trade goods, became the first large-scale export from North America to Europe. As early as 1614, twenty-five thousand animal pelts, mostly beaver, were funneled through Quebec to France, where they were worked into fashionable headgear.[14] Dutch traders at Fort Orange and New Amsterdam took in eight thousand pelts a year by the mid-1620s.[15] Thirty years later, six times that amount of furs were traded at Fort Orange alone.[16]

The traffic in European goods to the Five Nations Iroquois was not insignificant in the early seventeenth century. When the Dutch barber-surgeon Harman Meyndertsz van den Bogaert visited the Mohawk near the end of 1634, he saw a plethora of trade goods, including "good timber axes, French shirts, coats, and razors."[17] Twentieth-century archaeologists have found that objects of European origin comprised up to 15 percent of the total artifacts recovered from Iroquois village sites that were occupied from about 1600 to 1620 in upstate New York. On village sites occupied in the mid-seventeenth century, the percentage of European trade items is even greater, often representing more than 75 percent of the total number of artifacts.[18] And that is only what has been found. The most popular trade item, cloth, seldom appears in the archaeological record.[19] Because of the durability and usefulness of European wares, the occupants of these villages probably made it a point to take their metal goods with them when they moved to a new site.

In the first two decades of the seventeenth century, Iroquoian peoples often did not view European goods, such as kettles, axes, knives, and cloth, as finished products. These goods were viewed as raw materials, waiting to be shaped and manipulated into usable form and to be given by their human makers, through the act of creation, a piece of their soul, so that the finished artifact would accompany its maker into the afterlife.

Since Iroquoian peoples, as part of their traditional, or renewable, thought world did not extract finished products from the landscape of Huronia or Iroquoia, they did not at first—indeed they could not—view European goods as finished. They inhabited a thought world in which raw materials-wood, stone, and bone—were everywhere. All of these items, however, required shaping and manipulation by humans before they could assume a usable form. Given this context of their thought world, Iroquoian peoples could not see European goods as finished. Like everything else, European goods required human intervention and shaping and, in the process, the bestowal of a soul.

Since these goods were, for the most part, "incomparably better and more convenient," they were more desirable.[20] But because Iroquoian peoples had a different view of trade goods, they were not always utilized, let alone conceptualized, in the manner that their European manufacturers had intended.

Iroquoian peoples viewed European goods in two ways: as raw materials or as works in progress. First, while kettles, axes, and knives in their existing state were very useful, they could be—and often were, as far as Iroquoian peoples were concerned—improved upon. Kettles, often of copper, were frequently never used as cooking vessels.[21] Instead, they became another source of raw material. New copper kettles were often cut up and made into awls, arrowheads, knives, beads, and pendants.[22] Axes, while obviously useful in their manufactured form, also were treated as a form of raw material, often being transformed into knives and scrapers. One axe could easily be turned into two knives and one scraper. Other European goods, such as swords, were modified and used as fish spears. Knives could become harpoon points.[23]

Many of these goods, however, required no modification. Thus iron axes replaced stone ones. Shorter axes replaced clubs of wood and stone. Iron awls and needles made the construction of clothing and footwear easier. Awls were also used to punch holes in softer trade metals such as copper and brass. They also made the production of existing Native technologies easier, since they were used as drills to work bone and wood.[24] Ice picks made the breaking down of beaver lodges easier, steel knives replaced the sharp but brittle knives of flint, and steel fishhooks were far more durable than ones made of wood or bone. Copper pots and kettles replaced ones made of clay.[25]

Rarely, however, is the trade item that native peoples of the Northeast desired the most found in the archaeological record. Cloth, often of wool in the form of blankets or duffels, was the most traded item. Unlike animal skins, cloth remained soft and supple after getting wet and dried quickly. Like metal goods, Iroquians regarded woolen cloth as a raw material. By using metal scissors, needles, and awls, native peoples fashioned the new material into traditional garments such as leggings, breechcloths, dresses, and tie-on sleeves. Cloth also freed women from the laborious tasks of scraping, treating, and tanning animal hides.[26] At the very least, cloth reduced the number of hides they had to tan.

Iroquoian peoples modified cloth in a number of ways. European "bed-blankets, which they improve with trimming and wear double," were in use at almost all hours of the day, particularly during the winter.[27] One Dutch trader noted that Native peoples "trade their beavers for duffels cloth . . . which they consider better for the rain."[28] One Jesuit noted that one trade "blanket would serve to clothe by day and cover by night two Barbarians, during a whole winter." Another Frenchman saw Huron converts who, upon hearing the bell ring for morning mass, rose, and "in the turn of one's hand they had wrapped themselves in their blankets, which serve as garments and as beds." Thus attired, they proceeded straight to the chapel.[29] A Dutchman noted that "they use a good deal of duffel cloth, which they buy from us, and which serves for their blanket by night, and their dress by day."[30] Sometimes, however, the Iroquois would not modify cloth they obtained in trade. Johannes Megapolensis wrote that "they buy of us Dutchmen two and a half ells of duffel, and that they hang simply about them, just as it was torn off, without sewing it, and walk away with it."[31]

European traders learned early in their dealings with Iroquoian peoples that they were particular about the goods they would trade for. Defective or undesirable goods could not be fobbed off on them. Nor were they interested in acquiring, European notions to the contrary, baubles and trinkets.[32] A Dutch trader wrote to his superiors of the Mohawk's preference in blankets, "I have only about thirty pieces of cloth in colors that are in demand, that is, blue and standard gray; the rest which I have are all red, whereof I can sell a yard, because the Indians say that it hinders them in hunting, being visible too far off. They all call for black, the darker the better, but red and green they will not take."[33]

European traders also learned that Iroquoian peoples would refuse goods for reasons of their own. The Dutch agent who complained about the cloth sent back "110 defective kettles which cannot be sold here." Nor could the Native peoples be induced to pay more for certain items based on European notions of value: "We have . . . a number of copper kettles, which cannot be traded . . . they would not give for them more than the others."[34] In other words, Native peoples did not trade more pelts for a copper kettle because European traders, and the dynamics of a distant European economy, dictated that a copper pot should cost more than one made of brass; they traded for goods based on how they valued them. At times, however, there could be other reasons for refusing certain trade goods. During an epidemic in the 1630s, the Huron "decided no longer to use French kettles, imagining that everything which came in any way from us was capable of communicating the disease to them."[35]

Trade goods, in the eyes of Iroquoian peoples, required further human manipulation before they could be considered finished. Once manipulated, they became, like other goods, linked to the afterlife. Like goods made by Native peoples of native material, they now had a soul and could accompany their maker or owner to the Village of the Dead.

But as early as the 1630s, the Iroquoian thought world began to change. Unaltered trade goods, ones that had not been treated as raw material and made into other objects, began to be deposited into ossuaries during the Huron Feast of the Dead.[36] Unmodified metal objects of European origin such as kettles, iron knives, scissors, keys, awls, and bracelets have been recovered from Huron ossuaries dating to 1636.[37] European goods made of glass have also been found, including magnifying glasses, beads, and parts of wineglasses.[38]

This change in the way that European trade goods were used reflects that the Huron were beginning to view trade goods differently. In the older view, trade items had to arrive in their raw state in a Huron community and be manipulated into useful shapes before they could be considered to have souls. Judging from their actions in the 1630s, it appears that the Huron now began to believe that the manipulation of these items by human hands in Europe must have already given them a soul and hence the ability to accompany the dead into the afterlife. This new mode of thinking came about as Iroquoian peoples began to acquire and use more trade goods that they could not fabricate themselves. Gabriel Sagard noted that the Huron believed that the French were "endowed with the greatest mind" and that "they alone could make the most complicated things, such as axes, knives, kettles, etc."[39]

The Five Nations Iroquois noted European agency in the creation of trade goods even earlier, referring to the Dutch as *kristoni,* "metal-makers," and Europeans in general as *asseroni,* "ax-makers."[40] Similarly, Johannes Megapolensis noted that the Dutch were known to the Mohawk as *assirioni,* "cloth-makers," and as *charistooni,* "iron-workers, because our people first brought cloth and iron among them."[41]

Perishable trade goods supplemented and may have added a bit of novelty to the Iroquoian diet. Iroquoian peoples used "bread, peas, beans, prunes ... etc." to supplement their diet.[42] Preserved foods, such as sea biscuit, prunes, and dried peas and beans, allowed hunters to remain in the woods far longer in their quest for the furs that fed the supply of trade goods. Some Native peoples, however, complained about the trade in European foodstuffs, arguing, "the merchandise is often counterfeited and adulterated, and that peas, beans, prunes, bread, and other things that are spoiled are sold to them; and that it is that which corrupts the body and gives rise to the dysentery and other diseases which always attack them in the Autumn."[43]

Iroquoian peoples seemed to have believed that European foodstuffs, unlike other European trade goods, were devoid of spiritual power. Tools of European origin such as knives, axes, and magnifying glasses have been found in Huron ossuaries. Items of personal adornment, such as polychrome glass beads, have also been discovered.[44] But European food items were absent from the burials. The Jesuit Jean de Brébeuf, who witnessed the interment of Huron dead in the ossuary at Ossassané in 1636, saw Huron women place "some dishes of corn" on the pit after it was closed. In the days following the Feast of the Dead, "several other Cabins of the Village provided nets quite full of it [corn], which were thrown upon the pit."[45]

The absence of European victuals could simply indicate scarcity, but it could also indicate that these foods were seen in a different way than those Iroquoian peoples produced themselves. In this sense, the connection to the earth was still strong. Food that came from the earth of Huronia could be replicated in the Village of the Dead. And food from Huronia may have also represented food that the Huron regarded as being alive, or having a spirit, unlike the preserved foods of Europe. The corn that the Huron placed in the ossuaries could be consumed by the dead and used as seed when they reached the Village of the Dead. European foods such as bread and prunes could not be replicated there—the dead would be unable to grow them—so the living did not include them among the grave goods. Durable trade items, however, such as knives and axes, had an infinite number of uses and were very useful to the dead.

Both of the two largest groups of Iroquoian peoples, the Huron and the Five Nations Iroquois, initially saw European trade goods, the first few of which they began to acquire in the late sixteenth century, in a positive light.[46] But by the late 1630s and early 1640s, the Huron began to link trade goods to death and Christianity, while the Iroquois saw them—particularly firearms—as the tools that would enable them to remake their world for the better.

Unlike the Huron, who traded almost exclusively with the French, the Five Nations had an array of European trading partners, including the Dutch, Swedes, English, and French. The Huron never seemed to acquire trade goods in the numbers that the Iroquois did. Gabriel Sagard noted that the Huron used metal knives to make arrows but that they also used "sharp-edged stones" if they did not have a knife.[47] Even after the introduction of European goods, the Huron still used stone tools.[48] Nor, despite the acquisition of brass and copper pots and kettles, did pottery making cease among the Huron.

There are two probable reasons why older Native technologies survived among the Huron for as long as they did. First, because the Huron had only one European trade partner, the French, they did not receive goods in sufficient quantities. The French trading companies seemed to have had continual problems producing, procuring, and shipping enough goods for the fur trade. This in part may have been because they were not prepared for the volume of trade that they experienced in the early years of the seventeenth century.[49] The second reason for the shortage was the poor quality of French trade goods. Many metal goods, such as axes and kettles, were made by the French specifically for the trade with Native peoples and were often inferior to like goods sold in Europe. The substandard kettles quickly wore out, and the Huron would ask missionaries if they knew how to fix them. Axes also broke frequently, and the resulting scrap metal, like that of the poorly made kettles, would be reworked into other items. But it was the difficulty of acquisition and the poor quality of the trade items that they did acquire that compelled the Huron to keep their lithic technology well into the seventeenth century.[50]

Yet despite the difficulties in obtaining trade goods, a large array of European-made items were exchanged for animal pelts. A Jesuit wrote to his brother in the 1620s of two ships that had brought merchandise to trade with the Native peoples. Among the goods were "cloaks, blankets, night-caps, hats, shirts, sheets, hatchets, iron arrowheads, bodkins, swords, picks to break the ice in Winter, knives, kettles, prunes, raisins, Indian corn, peas, crackers or sea biscuits, and tobacco."[51] A later Frenchman wrote of Native peoples acquiring "Short and light fusees . . . Sword-blades to make Darts of . . . Caps of blew Serge. Shirts . . . of the common *Brittany* Linnen . . . Woolsted Stockins . . . Thread . . . Needles . . . *Venice* Beads," and a "small quantity of soap." Most ominously, this writer made an allusion at the end of his list to the growing traffic in alcohol, noting, "Brandy goes off incomparably well."[52]

The Huron never acquired trade goods in sufficient numbers to cause them to completely give up their lithic technology. Iroquois incursions in the late 1630s and early 1640s caused the Huron to begin questioning the value of the fur trade altogether. The trading trips along the St. Lawrence from Huronia to Montreal began to cost many Hurons their lives. Indeed, Jesuits wrote to France asking that something be done about the Iroquois menace, otherwise "we must soon expect to see their [the Huron's] trade with our French entirely broken off,—for the enemies become every year stronger and more formidable upon the river, which is the only road they have for access thither." As the Iroquois turned traveling the St. Lawrence into a year-round hazard, another Jesuit was moved to write, "There is hardly an open passage left for us to reach the Hurons." This same Jesuit later wrote in the *Relations* that the Iroquois "make incursions . . . and watch the Hurons at all places along the River,—slaughtering them, burning them, and carrying off their Peltry, which they go and sell to the Dutch, in order to have powder and Arquebuses, and then to ravage everything and become masters everywhere, which is fairly easy unless France gives us help."[53]

The frequency of the attacks began to take a psychological toll on the Huron. They, and many of the French, began to imagine that the Iroquois were everywhere. "There is," the Jesuit Hierosme Lalemant moaned, "no safety for a moment from an enemy hidden in the rushes along the banks of the river, or in the depths of the forest, which screen them from your sight while they can see you coming from a distance of four, five, or six leagues."[54]

Lalemant went on to point out the danger to the French trade that the Iroquois posed. Not only were they seizing furs bound for Montreal and Quebec, but also they made the "Hurons think of giving up the trade with the French, because they find that it costs them too dear, and they prefer to do without European goods rather than expose themselves every year, not to a death that would be endurable, but to fires and flames, for which they have a thousand times greater horror." If the French did not send help, Lalemant believed, the Huron could turn on the remaining Jesuits, who would "be abandoned to the fury of a desperate people, who will no longer be restrained from massacring us all by fear of losing their trade with the French."[55]

While trade goods, to some degree, represented a technological advance and a twist in the technological imagination, the Huron did not receive them in sufficient numbers to completely give up precontact technology. Nor, after their acquisition began to lead to death, did they consider them worth dying for. The Five Nations Iroquois, on the other hand, saw trade goods in a more positive light.

Trade goods, in many ways, helped to bring about both the destroyed and remade thought worlds. The quest to acquire European goods meant that Iroquoian peoples were separating themselves from the Earth. Rather than seek their substance and artifacts from the environments of Huronia and Iroquoia, they now sought goods of steel and cloth. In the process, they had to destroy elements of the old thought world and construct new ones. Perhaps nothing emphasizes this more than the need to give many European goods a soul. Hand in hand with the destroyed thought world went the remade one. But it was only for the Five Nations Iroquois that the remade thought world became a reality.

8

MAKING WAR LETHAL

IN THE STILLNESS OF A JULY MORNING IN 1609, NEAR the lake that now bears his name, Samuel de Champlain, armed with a harquebus into which he "put four bullets," approached to "within some thirty yards" of a loose formation of Mohawks. He stopped and "took aim with my arquebus and shot straight at one of the three chiefs, and with this shot two fell to the ground and one of their companions was wounded who died thereof a little later." Another Frenchman then fired at the Mohawk from the cover of the woods, "which astonished them again so much that, seeing their chiefs dead they lost courage and took to flight, abandoning the field and their fort."[1]

Many historians have tended to portray this brief firefight as the genesis of the long-term enmity between New France and the Five Nations.[2] But perhaps of far more significance, it also heralded a vast shift in the Iroquoian thought world. A new technology, one almost unrecognizably different from any possessed by Iroquoian peoples, had been introduced.[3] War, one of the most important aspects of the Iroquois thought world because of its destructive and reconstructive properties, would now be transformed. While the evidence of this vast technological shift should have been immediately visible when the Mohawk fled the battlefield in 1609, Champlain's Native allies did not grasp the encounter's significance on the level of technology. Rather than pursue their beaten foe, Champlain noted that they "wasted time in taking . . . [the Mohawk's] shields, which they had left behind, the better in order to run."[4]

Like other fighting men in different times and places, Champlain's Indian allies, despite the evidence of their own eyes, did not realize that their existing technology had just been eclipsed by another. Their bearing off the shields of their foes indicates that they saw this engagement only in the immediate sense of a tactical victory. It seems not to have occurred to them that the gunpowder technology that routed the Mohawk could one day be turned on them.[5]

Among Iroquoian peoples, there had been something of a brief technological interlude between the stone-tipped arrow and the explosive propelled leaden ball. Precontact wooden armor, which provided an Iroquoian warrior with sufficient protection against Native-made weapons, consisted of "a sort of armor and cuirass . . . on their back and legs and other parts of the body to get protection from arrow-shots." Iron arrowheads, however, made for the fur trade by Europeans, made Native arrows more lethal and reduced—indeed, nearly eliminated—the protective properties of wooden armor, Gabriel Sagard noted that wooden armor was "proof against those sharp-pointed stones, yet not against our Quebec iron heads when the arrows fitted with them are shot by the stout and powerful arm such as that of a savage."[6]

The iron-tipped arrow, however, merely echoed a familiar technology, albeit in a much improved form. The firearm, while it served the same purpose as the bow and arrow, represented a shift in the technological imagination of Iroquoian peoples.[7] It killed loudly, introducing a new element of fright, and death by these weapons seemed to be instantaneous. But most important, it killed more men.

While Champlain's brief firefight led Native warriors to begin discarding their armor, it still remained in use for at least three more decades. Both Iroquois and Huron warriors continued to wear armor into battle. However, European technology made set-piece battles in which the participants went at each other toe to toe no longer feasible. Stealth now became more important, and Iroquoian warriors stopped wearing bulkier pieces of armor. The type of armor retained for use in battle tended to be pieces that could, its wearers hoped, nonetheless serve a useful purpose. While warriors realized they could encounter foes bearing firearms, armor could still offer them some protection from stone-tipped arrows, knives, and clubs. As late as 1637, the Jesuit François Joseph Le Mercier observed the Huron making wooden shields to carry into battle against the Iroquois. Another Jesuit witnessed a 1642 attack on a French redoubt, during which a charging Iroquois warrior "received seven leaden balls in his buckler, and as many in his body." His companions "dropped their shields, trusting more to their feet for safety than their bucklers."[8] A few years later, the same Jesuit took note of a small Huron war party setting out for "the country of the Hyroquois" in the winter of 1642–43. While some members of the troop carried firearms, others wore armor "stitched, and interlaced with small sticks" that covered the trunk of the body. Others carried "shields made of wood."[9] For the Huron, this winter war party ended in disaster. Planning to attack the Iroquois during their winter hunt, the Huron found themselves surprised and slain by their intended victims. The sole survivor, a woman, spent thirty days in the woods, eluding the Iroquois. Clad in only half a blanket and not daring to make a fire lest her pursuers discover her, she made her way back to Montreal.[10]

The use of armor at such a late date by Iroquoian warriors indicates that it still may have been useful. Perhaps the enemy did not always have European weaponry. Another, perhaps more likely, explanation is that wearing armor or carrying a shield gave a warrior some degree of psychological comfort, a feeling that maybe, with some luck, his armor might stop or deflect the lead balls and steel blades that would otherwise penetrate his body.

Firearms, however, were not the only European contribution to the more lethal battlefield of the American forests. Metal axes and hatchets replaced the traditional war club and made hand-to-hand combat more deadly. European-made axes also contributed to the elimination of wooden armor. Unlike the native-made clubs of wood and stone, steel ax bits easily cleaved their way through native armor at one blow, inflicting grievous, and oftentimes fatal, injuries.

Yet while the steel ax negated wooden armor as a form of protection, it facilitated the making of another sort of battlefield defense. Native warriors discovered that steel axes not only made excellent weapons, but they also used them as tools to hastily build battlefield fortifications. European observers, many of them military men, found the skill and speed native warriors displayed in constructing these redoubts impressive.

The Mohawk demonstrated their engineering abilities during a standoff between themselves and the French on the Richelieu River in the early 1640s. As daylight began to fade, the French force, aboard armed boats,

An Illustration by Jesuit Missionary Francesco Bressani of a Huron or Iroquois Warrior Carrying a Musket while Wearing Wooden Armor. Despite the fact that guns rendered wooden armor ineffective, it remained in use for years after the introduction of firearms. From *Novae Franciae Accurata Delineatio* (1657). Courtesy of the National Library and National Archives of Canada.

tensely waited, trying to anticipate the next move of the Iroquois force on the shore. Just as night fell, "suddenly was heard so horrible and frightful an uproar and clashing of hatchets, a fall and wreck of so many trees, that it seemed as if the whole forest were being overthrown." The next morning, the French found themselves facing an Iroquois fort on the shore, flying an Algonquin scalp as a flag. After a day of exchanging fire with the French, the Iroquois withdrew under cover of darkness. When the French went ashore, they discovered that the Iroquois had built not just one but two solid forts. They found the second fort "hidden further in the woods, but so well constructed and so well supplied that it was proof against all our resources." The next year there occurred yet another example of how the Iroquois used steel axes in hastily constructing fortifications. A small group of Iroquois, cornered by a superior French force, "in four minutes erected a small fort." Iroquois warriors also built forts in enemy territory, concealed them, and used them as bases from which to strike at their enemies.[11]

Most, but not all, Iroquoian villages were surrounded by circular wooden palisades as protection from enemy attack. European axes and military advice made these palisades more secure and, in theory, rendered villages less vulnerable to enemy attack.[12] Although the laws of the Society of Jesus prevented him from bearing arms, the Jesuit Jean de Brébeuf advised the Huron of the advantages of straight-line fortifications over circular ones. "We have told them ... henceforth, they should make their forts square, and arrange their stakes in straight lines; and that, by means of four little towers at the four corners, four Frenchmen might easily with their arquebuses or muskets defend a whole village."[13]

The Huron also began to use larger saplings in the construction of their palisades, a change made possible, in all likelihood, because of European tools such as steel axes. The Huron also, apparently on their own initiative, modified French suggestions for fortifications and built some that were quadrilateral in shape, making it possible for two men with muskets to defend a village.[14] The clever layout of these fortifications probably reflected a lack of firearms on the part of the Huron. These innovations in village fortification had the consequence of creating a sense of false security for their inhabitants, which the Iroquois would eventually take advantage of.[15]

Firearms, far more than any other form of European technology, brought about the most changes in Iroquoian warfare. The shock they caused in terms of noise and casualties made a great impression on Native Americans. While the noise of firearms is often cited as a source of terror, more significant to Native peoples may have been the seemingly instant lethality of these weapons. Launching one or more lead balls, ranging in size from .56 to .68 caliber, firearms caused battlefield injuries that were far more devastating than anything Native warriors had previously experienced.[16] The specter of mass casualties upset traditional notions of warfare.[17] While the Iroquois fled the field in terror at the conclusion of their 1609 confrontation with Champlain, apparently it did not take them long to determine what these new weapons could and could not do. In an attack on an Onondaga fort in June 1610, Champlain observed that the

Onondaga "out of fear, thinking these shots to be irresistible . . . would throw themselves upon the ground when they heard a report."[18] While an element of fear was probably present, in all likelihood the Onondaga were simply taking cover. They had doubtless ascertained that the flight of a ball from a harquebus followed a straight-line trajectory. They were simply doing what soldiers on a modern battlefield do: they dropped to the ground to make a smaller target, or they placed a good-sized tree or rock between themselves and the French who were shooting at them. A Dutch observer in 1624 noted that the Mohawk had no firearms and that "whole troops run before five or six muskets. At the first coming (of the Europeans) they were accustomed to fall prostrate on the ground at the report of a gun."[19] Only two years later, however, firearms seemed to present no particular terror to the Mohawk. A party of seven Dutchmen from Fort Orange set out to assist the Mahicans in their war against the Mohawk. The Mohawk, armed with bows and arrows, attacked the combined Dutch-Mahican force and killed four of the Dutch, one of whom they "devoured, after having well roasted him." A few days after the incident, an official of the Dutch West India Company arrived at Fort Orange and, upon hearing of the conflict, set out to mend fences with the Mohawk. He visited the Mohawk, who said that "they wished to excuse their act, on the plea that they had never set themselves against the whites, and asked why the latter had meddled with them; otherwise, they would not have shot them."[20]

After this incident, the Dutch West India Company adopted a policy of noninterference with the Five Nations.[21] Official Dutch policy, for the most part, attempted to keep firearms out of the hands of Native peoples.[22] However, once independent Dutch traders learned of the Mohawk's willingness to travel to the New England colonies and pay up to twenty beaver pelts for a musket, an illicit trade quickly developed. The Mohawk no longer had to travel as far and could obtain guns for roughly the same price—or lower—as they paid the English. By 1638, "the traders coming from Holland soon got scent of it [the trade], and from time to time brought over great quantities, so that the Mohawks in a short time were seen with firelocks, powder, and lead in proportion."[23]

Although Iroquoian warriors greatly prized guns, they would not buy just any firearm. They critically assessed the available weapons against their needs and found many European firearms lacking. In the early seventeenth century, European firearms used two basic types of ignition systems. One form was the matchlock, and the other was one of the several varieties of flint-activated guns that for simplicity's sake are known as flintlocks. The matchlock received its name because it required a match, a lit piece of cord treated with saltpeter or gunpowder—so that the match would burn slowly—to fire the weapon. The weapon had to be primed before firing and the match lit, and kept lit, by the musketeer, for if an enemy suddenly came upon him, he likely would not be given a chance to kindle a fire. A musketeer usually lit both ends of the match as a precaution against one end going out. Matches burned at a rate of approximately nine inches an hour, so if a musketeer took the precaution of lighting both ends, he expended a foot and a half of the specially treated cord each hour. All of this meant that one had to carry a large quantity of match in the field. On top of all this, a man carrying a matchlock constantly had to check the match to ensure that it remained lit and to blow away the ashes. When it came time to fire his weapon, the musketeer clamped the match into a "serpentine," a hammer that guided the match to the touchhole and set off the weapon.[24] For Iroquoian warriors, the matchlock had too many drawbacks to be considered as a primary weapon. If the match became wet, the weapon was useless, except perhaps as a club. The smell of burning saltpeter, as well as the glow from the match at night, gave away one's position.[25] It also made the weapon less than useful for hunting. Game animals would smell the burning match and avoid the hunter's location. The fourteen separate steps required to load and fire the weapon made it impractical for Iroquoian warriors. Moreover, the combination of a smoldering match in close proximity to volatile black powder made the process of loading a matchlock hazardous.[26]

Iroquoian warriors found flint weapons to be far more useful. These weapons did not use a match to fire. To fire a flintlock, one pulled the trigger, which thrust the cock, a hammer griping a flint, forward, where it struck a piece of steel called the battery. The resulting sparks fell into the touchhole, igniting the powder and firing the weapon.[27] While these weapons cost more than the matchlock, Iroquoian warriors quickly recognized that the flintlock was the superior weapon. Indeed, few matchlocks, or parts of them, are found in the archaeological record, while many parts of flintlock weapons have been found on Iroquois and Huron sites.[28] The flintlock lacked the disadvantages that plagued the matchlock. It was also a much safer weapon, since it did not require a burning object to be in close proximity to gunpowder. Based on the archaeological evidence, it appears that Iroquoians simply refused to trade for matchlocks—even though most European armies used them at the time—because of their shortcomings.

Just as Iroquoians refused to trade for cloth or metal goods that did not meet their criteria, so, too, did they refuse to accept a form of European technology that they viewed as imperfect and impractical. While the matchlock was impressive—it was loud, and it killed men in a seemingly instantaneous fashion—it had too many drawbacks to be useful in war or on the hunt. Iroquoian warriors would continue, for the most part, to carry bows until flintlocks became available.

There has been a minor debate in academia over the effectiveness of European guns versus Native-made bows.[29] While bows did have a higher rate of fire then muzzle-loading weapons and were very effective, Native peoples, despite the advantages that modern scholars have enumerated, chose to replace them with guns.[30] Some years ago, Francis Jennings placed the controversy in its proper perspective. While scholars have argued that guns were not as efficient as bows, Jennings noted that "records clearly show Indians everywhere were demanding guns in trade, not only for war but for the hunt as well. It is not necessary to rely on argument. They were vocal and explicit about this demand."[31]

While it is not known how many guns the Iroquois had at a given time, it is possible, based on the sources, to make a guess. An anonymous Dutch source claims that the Mohawk, as of 1638, had four hundred firearms and a large quantity of powder.[32] In June 1641, a force of five hundred Iroquois appeared at Montreal to treat for peace with the French. One of their captives, a French soldier, reported that in this party there were "thirty-six arquebusiers, as skillful as the French."[33] This figure is at odds with other sources, and the Iroquois may have been short of, or felt they were short of, firearms. In exchange for this purported "peace" that the Five Nations offered the French, they expected to be supplied with arquebuses. Yet only two years later, the Jesuits claimed that the Iroquois had three hundred guns. By the end of the 1640s, the Iroquois had at least a thousand firearms. The thousand-man Iroquois army that devastated Huronia in the spring of 1649 had "mostly firearms."[34]

Not only did the Iroquois have firearms, they had also, interestingly enough, acquired a degree of skill in handling them that sometimes surpassed that of Europeans. Iroquoian warriors taught themselves one thing with firearms that Europeans did not teach their own soldiers: how to aim.[35] The Jesuit Isaac Jouges, writing from his captivity in Iroquoia in the early 1640s, warned his fellow missionaries that Iroquois war parties had muskets and that "they are skilled in handling them."[36] A Dutch source in 1650 claimed that Native peoples were "exceedingly fond of guns, sparing no expense for them; and are so skilful in the use of them that they surpass many Christians."[37] Baron Lahonton, writing in the early eighteenth century, claimed that "the Strength of the *Iroquese* lies in engaging with Fire-Arms in a Forrest; for they shoot very dexterously."[38] Despite Europe's wars, few colonists had extensive training in the use of guns. Indeed, a recruit may have had only a few days' training in which he struggled to master the myriad steps required to load and fire a matchlock before his commanders dispatched him to the front.[39]

The image of Daniel Boone or Natty Bumpo—that of an unerring marksman—that many Americans have of early frontiersmen is a treasured piece of American mythology. Many early settlers did, out of necessity, develop considerable skill with firearms; however, while some owned weapons, many of the first colonists were coming from cultures that restricted the use of guns. Few people in Europe hunted, and hunting laws were usually intended to preserve game for the upper classes. In the first half of the seventeenth century, an Englishman needed an annual income of at least 100 pounds before he was permitted to own a firearm. Even if he met the income requirements and owned a gun, it was unlikely that an upper-class Englishman would fire the weapon very often. Guns were thought to be "unsporting." It was far more respectable to use other animals—such as hounds or falcons—to hunt game. Nor did poachers use them; the sound of a gun would have given away their presence. Thus most colonists' experience with weaponry was limited to any prior military service they may have had in the Old World or to the infrequent drills they participated in as part of the colonial militia.[40]

Unlike the Dutch, who officially limited the gun trade but understood that they could not stop independent traders, the French were actually able to limit the sale of firearms to Native peoples. The English and the Swedes, like the Dutch, were unable to control the gun trade. In this respect, the government of New France was unique. Geographic barriers prevented other European powers from making contact with the Huron. And the Five Nations, sitting athwart the routes that the Dutch, English, or Swedes would have had to use to reach Huronia, surely would have vetoed any such attempt. Whereas the Five Nations could always obtain firearms from one

European trading partner or another, the geographic location of the league denied the Huron and other Native allies of the French access to Fort Orange.[41] Initially, the French attempted to link firearms, as they did other forms of European technology, to conversion to Christianity. "The use of arquebuses . . . granted to the Christian Neophytes," one Jesuit wrote, "is a powerful attraction to win them."[42]

Doubtless, firearms probably did attract converts. But the realities of warfare and the inability of the French to transport goods in large quantities quickly made the policy of trading arms only to converts obsolete. The Jesuit Barthelemy Vimont, having observed a 1642 skirmish between Iroquois and Algonquin Christians, believed that the Algonquins would have killed most of the Iroquois had they enough powder, and his remarks reveal much about the French arms trade: "We have always been afraid to arm the savages too much. Would to God that the Hollanders had done the same, and had not compelled us to give arms even to our Christians."[43]

The French continued to come up short in the colonial arms race that Vimot describes. It may very well have been a common attitude among the French that firearms should be difficult for Native peoples to acquire. But Vimot's remark also reveals that the French realized that in order for their Native allies to be a match for the Iroquois, they must have European weaponry, even if the French had to give, rather than trade, muskets to their allies.

In theory, the Huron should not have been lacking firearms. But poor-quality weapons, unreliable transport from the Old World, and steep prices for these weapons posed problems in obtaining muskets. Equally important is that frequent Iroquois attacks on Huron trading canoes doubtless resulted in the loss of trade goods, and some of these goods may have been firearms.[44] In a representative 1642 incident, forty Iroquois, all equipped with firearms, waylaid thirteen Huron canoes on the St. Lawrence, near Montreal. The sixty Hurons defending the canoes had only bows and arrows, and the Iroquois took twenty-three of the Huron captive.[45] Because of their lack of firearms, the Huron began encouraging armed Frenchmen to accompany them on their trading voyages.[46] The protection that armed Europeans offered may have been a factor in lifting the Huron's prohibition on allowing Europeans to accompany them along trade routes.[47]

Each year in the 1640s, as the Huron attempted to ferry their peltries to Montreal, they found themselves ambushed by the Iroquois, who "now use firearms, which they buy from the Flemings. . . . A single discharge of fifty or sixty arquebuses would be sufficient to cause terror in a thousand Hurons."[48] In the French sources, the Huron tend to be portrayed as being afraid of firearms, while the Iroquois, with the notable exception of their first encounter with Champlain, did not seem to have any particular fear of firearms.

There are two possible reasons why the Huron feared guns while the Iroquois did not. One reason for this may be that as late as the 1640s, the Huron had difficulty obtaining European trade goods, including guns, and were forced to use lithic technology at this late date.[49] A second part of the answer may be that the Iroquois made efforts—and had the opportunity—to familiarize themselves with firearms far more often than did the Huron. In the 1626 clash with the Dutch, the Mohawk only had bows and arrows, but they still won.[50] Harmen Meyndertsz van den Bogaert, visiting the Oneida and Mohawk in 1634–35, noted that they had no guns, but they obviously knew of them. On two different occasions, the Mohawk, and later the Oneida, for no discernable reason imploredVan den Bogaert and his companions to fire their weapons.[51] While there may have been a novelty factor at work—perhaps the Iroquois knew of firearms, but most of them had not seen one in use—this firing of guns may have been analogous to modern military training. Present-day recruits crawl under machine-gun fire to familiarize themselves with the report of the weapon and the sounds of combat. This sort of training could have been true of seventeenth-century Mohawk as well. If the Mohawk could familiarize their warriors with the report of the weapons, they would, in theory, not panic when they encountered them in combat. Firearms, particularly if fired from an ambush, could still startle them, but recognizing the report, they would not flee the battlefield in terror. Another possibility is that they could have observed the Dutchmen reload their weapons after firing. This could have served two purposes. First, this gave them a practical demonstration on how to reload the weapon, and second, it gave them a sense of how long it would take a foe to bring his gun back into action after firing it.

These lessons took on added meaning for Iroquoian peoples when European weaponry began to alter their traditional view of warfare. While captives remained the primary stimulus for war, combat itself, because of European weaponry, had become more deadly. European diseases and the need for European trade goods made war more frequent. Epidemics of European diseases such as smallpox increased the number of dead in Iroquoian communities and necessitated the taking of more captives to replace them.[52] While most epidemics no doubt went unreported, some found their way into the record. When Van den Bogaert visited a Mohawk village in late 1634, he found a chief "living one quarter mile from the fort in a small cabin because many Indians here in the castle had died of smallpox."[53] Jesuits learned of epidemics among the Five Nations in 1647 from escaped prisoners.[54]

European diseases and European weaponry made for a strange paradox. Death from disease meant that the dead had to be replaced by captives. But the use of firearms increased the number of casualties, making the taking of captives less likely. The lethality of guns meant that men, and sometime women and children, who could have been captured instead died in battle and did not return to Iroquoian villages for torture or adoption. Guns also meant that when women encouraged their kinsmen to go to war and bring back captives to replace the dead, they must have realized that the odds of their male kin returning from war decreased as firearms became more available to their enemies. European weaponry created a cycle of increased warfare. More men, because of firearms, died on the battlefield. In turn, Iroquoian clans sought to make up these deaths through adoption. But the primary mode of adoption, warfare, meant that men seeking captives were far more likely to be killed themselves and thus would have to be replaced by more adoptees.

The increased lethality of warfare meant that Iroquoian warriors now had to fight in different ways. Tactics changed quickly. Champlain had encountered Mohawk warriors who chose to fight in the daytime and in the open, eschewing the use of cover and concealment.[55] Champlain's object lesson as to the lethality of firearms changed the way that Iroquoian warriors fought. Except for ambushes on targets of opportunity, such as fur-bearing canoes, attacking warriors now chose to initiate combat during the hours of darkness. This helped an attacking force achieve surprise, and it reduced casualties because it gave the enemy a more difficult target. But it also created difficulties in command and control for the leaders of war parties.[56]

So well did the Five Nations Iroquois adopt these new weapons and tactics that a Jesuit priest, writing from Huronia in 1640, begged Cardinal Richelieu to do something about the Iroquois and the Europeans who traded with them. Pointing to the effects that this trade had on the Huron, he noted "that in less than ten years they have become reduced from thirty thousand to ten thousand; so that if in the past, when their numbers were great, they were unable to resist their enemies, what can we expect for them in the future?"[57] Shortly after this Jesuit wrote Richelieu, the governor of Canada, Charles de Huault de Montmagny, rejected peace overtures from the Five Nations. Two fears prompted the French to rebuff the Iroquois. If they negotiated a peace with the Iroquois separate from their Native allies, the French feared that the Iroquois would fall upon France's Native allies "who surround us on all sides . . . should we abandon them, they would give us more trouble than the Hiroquois." But the French had another, greater fear; "if the Hiroquois had free access to our ports, the trade . . . would be entirely stopped."[58]

The governors of New France realized that they could not make peace with the Five Nations. On the one hand, any such peace would not include their Native allies, who the Iroquois would be free to attack without fear of French interference. The Iroquois could also make peace with the Huron and Algonquin peoples who traded with the French and allow them to pass through Iroquoia, for a price. This unlikely scenario would have given the Huron and Algonquins access to Fort Orange and the superior trade goods available there. The third and most likely thing the Iroquois would do was to continue to seize and sell Huron and Algonquin peltries to the Dutch. Thus the French could not, during the course of the seventeenth century, consider a true peace with the Five Nations without undermining the economy of Canada.

Within a year after the rebuff of the Five Nations' peace overtures, Vimot, reporting on the state of Jesuit missions to his superiors in France, noted that "danger will not be averted from our colony, until the Hiroquois are either won over or exterminated." He also noted the continuing efforts of the Iroquois to wreck the French fur trade. "They block all roads leading to our great river; they . . . threaten to ruin our whole country."[59]

Indeed, the Iroquois raids and pirating of Huron furs proved so costly that by the mid-1640s the Huron seriously considered "giving up the trade with the French, because they find it costs them too dear, and they prefer to do without European goods rather than to expose themselves every year."[60] This represents an unusual change in way that the Huron viewed European trade. Whereas other Native peoples attempted to acquire more trade goods by expanding their role in the fur trade, the Huron, because of Iroquois aggression, now contemplated dropping out of the trade. This would have meant no more trade goods and more reliance on lithic technology, which the Huron apparently still had. The Huron, however, did not cease trading with the French, but it is significant that some of them at least voiced the thought. It is possible, of course, that they spoke of stopping the fur trade in an effort to gain French assistance against the Iroquois.

For the Huron, European technology and trade goods meant death. But the lack of trade goods also meant that some material aspects of the renewable world, such as stone tools, survived. At the same time, this lack of goods, particularly weapons, placed them at a severe disadvantage in their conflicts with the Iroquois.

For the Five Nations, the use of deadly new technologies such as firearms and steel axes tied a strong traditional, but largely theoretical, strand of the renewed thought world to their remade thought world. The extension of the Great Peace was one of the main precepts of the Deganawidah epic, the founding myth of the Iroquois League. Other peoples would be invited to join the league. If they refused to join, they should then be forced into the Longhouse—the Iroquois metaphor for the League. Prior to the Iroquois superiority in firearms, the Iroquois often got as good as they gave in battle with Native foes, with the result that the hoped-for extension of the Longhouse did not occur to any great degree. Firearms changed this. While combat became more deadly, innovations in the way that the Iroquois fought in the 1640s made the incorporation of other peoples into the Five Nations on a large scale a reality.

By the late 1640s, the Iroquois mode of warfare had undergone a drastic change. The destruction of Huronia in March 1649 and of other smaller groups of Iroquoian-speaking peoples in the 1650s demonstrates that the Five Nations had created concepts of warfare that, for the most part, were new to Native peoples in the Northeast. While captives remained the primary impetus for warfare, the Five Nations Iroquois, while not taking territory in the European sense, were effectively gaining control of previously contested areas.

The manner in which Iroquoian peoples regarded war underwent a radical change in less than half a century. War changed from the open, highly ritualized, largely nonlethal skirmishes between warriors seeking honor and captives to large-scale campaigns that had strategic, economic, and military objectives. Warfare was also where the renewed and remade worlds of the Huron and Five Nations blended. Elements of the remade world, such as the elimination of rival fur traders, came to be seen as strategic goals. Aspects of the renewed world, such as honor and especially the taking of captives, remained an important and necessary goal of Iroquoian warfare.

9

THE DESTRUCTION OF THE HURON AND REMAKING OF THE FIVE NATIONS

BY THE LATE 1640S, THE HURON HAD BEGUN TO DISINtegrate from within and without. Christianity, and the divisions that it caused, split the Huron into two diametrically opposed factions. So riven were the Huron by internal strife that many traditionalists now began to consider that which had once been unthinkable: they would leave Huronia—their family, friends, and community—and join the Five Nations Iroquois. The attacks by Iroquois warriors increased as the 1640s wore on and contributed to the debilitated state of Huronia. The Iroquois attacks further persuaded Huron traditionalists that perhaps they would be better off if they went to live among the Five Nations.

European contact and Christianity resulted in the Huron splitting themselves along religious lines. The Five Nations, however, through the selective use of European technology and their successful quest to gain control of the Great Lakes fur-trading routes, seemed by the mid-seventeenth century to be more united than ever. At the same time, the Five Nations' acquisition of European weaponry gave them a decisive edge over their Native foes. Because of these new weapons, the Iroquois' long-cherished traditional goal, the incorporation of other peoples into their confederacy, which they metaphorically described as the White Roots of Peace, now seemed to be becoming a reality.

The Five Nations' use of European technology and armament would result in dramatic changes in the way that they fought wars. The Huron, ironically linked mythologically to the Five Nations, had the misfortune of being the first people to experience how dramatic these changes were. The Iroquois would now show themselves more willing to fight far from home, and, most disconcerting to their Native foes, the Iroquois would display a hitherto unknown willingness to absorb large numbers of casualties in order to obtain a desired military objective.

In the summer of 1648, the Iroquois first revealed these new commitments. The Five Nations began a series of military operations that would culminate in the destruction, dispersal, and absorption of the Huron by the Five Nations. These operations represented a drastic departure from previous Iroquois strategy. Rather than a few warriors attacking fur-laden canoes, the Iroquois now appeared in Huronia in large numbers and assaulted entire villages. They also, despite having many of their number killed or captured, no longer broke off actions unless the tactical situation warranted it. Indeed, in what can only be considered a radical change, the Iroquois now only broke contact with an enemy when they had secured their objectives or when victory—now construed in European, not Iroquoian, terms—was not possible.

This sort of warfare required large forces; previously, the Iroquois preferred to fight in small groups. But warfare, with the intent of eliminating an enemy or forcing an enemy to desert its territory, was not unprecedented in the Five Nations' history.[1] In the late sixteenth century, the Mohawk warred on peoples to the north of them in an attempt to open a corridor to European traders in Canada.[2] In the 1620s, two decades before the Iroquois began their sustained campaign against the Huron, the Mohawk viewed the trading relationship between their old enemies, the Mahican and the Dutch, with growing concern. Should hostilities erupt, the Mohawk feared that the Dutch would choose to trade only with the Mahicans, thus depriving the Mohawk of European goods. The Mohawk's solution was to drive the Mahicans from the Hudson River Valley.[3]

By the 1620s, the Mahicans had situated themselves close to the Dutch. Nicolaes van Wassenaer, in 1626, wrote that "opposite [of Fort Orange] is the fort of the Maykans [Mahicans], which they built against the Maquaes [Mohawks], a powerful people." Two years later, Van Wassenaer noted exactly how powerful the Mohawk were when he wrote that "war broke out between the Maikans [Mahicans] near Fort Orange and the Makuaes [Mohawks], but these beat and captured the Maikans and drove off the remainder who have settled towards the north by the Fresh River . . . and thus the war has come to an end."[4] A Dutch clergyman seconded Van Wassenaer's observations, commenting that the fur trade was "dull on account of the new war of the Maechibaeys [Mohawks] against the Mohicans at the upper end of this river. . . . The Mohicans have fled and their lands are unoccupied and are very fertile and pleasant."[5]

There was a precedent then, and recent precedent in the history of the Five Nations, to use force against peoples who they thought threatened their economic or political interests. Through warfare, they forced these peoples to move, and in accordance with Iroquoian tradition, they captured and adopted large numbers of these dispersed enemy populations.

The Mohawk, the easternmost of the Five Nations, also had the example of the brief, bitter war between the Pequot and the British colonies of New England. The colonial forces had demonstrated that Native palisades were no match for the European weaponry.[6] The Mohawk knew what had happened at the Pequot fort on the Mystic River. Indeed, the Mohawk captured Sasacus, the Pequot leader, and "cutt of his head, with some other of the cheefe of them."[7] The Mohawk also seized the considerable amount of "wampom . . . to the value of five hundred pounds."[8] It is entirely possible that the events that occurred on the Mystic River in 1637 became incorporated into the Five Nations' new military strategy. Like the New Englanders, they had the military technology to reduce Native palisades. They also had, in their quest to seize the northern fur-trading routes, a powerful incentive to unleash that technology and their newly developed tactics on any Native group that stood in their way.

In the summer of 1648, large numbers of Iroquois warriors began to appear in Huronia. While their mission incorporated many of the traditional aspects of Iroquoian warfare, such as the acquisition of captives, they also carried out tasks that, while not unknown to the Iroquois, were unusual. Their missions went far beyond the taking of captives and the pillaging of fur-trading canoes. These warriors sought to eliminate entire Huron communities.

These large military operations attested to a higher level of organization than any previous Iroquois military efforts. These operations were not, as the Iroquois had done in the early and mid-1640s, a few warriors attacking fur-laden trading canoes. These were large—hitherto unknown—numbers of Iroquois warriors. While perhaps they could not be called armies in the European sense, their numbers, organization, planning, and leadership did demonstrate a definite sort military organization. A high level of organization was required, because these Iroquois armies needed to have the ability to operate far from home without supplies or reinforcement for long periods of time.

If the Iroquois could gain effective control over Huronia, they believed they could funnel the furs of the Great Lakes to Fort Orange, thus bypassing the French. This would not only strengthen the Iroquois by virtually assuring their economic ties to the Dutch, it also would deal an economic deathblow to New France. With New France no longer a viable entity, Native peoples would then have to trade with either the New England colonies or New Netherlands. For most of the tribes that occupied the prime beaver-hunting grounds of the Canadian Shield and the upper Great Lakes, access to these European traders would be blocked by the geographic location of the Iroquois League.

To achieve this objective, the Five Nations began a series of campaigns in the late 1640s and early 1650s designed to cripple the Huron and, by extension, the French fur-trading concerns. These Iroquois incursions into Huronia probably succeeded beyond their wildest hopes. In part, this success was possible because the Five Nations had adopted several principles of European warfare.[9]

In early July 1648, a large force of Iroquois warriors learned from their Huron prisoners that most of the warriors of the village of St. Joseph were either hunting or at war.[10] Taking advantage of the warriors' absence, the Iroquois lunged out of the cornfields and forests that bordered the northern edge of the village. The Jesuit Father Antoine Daniel had just finished morning mass when his flock heard the cry, "To arms! And repel the enemy!"[11] They then heard another set of cries—those of the Iroquois warriors who had breached the walls of the town.[12] Father Daniel led the resistance to the invaders, exhorting the Huron, both Christians and traditionalists, to hurl back the Iroquois. He preached during the melee "of contempt for death, and of the joys of Paradise, with such ardor of soul that he seemed ready to enjoy its bliss."[13] During the fray, the Huron sought the supernatural protection of baptism from Father Daniel.[14] Unable to baptize all of the Huron at once, Father Daniel "was forced to dip his handkerchief in the water and baptize by sprinkling the multitude who thronged around him." When it became apparent that the town would be lost, Father Daniel went in to the remaining longhouses and baptized the sick and the aged. He then proceeded to the church, where the remainder of his flock had gathered. Telling the converts to flee, the good father walked out of the church toward the Iroquois warriors, who, baffled at the Jesuit's behavior, "stop[ped] in astonishment." The warriors quickly recovered, however, and "they transfixed him with a thousand arrows." One Iroquois ended Father Daniel's miseries with "a mortal wound from an arquebus shot." The Iroquois vented their fury on the dead priest. They stripped his body and "exercise[d] upon him a thousand indignities" before they consigned his corpse to the flames of his church.[15]

The Iroquois then fanned out into the forest, seeking out the women and children who had fled during the battle. Many reached other Huron villages and safety, but others, "especially mothers,—at every step delayed by the babes at their breast, or by those whose childish years—as yet unaccustomed to prudent fear—betrayed their hiding places." The Iroquois killed the old and the sick on the spot, set fire to the village, and took seven hundred Huron, mostly women and children, back to Iroquoia with them as captives.[16]

St. Joseph was the first in a short, sharp series of disasters that the Five Nations inflicted on the Huron in the mid-seventeenth century. St. Joseph had been one of the larger Huron villages. Between the dead and the captives that the Iroquois carried off, the Huron had lost a tenth of their population.[17]

For the better part of the decade of the 1640s, the Five Nations' warriors had contented themselves with attacking and pillaging Huron fur-trading canoes. Until the assault on St. Joseph, they had made no effort to take a Huron village. This attack on a fortified village interjected a new mode of warfare into the Huron-Iroquois conflict.

In their spring 1649 campaign, the Five Nations displayed a level of unity that they had not heretofore exhibited. During this campaign and their following efforts to destroy the Huron confederacy, they displayed a high level of organization and cooperativeness. These were campaigns that required planning and leadership. Operating at a time of year in which neither they nor the Huron normally fought, far from home, and traveling in poor weather conditions, the Five Nations began their final effort to destroy the Huron and to remake their own world.

In the view of the Five Nations, the destruction of the Huron and their own remaking had to go hand in hand. On the strategic level, the destruction of the Huron would deprive New France of a reliable ally, and the Five Nations could divert northern furs through Iroquoia. On another level, they would obtain captives—Iroquoian-speaking ones to boot—who would replace their own dead.

In the predawn hours of March 16, 1649, small elements of a force totaling one thousand Seneca and Mohawk warriors reconnoitered the palisade and defenses of the village of St. Ignace in central Huronia. The Huron believed that their stockade, built with French help, was "impregnable." But, discovering a weakness in the walls, the Iroquois quietly made a breach and "secretly and promptly" before daylight made themselves "master of the place before people had put themselves on the defensive." The warriors killed "part of the Hurons" and made captives of the rest. Having captured St. Ignace intact, the Iroquois seized the food provisions and decided to use the village as a fortified base for the remainder of their campaign against the Huron.[18]

The Jesuit Paul Ragueneau wrote that this large Iroquois war party had left "their country in the Autumn, hunting in the forests throughout the Winter, and had made over the snow nearly two hundred leagues of a very difficult road, in order to come and surprise us."[19] Historians, almost without question, have accepted Ragueneau's assertion that the Iroquois wintered undetected in the forests of Huronia.[20] But Pere Ragueneau had no way of knowing if the Iroquois had really spent the winter there.

Another, more likely scenario is that the Iroquois warriors gathered in western Iroquoia, the lands of the Seneca, in mid to late February. From there, they traveled overland to attack St. Ignace and St. Louys. The reason why this stratagem seems more likely is that the Iroquois plan placed a premium on surprise. If the Iroquois army had been detected, deep as they were in enemy territory, they ran the risk of incurring significant losses—something Iroquoian war chiefs always tried to avoid—or even total destruction. While the Five Nations were now willing to absorb losses, they were not willing to incur casualties needlessly. Therefore, it is far more likely that the Iroquois chose to limit the amount of time they spent in Huronia in the days prior to assaulting the villages. The longer they remained in Huronia, the greater the odds of their being detected. In turn, detection, at the very least, would have meant the failure of their mission. Nor was the fear of detection unfounded. The Huron had warriors in the field looking for signs of Iroquois war parties.[21]

Despite their swift and generally silent takeover of St. Ignace, the invaders had lost the element of surprise. "Three persons alone escaped, . . . in order to give warning . . . to the . . . neighboring Village, called St. Louis, not more than three miles distant." The escapees fled to the village of St. Louys and warned the populace. On the orders of their headmen, about five hundred women and children fled St. Louys for the safety of the fortified Jesuit mission at St. Marie. Those too elderly and ill to flee remained in the village. Eighty to one hundred warriors remained behind to defend St. Louys as well as the Jesuits Jean de Brébeuf and Gabriel Lalemant.[22]

The Iroquois moved quickly to follow up on their success at St. Ignace. Leaving three hundred warriors to secure their newly won base, the rest of the Iroquois army attacked St. Louys at daybreak.[23] The Huron defenders threw back the first two Iroquois assaults, killing some thirty warriors in the process. "But, finally, number has the advantage,—the Iroquois having undermined with blows from their hatchets the palisade of stakes, and having made for themselves through considerable breaches."[24] By nine o'clock in the morning, St. Louys was in flames. The Iroquois seized many of the defenders as prisoners, including Brébeuf and Lalemant, and marched them back to St. Ignace. The wounded Huron warriors were slain on the spot, as were the old and sick.[25]

The Iroquois returned to St. Ignace to regroup and to prepare for the next phase of their operation, an assault on St. Marie. While they planned their next move, they amused themselves by slowly torturing Brébeuf and Lalemant to death. Huron traditionalists who had been captured and naturalized among the Iroquois played a major role in the killing of the two Jesuits. During his long years of service among the Huron, Brébeuf had made many enemies. The traditionalist Huron among the Iroquois regarded the Jesuits and Christianity as the cause of their people's misfortune. Irritated at hearing Brébeuf preach to the Huron converts they had captured, a former Huron Christian, now a naturalized Iroquois, poured several kettles of boiling water over Brébeuf, mocking the rite of baptism, and told him to "go to Heaven, for thou art well baptized." Because Brébeuf had been among the Huron far longer than Lalemant, he was the object of most of the torturer's rage, who cut off Brébeuf's tongue and lips and hacked flesh out of his thighs and calves, which the Iroquois and their Huron adoptees roasted and devoured in front of him. Lalemant came off comparatively easy, having been burned by a girdle of flammable bark and pitch. Lalemant died the morning of March 17, while Brébeuf expired late on the afternoon of the previous day.[26]

On the night of the March 16, a few hours after Brébeuf had breathed his last, the Iroquois reconnoitered the defenses of St. Marie. They attacked the morning of the 17th, but with only two hundred warriors. Unbeknownst to the attackers, however, three hundred Huron had made an overnight march from the village of Ossosane to reinforce St. Marie. Within sight of the walls of the mission, this force intercepted the Iroquois. The tables turned temporarily. The remnants of the Iroquois advance party took refuge behind the scorched palisades of St. Louys, and the Huron took thirty Iroquois warriors captive. But the melee was far from over; five hundred Iroquois set out from their temporary base at St. Ignace to rescue their comrades trapped in St. Louys. By now, there were now only a 150 Huron left out of the 300 who began the battle. As the battle raged throughout the afternoon and into the night, the Iroquois lost one hundred more men, but they destroyed the remainder of the Huron force from Ossosane, who had hoped to rescue St. Marie.[27]

The Jesuit Paul Ragueneau surveyed the countryside from the walls of St. Marie on the next day, March 18. He noted that "the whole day passed in profound silence on both sides,—the country being in terror and in the expectation of some new misfortune."[28] Possibly the Huron had decided to take refuge at St. Marie while they waited for reinforcements. The Iroquois spent the day assessing their situation. They had lost anywhere from 140 to 350 men; they were far from home, and reinforcement was not possible. They may have thought of attempting to take St. Marie again but vetoed this idea. They had no idea how many warriors were in the mission. Even if they did outnumber them, surely by now other Huron warriors were en route to augment those already within the walls of St. Marie.

On March 19, it became apparent that the Iroquois had made their decision. They began a disorganized retreat, "driving forth in haste a part of their captives, who were burdened above their strength, like packhorses, with the spoils which the victorious were carrying off." Captives who would have slowed down their retreat—the old, the sick, and the very young—were "attached . . . to stakes fastened in the earth, which they . . . arranged in various cabins. To these, on leaving the village, they set fire on all sides,—taking pleasure . . . in feasting upon the frightful cries which these poor victims uttered in the midst of those flames."[29]

One Huron woman escaped the fire and fled to the village of St. Michel, seven miles southwest of St. Ignace.[30] There she alerted the populace to the Iroquois presence. Seven hundred Huron set out from St. Michel in pursuit of the Iroquois. Despite following the Iroquois for two days, they were unable, or perhaps unwilling, to engage them, "partly [from] want of provisions, partly the dread of combatting without advantage an enemy encouraged by his victories, and one who had mostly firearms, of which our Hurons have very few,—all these things obliged them to retrace their steps, without having done aught."[31]

This spring 1649 campaign, which consisted of three different battles fought in the space of two days, unveiled several different aspects of a new mode of Iroquois warfare. The timing of the attack differed from anything the Iroquois had done in the past. While winter war parties were not unknown to the Iroquois and Huron, this assault took place in mid-March and prior to planting, when food reserves would have been at their lowest. Snow was still on the ground in March 1649. But the Iroquois took a tremendous risk with the weather. Had there been a sudden thaw, a distinct possibility that time of year, travel by foot would have been treacherous. The Iroquois retreat from Huronia would have been exhausting and perhaps impossible. The landscape would have turned to mud and slush and rendered snowshoes useless.

Other differences included the way that the Iroquois now fought. For the first time, the Iroquois placed a thousand fighting men in the field at once.[32] Another difference, to which the Huron may not have been able to adapt, was the Iroquois' new practice of fighting during the hours of darkness. The assault on St. Ignace took place in the dark, and the Iroquois fought the Huron well into the night of the second day of battle, eventually killing or capturing all three hundred Huron reinforcements from Ossosane.

The Iroquois also behaved in ways that indicated that they were thinking of the next battle, not just this one. When they withdrew, the Iroquois burned more than the captives who would have slowed their withdrawal; they also destroyed the provisions that they and their captives—who were used as pack mules—could not carry off. In all likelihood, they destroyed or claimed the Huron's seed corn as part of their booty, making it impossible for the survivors to plant crops for the coming year.

The battle had an unprecedented number of casualties on both sides. Iroquois losses numbered anywhere from 140 to 350. Estimates of Huron losses ranged from 630 to 880. Out of these, between 230 and 480 were warriors, both Huron and Iroquois.[33]

The number of casualties points out what the foes of the Five Nations may have seen as a disturbing shift in the Iroquois battle strategy. The Iroquois, it now appeared, were willing to absorb large numbers of casualties so long as these large war parties brought home sufficient numbers of captives to replace the losses. The casualty ratio of the victorious Iroquois in March 1649, anywhere from 15 to 35 percent, would have been considered disastrous only a few years earlier.

The Iroquois attacks had profound psychological effects on the Huron. Realizing that if the Iroquois followed up on these attacks they would be unable to grow the crops necessary to sustain themselves, the Huron began a mass exodus from Huronia. In the two weeks following the assaults on St. Ignace, St. Louys, and St. Marie, the Huron abandoned and burned "fifteen villages . . . the people of each scattering where they could,—in the woods and the forests, on the lakes and rivers, and among the Islands most unknown to the enemy." Still others sought refuge among the Neutral and Tobacco tribes. Some fled north, where they attempted to settle on the small islands in the northern part of Georgian Bay. Others fled to Quebec, where they could live near the French.[34]

The Jesuits attempted to induce the Huron to move to Manitoulin Island, located in northern Lake Huron. The Huron, however, refused. In all likelihood, their refusal was based on the island's location. The frost-free season there was too short for them to rely on corn for subsistence.[35]

Large numbers of Huron choose to flee to Ganoendoe, or Christian Island, in Lake Huron, approximately twenty-five miles west of mainland Huronia. A few Huron had settled on Ganoendoe as early as 1648, and the Jesuits had sent a mission to them.[36] Unbeknownst to the Huron who flocked there, and to the Jesuits who followed them, Ganoendoe would become the graveyard of their nation.

At first glance, Ganoendoe seemed to be much like the rest of Huronia. The Huron had always selected their village sites for defense and for the quality of the soil. In these two respects, Ganoendoe seemed to fit the Huron's needs. The soils of Ganoendoe, in the words of the Jesuits, "could have returned with interest what we desired—indeed, more than a hundredfold." Ganoendoe, the Jesuits thought, helped provide for its own defense, since "the ground furnished to us, without digging, the stone and cement we needed to fortify ourselves against our enemies."[37]

But Ganoendoe was not like the rest of Huronia. In Huronia, the Huron often reused village sites every half century or so. This allowed them to use the same plot of earth without having to fell very large trees. Ganoendoe was very different; it was truly an untouched wilderness. It seemed to the Jesuits that "these grand forests, which, since the Creation of the world, had not been felled by the hand of any man, received us as guests." Ganoendoe, "a thick forest, unprepared in any way for tillage," was outside the renewed world of Iroquoian peoples.[38] Unlike Huronia, humans had not manipulated the lands of Ganoendoe. The Huron, like the Jesuits, viewed the island as a wilderness. Having lost many men in the Iroquois attacks of 1648–49, many Huron families were unable to do the heavy work associated with clearing forests.

While the Jesuits could acquire some food for the Huron who flocked to Ganoendoe, it was far too little. They gathered "five or six hundred bushels of acorns," and they sent canoes to procure some fish from Algonquin peoples farther north.[39] But hunger stalked the Huron, and in the end, many resorted to cannibalism. Jesuits wrote with horror that the Huron's "famished teeth ceased to discern the nature of what they ate. Mothers fed upon their children; brothers on their brothers; while children recognized no longer, in a corpse, him whom, while he lived, they had called their Father."[40]

Nor had the Five Nations finished with their military strikes against the Huron. On March 25, 1650, slightly more than a year after the destruction of St. Ignace and St. Louys, another Iroquois army, using the same tactics of surprise and fighting at nighttime that had worked so well for them the previous year, appeared in Huronia. Paul Ragueneau expressed surprise that the Iroquois "marched over nearly two hundred leagues of country, across ice and snow, crossing mountains and forests full of terrors." This army "surprised, one nightfall, our Christians camp, and perpetuated in it a cruel butchery." In mid or late April, "two powerful war-parties" of Iroquois warriors were ravaging what was left of Huronia. The two large parties worked in tandem; the first was to "pluck up their Indian corn, and to lay waste to the country." The second war party was to "cut down everything that escaped the fury of the first."[41]

After a year of famine and death, most of the Huron resolved to leave Ganoendoe and set in motion the Huron diaspora. Most set out in small groups to live in the forests of central Ontario, north of Lake Huron. Others went north and west to Lake Michigan and Lake Superior. Still others chose to head south and join the Susquehannock.[42] Others, however, spoke of going to the Iroquois, "taking their wives and children, and throwing themselves into the arms of the enemy,—among whom they have a great number of relatives who wish for them, and counsel them to make their escape as soon as possible from a desolated country, if they do not wish to perish beneath its ruins."[43] During their campaigns against the Huron, the Iroquois had carried off many captives; for their relatives on Ganoendoe, going to Iroquoia seemed to be the only chance of families being reunited.

The Iroquois encouraged the Huron to give up and settle among them. In the fall of 1650, the Onondaga built a fort on the mainland across from Ganoendoe.[44] There were minor skirmishes between the Iroquois at this fort and the Huron, but it is possible that the Iroquois had another mission: to convince the Huron that since their nation was destroyed, they should cast their lot with the Five Nations. In one instance, the Iroquois proposed peace to the Huron at Ganoendoe. The Huron pretended to accept and went through the motions of preparing to move "in company with the Iroquois to a country which they should no longer look upon as hostile." The Huron, suspicious of the Onondaga's intentions, lured thirty of them into their fort where "they seized and killed the treacherous enemies, who were biding their time to carry out the same plan, but were forestalled."[45] While the Huron's wariness of the Onondaga is understandable, in this case they may have been wrong. The Iroquois seemed to be making a serious effort at this time to lure the remnants of the Huron to their country. Those Huron who did go to the Iroquois country sometimes lived in villages "apart from the Iroquois, satisfied to be united with them in good feeling and friendship." A Jesuit noted that "the former inhabitants [of] the villages of saint Michel and saint Jean Baptiste,—which, before our misfortunes, were two of our Huron Missions,—when they saw that there was no end to their evils, [they] went of their own accord to a Tribe of our enemies, the Iroquois, and now live as peacefully with them as if they had never been at war."[46]

The Iroquois made continuing efforts to induce the Huron to come and live among them. Indeed, at one point the Onondaga and Mohawk were competing with each other in their attempts to have the Huron at Quebec come and join them. One Iroquois leader told the Huron that in Iroquoia "were already [your] kinsfolk who had been formerly carried away captive, and who bore [your] absence only with regret and inconsolable sadness." The Iroquois speaker went to say that the Huron's relatives "were waiting for them with love, and would receive them with joy."[47] In 1654, a Mohawk delegation visited Quebec and convinced some Huron to come and live among them. Their spokesman employed a bit of revisionist history as he attempted to have the Huron move to Iroquoia:

> My brother, it is to thee that my words are addressed. Four years ago, thou didst beg me to take thee by the arm, to raise thee and bring thee to my country; thou didst sometimes withdraw it when I wished to comply with thy request; that is why I struck thee on the head with my hatchet. Withdraw it no more; for I tell thee in earnest to get up. It is time for thee to come.... Fear not; I no longer look upon thee as an enemy, but as my relative; thou shalt be cherished in my country, which shall also be thine.[48]

The Mohawk orator, however, realized that there were other audiences, besides the Huron, that needed to be swayed. Turning to the French governor, he offered him some advice, along with an implied threat: "Onontio, open thine arms and allow thy children to leave thy bosom; if thou shalt hold them so closely any longer, it is to be feared that thou mayst be wounded when we wish to strike them when they deserve it." The speaker then made a tempting offer to his third audience, the Jesuits: "I know that the Huron loves prayer, that he invokes him who has made all, that he clasps his hands when he asks anything of him. I wish to do as he does. Permit Father Ondesonk to come with us and instruct us in the Faith."[49]

Many of the Huron did accompany the Mohawk back to Iroquoia. To many, it seemed to be the only way that they could, in a way, be whole again and shake off an incredible melancholy that seemed to have afflicted the Huron. Two old Huron captains told the Jesuits that "thine eyes deceive thee when thou lookest on us; thou believest that thou seest living men, while we are but specters, the souls of the departed. The ground thou treadest on is about to open under us, to swallow us up ... that we may be in the place we ought to be, among the dead." During a meeting with the governor of New France, a Huron leader moaned: "We have been dead for four years, ever since our country was laid waste. Death follows us everywhere, and is always before our eyes."[50]

Perhaps one lone Huron, encountering a party of Iroquois warriors, said it best. He told them that "the country of the Hurons is no longer where it was,—you have transported it into your own: it is there where I was going, to join my relatives and compatriots, who are but one people with yourselves: I have escaped from the phantoms of a people who are no more."[51]

For the Five Nations, the destruction of the Huron facilitated their own renewal. In the destruction of the Huron, one sees the Iroquoian themes of death and resuscitation writ large. The mass adoption of Huron to replace dead Iroquois warriors echoed the first condolence that Deganawidah had performed on Hiawatha. And in the process of renewing themselves with the use of European technology, the Iroquois retained one the league's oldest traditions, the making of enemies into Iroquois, which had been first carried out when Deganawidah and Hiawatha sang the six songs and combed the snakes from Atotarho's hair.[52]

But not all of the Huron went to live among the Iroquois. Some Huron went south and lived among the Susquehannock. Others went west and lived in the areas around Lake Michigan and Lake Superior. In their diaspora, the Huron were spread all over northeastern America, and their dispersal had consequences that would be felt for the next century and a half by the French, the British, and later, the Americans.

EPILOGUE

IN THE DECADE FOLLOWING THE DESTRUCTION AND dispersal of the Huron, the Five Nations seemed to be on the verge of making the extension the White Roots of Peace a reality. The growth of the White Roots of Peace followed the Iroquoian paradox: peace through warfare. Some historians have attributed economic and traditional motivations—control of the fur trade and the continuing need for captives—to the wars that the Five Nations fought against other Native peoples in the mid to late seventeenth century.[1] They are, to some degree, correct. But there is another aspect of these wars that should be considered. The Five Nations, it could be argued, were attempting to create a *Pax Iroquoia* for Iroquoian peoples. While Algonquin peoples were incorporated into the Longhouse during the 1650s and later, the Five Nations seem to have focused their first efforts on other Iroquoian peoples.[2]

In the years after the destruction of Huronia, the Five Nations launched military campaigns against the Petun, the Neutrals, and the Erie, all three of whom were Iroquoian-speaking peoples. Iroquois armies, variously reported to number between six hundred and fifteen hundred, attacked and dispersed the Erie in December 1649 and again in 1653.[3] The Neutrals were destroyed and dispersed by the Five Nations in 1650 and 1651.[4] In each case, just as the Iroquois did with the Huron, they carried many of these people off into captivity.[5]

There are several possible reasons why the Five Nations targeted other Iroquoian peoples in the early 1650s. One reason may have reflected Five

Nations' ideology that all Iroquoian peoples were meant to be included in the Longhouse. They were, after all, like the Five Nations themselves, the descendants of Aataentsic. Second, the Five Nations may have made the assumption that assimilation would be easier for these culturally related peoples. They already spoke one dialect or another of the Iroquoian language, and they came from similar cultures. Yet a third reason may have been the Five Nations' knowledge that the former communities of their Huron, Erie, and Neutral captives were either destroyed or dispersed. Fleeing, their captors may have thought, was not an option. The captives' former communities did not exist, and their relations were spread all over the Northeast. In practical terms, there was no place to which they could flee.

Several historians have noted the disruption that mass adoptions caused the Five Nations in the 1660s and later.[6] It is possible that the Five Nations anticipated that large numbers of adoptees could create internal problems within their communities. Their focus on incorporating other Iroquoian peoples could have been an effort to minimize or mitigate the internal turmoil they thought these adoptions would cause.

The Iroquois also continued their efforts to bring the Huron into the Longhouse long after the destruction of Huronia. In 1657, the Mohawk obtained a public declaration from the French that the latter were not responsible for the Huron. The Jesuit Simon Le Moyne opened a conference and, speaking for the governor of New France, released the Huron to the Mohawk, who were encouraging the Huron to move to Iroquoia:

> Onontio loves the Hurons. They are no longer children in swaddling-clothes, but are old enough to be out of tutelage. They can go where they wish, without being hindered in any way by Onontio. He opens his arms to let them go. For my part, I am quite ready to follow my flock, when he who governs me permits me to do so. I shall teach thee also, my Agnieronon brother, how to obey God and how to pray to him.[7]

Many of these Huron did not want to leave Quebec, but recognizing that the French would make no effort to defend them, they resigned themselves to accompanying the Mohawk back to Iroquoia.

A month later, in June 1657, the French, hoping to strengthen their fragile peace agreement with the Five Nations, encouraged fifty Huron to heed the Onondaga's pleas to come and live among them. Accompanied by the Jesuit Paul Ragueneau, the Huron set off for Iroquoia in July with a party of about forty-five Onondaga and Seneca warriors.[8] During the journey, however, the Iroquois attacked and killed the Huron men and treated the women and children as prisoners of war. Ragueneau, witnessing the event, told the French accompanying the Huron not to interfere.[9]

Due to the interconnectedness of the Northeast, these incidents probably became common knowledge among the Huron who were dispersed among the upper Great Lakes during the late seventeenth and early eighteenth centuries. Because of this apparent betrayal, these people, many of whom by the 1730s and 1740s became known as the Wyandot, came to distrust the French.[10] They recognized that as far as the French were concerned, they were economically disposable. Once they were dispersed and could no longer contribute effectively to the economy of New France, they became politically disposable as well. The dispersal of the Huron meant that they no longer had any value to the French as political or military allies. The fur trade undergirded New France's economy. As long as the Iroquois continued to raid other Native fur traders, New France, economically, was on shaky ground. Badly needing to secure a peace agreement with the Five Nations, the French were more than willing to surrender the politically now less than useful Huron.

Other Huron were incorporated into the various tribes of the Ohio country and the Great Lakes.[11] Having been "sold out," as they saw it, by the French and the Jesuits, the Huron remnants and those who reconstituted themselves as Wyandot actually began to think in terms more characteristic of pre-1650 Five Nations peoples. They began to pursue the acquisition of European technology, while encouraging resistance to European territorial intrusions and disdaining conversion to Christianity. Within their new communities, the Wyandot encouraged Native peoples' resistance to the Europeans.

Examples of the Wyandot's resistance to Europeans appeared in the 1740s, when they resisted French overtures to fight on their behalf in one of their many imperial wars.[12] In the 1760s, many Wyandot in the Ohio country became followers of the Delaware prophet Neolin. Neolin preached the concept of unity, that Native peoples must regard themselves—regardless of tribal affiliation—as more like each other and different from Europeans. A key component of his message—which he later amended somewhat—was a return to the old ways and a rejection of European technology and religion. The Ottawa leader Pontiac incorporated Neolin's teachings into his military efforts to eject the British from the

Ohio country in the 1760s. Many Wyandot joined Pontiac in actively resisting British encroachment in the region.[13]

In the 1790s, the Wyandot fought the Americans at the battle of Fallen Timbers. In the early nineteenth century, the Wyandot took part in the unification movements in the Ohio country that were led by the Shawnee Tecumseh and his brother, Tenskwatawa. Many Wyandot fought at Tippecanoe and later with Tecumseh in Canada.[14]

Ironically, as the Wyandot became more militant toward European intrusions and resistant to Christianity, the people who had dispersed their Huron ancestors became more accommodating toward Europeans, and many became Christians. In another twist of irony, the Five Nations found themselves, from the 1660s to the end of the seventeenth century, facing many of the same internal crises that wracked the Huron before 1650.

By the 1660s, the Five Nations' primary technological advantage—that of having more guns than their foes—had disappeared. Iroquois warfare had now come full circle. In precontact times, Five Nations' warriors got as good as they gave in battle; they could not, with technology equivalent to their Native foes, extend the Longhouse and incorporate other peoples on any great scale. But in the 1640s and 1650s, they used their technological advantage of greater firepower to destroy enemy communities and to carry off captives to replace the dead. Now their window of opportunity had closed. Native foes had firearms in sufficient numbers and could hold their own against Iroquois warriors. The extension of the White Roots of Peace ceased. Realizing that they could not continue to fight New France, especially after the arrival of regular French troops in the 1660s, the Iroquois entered into intermittent peace agreements with New France. Some of these agreements included the placement of Jesuit missions in the villages of the Five Nations.[15]

By permitting the Jesuits to come and live among them, the Five Nations discovered that many of the same evils that had plagued the Huron in the first half of the seventeenth century were now visited upon them. Christianity began to cause deep political divisions among Five Nations' peoples. Just as they had done with the Huron, the Jesuits encouraged Iroquois converts to separate themselves from their pagan relations and to live in Christian communities.[16]

Indeed, so successful were the Jesuits that many Iroquois left Iroquoia, settling at La Prairie la Madeleine, on the south side of the St. Lawrence, across from Montreal.[17] These people would form a separate community.

While they traded with their former kinspeople, they would no longer associate with them on a regular basis. Some would in time become allies of the French in their wars with the English colonies.[18]

While the Five Nations were weakened, their new European allies did not discard them. Unlike the defeated, dispersed Huron, the Five Nations, by virtue of their geographic position, were still very useful to the English, who had taken New Netherlands from the Dutch in 1664. Realizing that any French invasion force would attempt to use the Hudson River Valley to sever New England from the rest of Britain's North American colonies, the English cultivated the Five Nations' goodwill. The English viewed them—and, at this date, their inflated military reputation—as a shield for the colonies.[19] The Iroquois, in exchange, saw the colonies as a somewhat reliable source of the trade goods that they needed.

Realizing, however, that the English could not—indeed, would not—protect them from French military incursions, the Five Nations sought a peace agreement with both the French and the English that resulted in the Grand Settlement of 1701. In a series of diplomatic maneuvers, the Iroquois committed themselves to a path of neutrality in the colonial wars, and by ceding large parts of the former Huronia to the British at Albany, they obtained a promise of British military protection, while not committing themselves to the defense of the colonies.[20]

With the defeat of the French in 1763 and their subsequent withdrawal from North America, the Five Nations, like the Huron before them, were no longer useful to their European allies. For a brief period, during the American Revolution, the British rediscovered the usefulness of the Iroquois League, enlisting their aid against the Continentals.

For both the Huron and the Five Nations, the impact of technology and Christianity in the end had been the same. Technology gave the Iroquois the edge in their conflicts with other Native peoples and enabled them to achieve the long cherished traditional goal of extending the Longhouse. But the decision to take large numbers of casualties in their wars disrupted their society. And for the Five Nations, the acceptance of Christianity proved to be just as destructive and divisive as it had been for the Huron.

For both the Iroquois and the Huron remnants, the renewed world still existed. Both peoples still had intact, old, but often altered traditions and rituals and a relationship with the earth and other peoples in their communities. The destroyed world in time became a reality for both peoples.

Neither could continue their old relationship with the earth or with peoples in their communities, due to the influence of Christianity and the loss of old homelands. But the destroyed world, while tragic, was not a lasting world. The Five Nations' actively sought to remake their world, at the expense of the Huron and other Native peoples, during much of the seventeenth century. For many of the Huron, their destroyed world was the catalyst for their remade world. Many rebuilt their lives as captives in Iroquois communities, while other joined other Native communities in the Great Lakes and the Ohio country. Still others created for themselves a new cultural identity for themselves as Wyandot. In each case, they became part of a community that had, or developed, its own rituals and its own thought world. While the Five Nations did succeed for a time in remaking their world, they, too, went through the experience of the destroyed world in the years after the American Revolution. But they remade their world once again, using the religious catalyst envisioned by the Seneca Prophet Handsome Lake.[21]

NOTES

Introduction

1. Rueben Gold Thwaites, ed., *The Jesuit Relations and Allied Documents: Travels and Exporations of the Jesuit Missionaries in New France, 1610–1791,* 73 vols. (Cleveland: Burrows Brothers, 1896–1901), 27:247 (hereafter cited as *JR*). The beads that the French frequently referred to as "porcelain" were actually wampum, usually made from whelk shells. See also Francis Jennings, "The Earliest Recorded Description: The Mohawk Treaty with New France at Three River, 1645," in *The History and Culture of Iroquois Diplomacy: An Interdisciplinary Guide to the Treaties of the Six Nations and Their League,* eds. William N. Fenton, Mary A. Druke, and David R. Miller (Syracuse, N.Y.: Syracuse University Press, 1985), 127–31; Matthew Dennis, *Cultivating a Landscape of Peace* (Ithaca, N.Y.: Cornell University Press, 1993), 77–78.

2. "*Onontio*" is an Iroquoian term that Algonquins also began to use in their dealings with the French. The word means "big mountain" and was originally applied to Charles Jacques de Huault de Montmagny, who was the governor of New France from 1636 to 1648. Thereafter, Native peoples applied the term to his successors as well. See *JR,* 20:221. See also W. J. Eccles, *The Canadian Frontier 1534–1670* (New York: Holt, Rinehart and Winston, 1969), 201n.15; Richard White, *The Middle Ground: Indians, Empires, and Republics in the Great Lakes Region, 1650–1815* (New York: Cambridge University Press, 1991), 36.

3. Vimont in *JR,* 27:253. In all likelihood, the "collars" the French referred to are called belts and strings in other sources and by the Iroquois.

4. Ibid.

5. Ibid, 27:259, 261.

6. Ibid., 27:297.

7. William N. Fenton, *The Great Law and the Longhouse: A Political History of the Iroquois Confederacy* (Norman: University of Oklahoma Press, 1998), 198.

8. Ibid., 69.

9. Barbara Mann and Jerry Fields, "A Sign in the Sky: Dating the League of the Haudenosaunee," *American Indian Culture and Research Journal* 21, no. 2 (1997): 105–63.

10. I tend to favor a founding date ranging from the mid-fifteenth to the mid-sixteenth century; however, I do not believe that the date of the league's founding is as important an issue as some scholars have made it out to be. While the discussion is interesting, a definitive answer is not possible, and such debates tend to generate far more heat than light.

11. The versions rendered above of the Iroquoian cosmogonic myths are somewhat basic. There are several variations on the Iroquois and Huron creation stories. See J. N. B. Hewitt, *Iroquoian Cosmology* (1899 and 1926; reprint, New York: AMS Press, 1974), 141–339. Hewitt gives three different versions—Mohawk, Onondaga, and Seneca—of the creation myth. See also Hazel W. Hertzberg, "The World on the Turtle's Back," in *The Indian Peoples of Eastern America,* ed. James Axtell (Oxford: Oxford University Press, 1979), 173–78; Elisabeth Tooker, ed., *Native North American Spirituality of the Eastern Woodlands* (New York: Paulist Press, 1979), 33–55. For Huron versions, see Bruce Trigger, *The Children of Aataentsic,* 2 vols. (Montreal: McGill-Queen's University Press, 1976), 1:77–78. See also *JR,* 8:117–19; Nicholas Perrot, "Memoir on the Manner, Customs, and Religion of the Savages of North America," in *The Indian Tribes of the Upper Mississippi Valley & the Region of the Great Lakes,* ed. Emma Helen Blair, 2 vols. (1911–12; reprint, Lincoln: University of Nebraska Press, 1996), 1:31–36; Fenton, *Great Law,* 44–45; C. M. Barbeau, "Supernatural Beings of the Huron and Wyandot," *American Anthropologist* 16 (1914): 218–313. Perrot's version seems to be an amalgamation of several different creation myths and appears to mix elements of Iroquoian cosmology with that of Great Lakes Algonquins.

12. Gabriel Sagard, *The Long Journey to the Country of the Hurons,* ed. George M. Wrong, trans. H. H. Langton (1939; reprint, New York: Greenwood Press, 1968), 169–70. See also François Du Creux, *History of Canada,* trans. Percy J. Robinson, ed. James B. Conacher, 2 vols. (1951–52; reprint, New York: Greenwood Press, 1969), 1:111–15; Fenton, *Great Law,* 34–50; Hewitt, *Iroquoian Cosmology.*

13. Joseph François Lafitau, *Customs of the American Indians Compared with the Customs of Primitive Times,* ed. and trans. William N. Fenton and Elizabeth L. Moore, 2 vols. (Toronto: Champlain Society, 1974–77), 1:82. Lafitau's version of the Iroquoian creation myth differs from the others in several respects. Lafitau's version has six men who wandered on the wind before the creation of the earth. They sought a woman—they had none—to ensure the propagation of the species. Eventually, they heard of Aataentsic, found her, and one of the men seduced and impregnated her.

14. For Iroquoian peoples other than the Huron and Five Nations, see Marian E. White, "Erie" and "Neutral and Wenro," in *Handbook of North American Indians: Northeast,* ed. Bruce G. Trigger, vol. 15 of *Handbook of North American Indians,* William C. Sturtevant, gen. ed. (Washington D.C.: Smithsonian Institution, 1978), 407–17. For the purposes of this work, the term "Iroquoian" will refer to the Huron and the Five Nations collectively, the term "Huron" will refer to the Huron confederacy, while the

term "Five Nations" will be used for the Iroquois Confederacy, except when I am referring to the constituent tribes.

15. Conrad Heidenreich, *Huronia: A History and Geography of the Huron Indians, 1600–1650* (Ontario: McCelland and Stewart, 1971), 372.

16. The mythological Hiawatha of the Iroquois has nothing to do with the poem by Longfellow. Longfellow took the name of an Iroquoian person whom he learned of through Henry R. Schoolcraft's writings and somehow bastardized Hiawatha into an Ojibwe. See Robert F. Berkhofer, *The White Man's Indian: Images of the American Indian from Columbus to the Present* (New York: Knopf, 1978), 90.

17. Alvin Josephy, *The Patriot Chiefs: A Chronicle of American Indian Resistance* (New York: Viking, 1958), 18. In all likelihood, this foreshadowing that Deganawidah would cause the destruction of the Huron is a post-1649 invention. For an analysis of the Deganawidah epic, see Anthony F. C. Wallace, "The Dekanawideh Myth Analyzed as the Record of a Revitalization Movement," *Ethnohistory* 5 (1958): 118–30.

18. It is possible that the virgin birth aspect of the Deganawidah epic reflects postcontact Christian influences. See Josephy, *Patriot Chiefs,* 18. See also Paul A. W. Wallace, "The Iroquois: A Brief Outline of their History," *Pennsylvania History* 23, no. 1 (1956): 17.

19. Paul A. W. Wallace, *The White Roots of Peace* (Philadelphia: University of Pennsylvania Press, 1946), 6–7, 4; Fenton, *Great Law,* 193.

20. Wallace, *White Roots,* 11, 15–17, 22.

21. Ibid., 21, 24–25; Fenton, *Great Law,* 77–78.

22. Fenton, *Great Law,* 87, 95. Paul Wallace offers a slightly different version in *White Roots* (14).

23. Elisabeth Tooker, "Women in Iroquois Society," in *Extending the Rafters: Interdisciplinary Approaches to Iroquoian Studies,* ed. Michael K. Foster, Jack Campisi, and Marianne Mithun (Albany: State University of New York Press, 1984), 112–13.

24. Horatio Hale, *The Iroquois Book of Rites* (1883; reprint with new introduction by William N. Fenton, Toronto: University of Toronto Press, 1963), 121.

25. Trigger, *Handbook of North American Indians,* 15:344–46.

26. Jonas Michaëlius, "Letter of Reverend Jonas Michaëlius," in *Narratives of New Netherland 1609–1664,* ed. J. Franklin Jameson (New York: Scribner's, 1909), 128 (hereafter cited as *NNN*). See also A. Eekhof, *Jonas Michaëlius, Founder of the Church in New Netherland* (Leyden: A. W. Sijtoff's Publishing Company, 1926), 133–34.

27. Johannes Megapolensis Jr., "A Short Account of the Mohawk Indians, by Reverend Johannes Megapolensis Jr., 1644" in *NNN,* 172–73. See also Lois M. Feister, "Linguistic Communication between the Dutch and Indians in New Netherland 1609–1664," *Ethnohistory* 21, no. 1 (1973): 25–38.

28. James Axtell, *Beyond 1492: Encounters in Colonial North America* (New York: Oxford University Press, 1992), 153–54. See also James H. Merrell, *The Indians' New World: Catawbas and Their Neighbors from European Contact through the Era of Removal* (Chapel Hill: University of North Carolina Press, 1989), for another view of how European—Native American contact created a "New World."

Chapter 1. The Renewal of the Earth

1. See the introduction.

2. For a good example of this line of thinking, see Kirkpatrick Sale, *The Conquest of Paradise: Christopher Columbus and the Columbian Legacy* (New York: Knopf, 1990).

3. Lewis H. Morgan, *League of the Iroquois* (1851; reprint with an introduction by William N. Fenton, Secaucus, N.J.: Citadel Press, 1962), 175–76.

4. Chrestien Le Clercq, *New Relation of Gaspesia, With the Customs and Religion of the Gaspesian Indians,* trans. and ed. William F. Ganong (1910; reprint, New York: Greenwood Press, 1968), 122. Le Clercq described the gathering of sap among the Micmac, but the procedure of gathering sap was much the same in northeastern North America. See also Lafitau, *Customs,* 2:94.

5. H. W. Henshaw, "Indian Origin of Maple Sugar," *American Anthropologist,* no. 3 (1890): 341–51.

6. Morgan, *League of the Iroquois,* 180–86.

7. C. O. Willits and Claude H. Hills, *Maple Sirup Producers Manual,* rev. ed. (Washington, D.C.: U.S. Government Printing Office, 1976), 68–69.

8. Morgan, *League of the Iroquois,* 186–89.

9. Ibid., 190–97; Fenton, *Great Law,* 22.

10. Morgan, *League of the Iroquois,* 197–99.

11. Dean R. Snow, *The Iroquois* (Cambridge: Blackwell, 1994), 7.

12. Frank G. Speck, *Midwinter Rites of the Cayuga Longhouse* (1949; reprint with an introduction by William N. Fenton, Lincoln: University of Nebraska Press, 1995), 53–56.

13. Elisabeth Tooker, *The Iroquois Ceremonial of Midwinter* (Syracuse, N.Y.: Syracuse University Press, 1970), 43–46. See also Lynn Ceci, "Watchers of the Pleiades: Ethnoastronomy among Native Cultivators in Northeastern North America," *Ethnohistory* 25, no. 4 (1978): 309; Speck, *Midwinter Rites,* 145–46.

14. Karen Ordahl Kupperman, "The Puzzle of the American Climate in the Early Colonial Period," *American Historical Review* 87, no. 5 (1982): 1262–89.

15. Ceci, "Watchers," 306

16. William N. Fenton, "The Iroquois in History," in *North American Indians in Historical Perspective,* ed. Eleanor Burke Leacock and Nancy Oestreich Lurie (New York: Random House, 1971), 135. See also Fenton, *Great Law,* 20. Comparisons of the advantages and disadvantages of birch and elm bark as canoe-making material are found in Lafitau, *Customs,* 2:124–26.

17. For Huron population estimates, see Samuel de Champlain, *The Works of Samuel Champlain,* ed. H. P. Biggar, 6 vols. (Toronto: Champlain Society, 1922–36), 3:122, and Sagard, *Long Journey,* 92. The best guess for Iroquois population in this period is derived from Harman Meyndertsz van den Bogaert, "A Journey into Mohawk and Oneida Country, 1634–1635," in *In Mohawk Country: Early Narratives about a Native People,* ed. Dean R. Snow and William A. Starna (Syracuse, N.Y.: Syra-

cuse University Press, 1996), 1–13. Van den Bogaert counted a total of 180 longhouses in the villages he visited. Using these figures, José António Brandão, *"Your fyre shall burn no more": Iroquois Policy toward New France and Its Native Allies to 1701* (Lincoln: University of Nebraska Press, 1997), estimates that the combined Mohawk and Oneida population was between 7,380 and 9,840.

18. Champlain, *Works,* 3:122, 117, 48, 63.

19. Ibid., 3:125.

20. Stephen J. Pyne, *Fire in America: A Cultural History of Wildland and Rural Fire* (Princeton, N.J.: Princeton University Press, 1982), 71.

21. Ibid., 35–38.

22. Champlain, *Works,* 3:156; Sagard, *Long Journey,* 94.

23. Adriaen van der Donck, *A Description of the New Netherlands,* ed. Thomas F. O'Donnell (Syracuse, N.Y.: Syracuse University Press, 1968), 21. See also Arthur Caswell Parker, *Parker on the Iroquois,* ed. and intro. by William N. Fenton (Syracuse, N.Y.: Syracuse University Press, 1968), 21–22.

24. Van der Donck, *Description of the New Netherlands,* 21.

25. William Cronon, *Changes in the Land: Indians, Colonists, and the Ecology of New England* (New York: Hill and Wang, 1983), 47–51.

26. Champlain, *Works,* 3:117.

27. Cronon, *Changes in the Land,* 49.

28. Hu Maxwell, "The Use and Abuse of Forests by the Virginia Indians," *William and Mary Quarterly,* 2nd ser., 19, no. 2 (1910): 90. See also William Bullock, *Virginia Impartially Examined . . .* (London: John Hammond, 1649), 3.

29. Maxwell, "Use and Abuse of Forests," 90.

30. Nicolas Denys, *The Description and Natural History of the Coasts of North America (Acadia),* trans. and ed. William F. Ganong (1908; reprint, New York: Greenwood Press, 1968), 377 n.1. In a footnote, Ganong disputes Deny's description of the Acadian forests, stating that they "are dense, obstructed, and practically impossible for horses." Ganong may well be right, but his observations took place in the early twentieth century; Denys was describing the same area in the mid-seventeenth century.

31. Maxwell, "Use and Abuse of Forests," 90.

32. Cronon, *Changes in the Land,* 51.

33. William A. Starna, George A. Hamell, and William L. Butts, "Northern Iroquoian Horticulture and Insect Infestation: A Cause for Village Removal," *Ethnohistory* 31, no. 3 (1984): 205.

34. Heidenreich, *Huronia,* 175.

35. Ibid., 153, 163.

36. Ceci, "Watchers," 306. See also Fenton, "Iroquois in History," 136.

37. See William Beauchamp, "Onondaga Tale of the Pleiades," *Journal of American Folklore* 13 (1900): 281–82. For the lack of frost in May, see Van der Donck, *Description of the New Netherlands,* 62.

38. Ceci, "Watchers," 305–6.

39. E. B. O'Callaghan, ed., *Documentary History of the State of New York,* 4 vols. (Albany, N.Y.: Weed, Parsons, 1849–51), 3:20.

40. Gabriel Sagard, *Historie du Canada,* 4 vols. (Paris, 1865), 2:429–30.

41. Champlain, *Works,* 3:156. For the 120-day frost-free period, see James E. Fitting, "The Huron as an Ecotype: The Limits of Maximization in a Western Great Lakes Society," *Anthropologica* 14, no. 1 (1972): 9. See also Richard Asa Yarnell, *Aboriginal Relationships between Culture and Plant Life in the Upper Great Lakes Region* (Ann Arbor: University of Michigan, 1964), 133. The quote is from Sagard, *Long Journey,* 103–4.

42. *JR,* 8:99.

43. For May frosts in Huronia, see *JR,* 24:275. For September frosts, see Champlain, *Works,* 3:58.

44. Sagard, *Long Journey,* 103. Esther Louise Larsen, "Pehr Kalm's Description of Maize, How It Is Planted and Cultivated in North America, Together with the Many Uses of This Crop Plant," *Agricultural History* 9, no. 2 (1935): 107.

45. Both Champlain, *Works,* 3:156, and Sagard, *Long Journey,* 103, claim that Huron corn hills were one pace apart. Issack de Rasieres, "Letter of Issack de Rasieres to Samuel Blommaert, 1628(?)," in *NNN,* 107, observed Mohawk women planting corn in 1628 and noted that the hills were two and a half feet apart.

46. Larsen, "Pehr Kalm's Description," 107.

47. Sagard, *Long Journey,* 104.

48. Bruce G. Trigger, "Settlement as an Aspect of Iroquoian Adaptation at the Time of Contact," *American Anthropologist* 65, no. 1 (1963): 90.

49. Champlain, *Works,* 3:127, 128. See also Parker, *Parker on the Iroquois,* 76; Van der Donck, *Description of the New Netherlands,* 76–77; Sagard, *Long Journey,* 153.

50. Sagard, *Long Journey,* 105–6.

51. Champlain, *Works,* 3:129.

52. Sagard, *Long Journey,* 108, Champlain, *Works,* 3:129–30, and Lafitau, *Customs,* 2:63, also found the odor of "stinking corn" repulsive, and they also noted the apparent relish with which Iroquoian peoples consumed it.

53. Sagard, *Long Journey,* 105. Pierre Radisson, *The Explorations of Pierre Esprit Radisson,* ed. Arthur T. Adams (Minneapolis: Ross and Haines, 1961), had a different opinion of another variation of this dish made by Iroquois women in the form of a dumpling. Radisson regarded it as "the most delicious bit of the world" (37).

54. Sagard, *Long Journey,* 239. Translator George M. Wrong speculated that Sagard was describing the American pennyroyal (239n.4).

55. Champlain, *Works,* 3:51.

56. Heidenreich, *Huronia,* 180–81. See also *JR,* 15:153, 19:133; Champlain, *Works,* 3:124; Sagard, *Long Journey,* 92.

57. Van der Donck, *Description of the New Netherlands,* 30, 96; Lynn Ceci, *The Effect of European Contact and Trade on the Settlement Pattern of Indians in Coastal New York, 1524–1665* (New York: Garland Press, 1990), 115.

58. Megapolensis, "Short Account," 170.

59. Quoted in Ceci, *Effect of European Contact,* 117. See also Megapolensis, "Short Account," 171.

60. Ceci, *Effect of European Contact,* 119; O'Callaghan, *Documentary History,* 4:167.

61. See Ceci, *Effect of European Contact,* 115; Cronon, Changes in the Land, 45.

62. Sagard, *Long Journey,* 104.

63. Ibid.

64. Van der Donck, *Description of the New Netherlands,* 98.

65. Heidenreich, *Huronia,* 213. The high figure of thirty is from Sagard, *Long Journey,* 92. See *JR,* 10:275, 15:153, 19:133.

66. *JR,* 11:7. For Seneca village removals, see George R. Hamell, "Gannagaro State Historic Site: A Current Perspective," in *Studies on Iroquoian Culture,* ed. Nancy Bonvillain (Rindge, N.H.: Occasional Publications in Northeastern Anthropology no. 6, 1980), 94. See also Susan Bamann, Robert Kuhn, James Molnar, and Dean Snow, "Iroquoian Archaeology," *Annual Review of Anthropology* 21 (1992): 445–46.

67. Fitting, "Huron as an Ecotype," 11.

68. Champlain, *Works,* 3:124–25. A league is approximately 3 miles, or 4.8 kilometers.

69. *JR,* 6:29, 14:105.

70. Sagard, *Long Journey,* 94.

71. Champlain, *Works,* 3:156; Sagard, *Long Journey,* 94.

72. James A. Tuck, *Onondaga Iroquois Prehistory: A Study in Settlement Archaeology* (Syracuse, N.Y.: Syracuse University Press, 1971), 58.

73. Heidenreich, *Huronia,* 67, 109.

74. Champlain, *Works,* 3:70.

75. Van der Donck, *Description of the New Netherlands,* 81. See also Heidenreich, *Huronia,* 113; Frederick Houghton, "The Characteristics of Iroquoian Village Sites of Western New York," *American Anthropologist* 18 (1916): 513.

76. Champlain, *Works,* 2:90.

Chapter 2. The Renewal of Human Beings

1. *JR,* 26:157.

2. Ibid., 26:159.

3. Fenton, *Great Law,* 198–99.

4. Ibid., 137–38

5. Ibid. "Bare" in this context refers to the minimum.

6. Ibid., 737.

7. Ibid., 138.

8. Daniel K. Richter, *The Ordeal of the Longhouse: The Peoples of the Iroquois League in the Era of European Colonization* (Chapel Hill: University of North Carolina Press, 1992), 35.

9. *JR,* 10:225

10. Most European wars, while they may have contained the veneer of being for God or Crown, were usually about territory or the control of commodities.

11. Richter, *Ordeal,* 36–38.

12. Daniel K. Richter, "War and Culture: The Iroquois Experience," *William and Mary Quarterly,* 3rd ser., 40, no. 4 (1983): 535.

13. Sagard, *Long Journey,* 158–63.

14. Snow, *Iroquois,* 54–55.

15. Lafitau, *Customs,* 2:141–42.

16. Trigger, *Children of Aataentsic,* 1:68.

17. *JR,* 1:269–71. See also *JR,* 5:93–95.

18. Champlain, *Works,* 2:96–97.

19. Ibid., 2:97.

20. Ibid., 2:98.

21. Dennis, *Cultivating a Landscape,* 71–72.

22. *JR,* 11:99, 15:245. See also Robert Juet, "The Third Voyage of Master Henry Hudson," in *NNN,* 26; Johan de Laet, "New World," in *NNN,* 57.

23. *JR,* 1:271, 5:95.

24. Richter, *Ordeal,* 54–55. For battlefield use of wooden armor against European firepower, see chapter 8.

25. Van den Bogaert, "Journey," 6.

26. Champlain, *Works,* 2:83–84.

27. Ibid., 2:130. Trigger, *Children of Aataentsic,* 1:313, points out that Champlain spoke neither Huron nor Algonquin. One has to question whether his allies actually understood his "orders." It is entirely possible they tore down the barricade on their own initiative.

28. *JR,* 9:263.

29. Megapolensis, "Short Account," 175.

30. *JR,* 13:39, 9:265–67.

31. Ibid., 18:219.

32. Ibid., 35:249, 251.

33. Ibid., 35:255.

34. Ibid., 23:167.

35. Ibid., 22:289.

36. Ibid., 29:217, 32:209–11.

37. Ibid., 13:45–49.

38. Ibid., 13:53–55.

39. Ibid., 13:55.

40. Bruce G. Trigger, *The Huron: Farmers of the North* (New York: Holt, Rinehart, and Winston, 1969), 49

41. *JR,* 13:67–69.

42. Ibid., 13:69.

43. Ibid., 13:79.

44. Ibid., 10:29. See Thomas S. Abler, "Iroquoian Cannibalism: Fact not Fiction" *Ethnohistory* 27, no. 4 (1980): 309–16. See also Tuck, *Onondaga Iroquois Prehistory,* 113–14, for archaeological evidence of cannibalism.

45. Richter, *Ordeal,* 36. See also Nathaniel Knowles, "The Torture of Captives by the Indians of Eastern North America," *Proceedings of the American Philosophical Society* 82, no. 2 (1940): 152–56.

Chapter 3. The Supernatural

1. *JR,* 23:155, 15, 157, 159.

2. Trigger, *Children of Aataentsic,* 1:48; James Axtell, *The Invasion Within: The Contest of Cultures in Colonial North America* (Oxford: Oxford University Press, 1985), 15–16. See also Anthony F. C. Wallace, *The Death and Rebirth of the Seneca* (New York: Knopf, 1970), 73.

3. *JR,* 1:287.

4. Lafitau, *Customs,* 1:217, 236–37. See also Wallace, *Death and Rebirth,* 85.

5. For variance in spiritual beliefs, see the Onondaga, Seneca, and Mohawk versions of the Iroquoian cosmogonic myth in Hewitt, *Iroquoian Cosmology,* and the Seneca version in Tooker, *Native North American Spirituality,* 35–47. See also Trigger, *Children of Aataentsic,* 1:75–77.

6. *JR,* 1:283, 6:211–13, 5:165. See also Du Creux, *History of Canada,* 1:97.

7. Sagard, *Long Voyage,* 171; *JR,* 10:165–67.

8. Richter, *Ordeal,* 24.

9. *JR,* 17:165, 167. The term "seignior general" is French; possibly the woman used the term, but it is also possible that this was the nearest interpretation the Jesuits could come up with after she related her vision to them.

10. Ibid., 10:169–71. See also Du Creux, *History of Canada,* 1:115.

11. Anthony F. C. Wallace, "Dreams and the Wishes of the Soul: A Type of Psychoanalytic Theory among the Seventeenth Century Iroquois," *American Anthropologist* 60, no. 2 (1958): 246; J. N. B. Hewitt, "The Iroquoian Concept of the Soul," *Journal of American Folklore* 8 (1895): 110. See also Cornelius J. Jaenen, *Friend and Foe: Aspects of French-Amerindian Contact in the Sixteenth and Seventeenth Centuries* (New York: Columbia University Press, 1976), 57.

12. *JR,* 10:147.

13. Hewitt, "Concept," 110.

14. *JR,* 33:189.

15. Ibid., 15:179.

16. Ibid., 4:217.

17. Wallace, "Dreams," 237–38.

18. *JR,* 33:189.

19. Ibid., 10:173.

20. Ibid., 23:171–73.

21. Champlain, *Works,* 4:93–94.

22. Marc Lescarbot, *History of New France,* trans. W. L. Grant, 3 vols. (1907–14; reprint, New York: Greenwood Press, 1968), 3:31, 15.

23. Du Creux, *History of Canada,* 1:165–66; *JR,* 7:167–71.

24. *JR,* 17:213, 33:219.

25. Ibid., 33:221, 12:7–9.

26. Ibid., 33:221.

27. Ibid., 19:83, 8:123, 10:223.

28. Ibid., 14:37–39.

29. Ibid., 33:219.

30. Ibid., 14:39.

31. Ibid., 10:175–77, 17:177–79.

32. Ibid., 30:102.

33. Peter A. Timmins, *The Calvert Site: An Interpretive Framework for the Early Iroquoian Village* (Hull, Quebec: Canadian Museum of Civilization, 1997), 233. See also Sagard, *Long Journey,* 207; Richter, *Ordeal,* 24, 31.

34. Sagard, *Long Journey,* 209; *JR,* 39:31. See also Heidenreich, *Huronia,* 151.

35. Most literature dealing with the Huron refers to this place as the Village of the Dead. Literature dealing with the Five Nations Iroquois tends to use the term Land of the Dead. References to the afterlife in primary sources may use several variations of these terms.

36. Lafitau, *Customs,* 1:251–53.

37. *JR,* 10:145, 273; 15:183. See also Susan Pfeiffer and Scott I. Fairgrieve, "Evidence from Ossuaries: The Effect of Contact on the Health of Iroquoians," in *In the Wake of Contact: Biological Responses to Conquest,* ed. Clark Spencer Larsen and George R. Milner (New York: Wiley-Liss, 1994), 48.

38. Hewitt, "Concept," 108.

39. *JR,* 10:141–43, 16:191–93, 33:191; Hewitt, "Concept."

40. Sagard, *Long Journey,* 207.

41. *JR,* 1:261, 5:129, 6:209, 10:143.

42. Ibid., 10:141–45, 8:121; Sagard, *Long Journey,* 172; Du Creux, *History of Canada,* 1:118; Hewitt, "Concept."

43. *JR,* 8:21, 6:211. Throwing food into the fire was considered a form of feeding it to the dead.

44. Ibid., 13:151–53.

45. Ibid., 1:261, 5:129, 6:211, 16:195–97.

46. Ibid., 10:149–53; Du Creux, *History of Canada,* 1:120–21. Du Creux adds to the story somewhat, saying that after the young man secured his sister's soul in the pumpkin, Oscotarach gave him another pumpkin that contained the brain of his sister. Du Creux uses the term "gourds," while Brébeuf uses the term "pumpkin" in *JR.*

47. *JR,* 4:201, 10:269–71. See also Sagard, *Long Journey,* 207; Champlain, *Works,* 4:54–55.

48. *JR,* 10:147, 6:211.

49. Sagard, *Long Journey,* 205; Du Creux, *History of Canada,* 1:177.

50. The souls of tools and animals differed from those of humans. Only humans were believed to have multiple souls.

51. Among Iroquoian peoples, the Huron are the only ones known to have had a Feast of the Dead. Five Nations Iroquois were usually interred in permanent, single graves.

52. Sagard, *Long Journey,* 211; *JR,* 10:283–301. See also Champlain, *Works,* 3:160–63.

53. Sagard, *Long Journey,* 213–14. See also Trigger, *Children of Aataentsic,* 1:87.

54. Sagard, *Long Journey,* 213.

55. *JR,* 10:283–85.

56. Ibid., 14:51.

57. Åke Hultkrantz, *Soul and Native Americans* (originally published as *Conceptions of the Soul among North American Indians*), ed. Robert Holland. (1952; reprint, Woodstock, Conn.: Spring Publications, 1997), 80.

58. *JR,* 10:147. This contradicts the assertion by most Huron that the *atisken* was immortal, but it should be remembered that in Huron communities, one could encounter a multiplicity of spiritual beliefs.

59. Ibid., 16:177–79, 8:121.

60. For Dutch efforts, or lack thereof, to convert the Iroquois, see Megapolensis, "Short Account," 172–73; Michaëlius, "Letter of Reverend Jonas Michaëlius," 127–29. For the tribulations of Jesuits among the Iroquois, see *JR,* 24:270–97, 25:42–73, 28:104–35, 39:55–83, 29:45–63. For Dutch attempts to ransom Jesuit captives, see "Extract from a Letter of Arent van Corlaer (Curler), Director of the Colony of Rensselaerswyck, to the Patroon in Holland, June 16th 1643," in *Documents Relative to the Colonial History of the State of New York,* ed. E. B. O'Callahan, John Romeyn Brodhead, and Berthold Fernow, 15 vols. (Albany, N.Y.: Weed, Parsons, 1853–87), 13:15 (hereafter cited as *NYCD*).

Chapter 4. The Jesuit Assault of the Huron Thought World

1. *JR,* 9:17.

2. Axtell, *Beyond 1492,* 155–56.

3. The term "thought world" is Calvin Martin's. See Martin, "The American Indian as Miscast Ecologist," in *Ecological Consciousness: Essays from the Earthday X Colloquium,* ed. Robert C. Schult and Donald J. Hughes (Washington, D.C.: University Press of America, 1981). Martin, however, did not define the term "thought world," thus the definition presented in the text is my own. The other Iroquoian peoples who came under this Jesuit assault in the first half of the seventeenth century were the Neutrals, Petun, and Erie. The Five Nations Iroquois had fairly limited contact with the Jesuits until the 1660s with the exception of Father Isaac Jogues's two voyages to Iroquoia and the Iroquois prisoners of war who were baptized by Jesuits. See *JR,* 23:249–51, 28:137–41.

4. See Perry Miller, *The New England Mind:The Seventeenth Century* (New York: Macmillan, 1939); Miller, *The New England Mind: From Colony to Province* (Cambridge, Mass.: Harvard University Press, 1953).

5. See Rhys Isaac, *The Transformation of Virginia: 1740–1790* (Chapel Hill: University of North Carolina Press, 1982); Timothy Breen, *Tobacco Culture:The Mentality of the Great Tidewater Planters on the Eve of Revolution* (Princeton, N.J.: Princeton University Press, 1985).

6. See Carl Becker, *The Heavenly City of the Eighteenth Century Philosophers* (New Haven, Conn.: Yale University Press, 1932); Lucien Goldmann, *The Philosophy of the Enlightenment;The Christian Burgess and the Enlightenment,* trans. Henry Maas (London: Routledge, 1973).

7. Axtell, *Invasion,* 53.

8. Ibid., 38. See also Peter A. Dorsey, "Going to School with Savages: Authority and Authorship among the Jesuits of New France," *William and Mary Quarterly,* 3rd ser., 55, no. 3 (1998): 399–420. For Jesuit activity in Asia during the sixteenth century, see Anthony Reid, "Early Southeast Asian Categorizations of Europeans." See also Ronald P. Toby, "The 'Indianness' of Iberia and Changing Japanese Iconographies of Other," and Willard J. Peterson, "What to Wear? Observation and Participation by Jesuit Missionaries in Late Ming Society." All three essays are found in Stuart B. Schwartz, ed., *Implicit Understandings: Observing, Reporting, and Reflecting on the Encounters between Europeans and Other Peoples in the Early Modern Era* (New York: Cambridge University Press, 1994), 283, 327, 403–48.

9. *JR,* 34:123–25. See also Du Creux, *History of Canada,* 2:517–34; George T. Hunt, *The Wars of the Iroquois:A Study in Intertribal Trade Relations* (Madison: University of Wisconsin Press, 1940), 87–96; Bruce G. Trigger, *Natives and Newcomers: Canada's "Heroic Age" Reconsidered* (Montreal: McGill-Queen's University Press, 1985), 259.

10. Axtell, *Beyond 1492,* 163–65.

11. Interestingly enough, it was at about this time that cosmology, of the religious sort, was beginning to fall out of favor in Europe. The Enlightenment instigated a search for a more rational, or at least nonreligious, explanation for the existence of the world and the beings that live in it.

12. See James Axtell, *After Columbus: Essays in the Ethnohistory of Colonial America* (Oxford: Oxford University Press, 1988), 100–124. See also Jaenen, *Friend and Foe,* 41–83; Trigger, *Natives,* 294–96; Allen W. Trelease, *Indian Affairs in Colonial New York: The Seventeenth Century* (1960; reprint with an introduction by William A. Starna, Lincoln: University of Nebraska Press, 1997), 172.

13. Sagard, *Long Journey,* 74.

14. *JR,* 13:221.

15. Sagard, *Long Journey,* 207.

16. *JR,* 10:121.

17. Axtell, *Invasion,* 108.

18. Trigger, *Natives,* 256. See also Trigger, *Children of Aataentsic,* 1:75; Axtell, *Invasion,* 107.

19. *JR,* 17:137, 139.

20. See chapter 5.

21. Trigger, *Natives,* 254.

22. Axtell, *Beyond 1492,* 156–57.

23. *JR,* 8:147

24. Ibid., 17:127.

25. Axtell, *Beyond 1492,* 160; Axtell, *Invasion,* 100–102. See also Trigger, *Children of Aataentsic,* 2:125; *JR,* 17:119, 30:67.

26. Du Creux, *History of Canada,* 1:160; *JR,* 7:95.

27. *JR,* 30:67. See also Axtell, *Invasion,* 102.

28. *JR,* 17:49.

29. Du Creux, *History of Canada,* 1:188–89.

30. Lescarbot, *History,* 3:28.

31. Sagard, *Long Journey,* 173.

32. Quoted in Axtell, *After Columbus,* 90.

33. See Martin McLuhan, *The Gutenberg Galaxy: The Making of Typographic Man* (Toronto: University of Toronto Press, 1962); Walter J. Ong, *The Presence of the Word: Some Prolegomena for Cultural and Religious History* (New Haven, Conn.: Yale University Press, 1967); Ong, *Orality and Literacy: The Technologizing of the Word* (New York: Methuen, 1982). See also Jack Goody, ed., *Literacy in Traditional Societies* (Cambridge: Cambridge University Press, 1968); Harvey J. Graff, *The Legacies of Literacy: Continuities and Contradictions in Western Culture and Society* (Bloomington: Indiana University Press, 1987).

34. *JR,* 11:195. See also Du Creux, *History of Canada,* 1:188–89; Lescarbot, *History,* 3:128.

35. *JR,* 10:259.

36. Axtell, *After Columbus,* 92–93.

37. John Heckewelder, *History, Manners, and Customs of the Indian Nations Who Once Inhabited Pennsylvania and the Neighboring States* (1876; reprint, New York: Arno Press, 1971), 319.

38. *JR,* 11:211–13.

39. Ibid.

40. Ibid., 15:229.

41. Axtell, *Invasion,* 86.

42. Axtell, *Beyond 1492,* 160.

43. *JR,* 15:121.

44. Ibid., 17:135.

45. Ibid., 11:109.

46. Ibid., 30:63.

47. Axtell, *Invasion,* 99–100; Axtell, *Beyond 1492,* 159.

48. *JR,* 21:207, 34:169.

49. Elisabeth Tooker, *An Ethnography of the Huron Indians, 1615–1649* (Washington, D.C.: Bureau of American Ethnology, 1964; reprint, Syracuse, N.Y.: Syracuse University Press, 1991), 119.

50. *JR,* 1:289–91.
51. Ibid., 13:149–51.
52. Ibid., 17:151–53.
53. Ibid., 13:177.
54. Trigger, *Children of Aataentsic,* 2:122.
55. *JR,* 8:147.
56. Ibid., 13:135.
57. Ibid., 13:127, 15:71.
58. Ibid., 25:129, 14:199.
59. Ibid., 1:283, 6:211–13, 5:165. See also Du Creux, *History of Canada,* 1:97.
60. *JR,* 20:199.
61. Ibid., 15:51.
62. Ibid., 8:267–69.
63. Ibid., 11:125.
64. Ibid., 16:161.
65. Ibid., 23:189.
66. Ibid., 30:29, 15:51, 20:27–31.
67. Ibid., 18:41, 20:33.
68. Ibid., 16:39.
69. Ibid., 11:239, 19:223.
70. Ibid., 29:277. See also Du Creux, *History of Canada,* 2:418–19.
71. *JR,* 10:261, 23:31.
72. Ibid., 20:195, 25:263, 23:127.
73. Du Creux, *History of Canada,* 2:504.
74. *JR,* 25:157.
75. Ibid., 26:175–79.
76. Ibid., 23:31.
77. Ibid., 23:125.

Chapter 5. Alcohol and the Supernatural

1. *JR,* 9:205–7.
2. Ibid., 9:207.
3. For a discussion of the similarities of writing to witchcraft, see chapter 4.
4. *JR,* 9:207.
5. Ibid., 9:203, 205.
6. Le Clercq, *New Relation,* 255.
7. Juet, "Third Voyage," 22. See also E. B. O'Callaghan, *History of New Netherland; or, New York under the Dutch,* 2 vols. (1845; reprint, Spartanburg, S.C.: Reprint Company, 1966), 1:38.
8. David Pietersz de Vries, "Korte Historiael Ende Journaels Aenteyckeninge," in *NNN,* 216.
9. *JR,* 52:193.

10. "Kiliaen van Rensselaer to Willem Kieft, June 8, 1642," in Kiliaen Van Rensselaer, *Van Rensselaer Bowier Manuscripts,* trans. and ed. A. J. F. Van Laer (Albany: State University of New York, 1908), 621 (hereafter cited as *VRBM*).

11. Radisson, *Explorations,* 4, 38.

12. DeVries, "Korte Historiael," 216.

13. *JR,* 27:119. The chevalet was a common punishment in European armies in the seventeenth and eighteenth centuries. In English-speaking armies, the punishment was often called "riding the wooden horse." The offender was set on a device, something like a sawhorse, for several hours. The portion he sat on came to a point, and muskets or cannonballs might have been tied to his feet to increase his discomfort.

14. For more on the European mode of consuming alcohol, consult Peter C. Mancall, *Deadly Medicine: Indians and Alcohol in Early America* (Ithaca, N.Y.: Cornell University Press, 1995), 14–19.

15. Axtell, *Invasion,* 64.

16. *JR,* 38:257.

17. Axtell, *Invasion,* 64.

18. *JR,* 22:243.

19. See chapter 3.

20. Mancall, *Deadly Medicine,* 74–75.

21. Trigger, *Natives,* 205.

22. Tooker, *Native North American Spirituality,* 84–85.

23. *JR,* 11:195.

24. R. C. Dailey, "The Role of Alcohol among North American Indian Tribes as Reported in the Jesuit Relations," *Anthropologica* 10, no. 1 (1968): 50.

25. *JR,* 11:195, 197; 6:251.

26. Ibid., 6:253; Dailey, "Role of Alcohol," 45.

27. Edmund S. Carpenter, "Alcohol in the Iroquois Dream Quest," *American Journal of Psychiatry* 116, no. 2 (1959): 148.

28. *JR,* 5:49.

29. DeVries, "Korte Historiael," 216.

30. *JR,* 5:49–51, 231.

31. François Vachon de Belmont, "Belmont's History of Brandy," ed. Joseph P. Donnelly. *Mid-America* 34, no. 1 (1952): 45. See also Mancall, *Deadly Medicine,* 79–82.

32. *JR,* 22:243.

33. Belmont, "Belmont's History," 45, 52.

34. *JR,* 5:231.

35. Ibid., 5:51.

36. Ibid., 22:241, 26:121–23. It is unlikely that the assailant actually fired "three or four shots" from an arquebus. The weapon took a long time to load, and given the probable level of intoxication of the user, it would have taken even longer or would have been impossible. It is possible that the weapon was already loaded with three or four balls of shot, and he discharged all of them at once in the face of the boy.

37. Ibid., 9:203.

38. Ibid., 5:51, 29:153–55.

39. Ibid., 5:231.

40. René de Bréhant de Galinée, "The Journey of Dollier and Galinée, by Galinée, 1669–1670," in *Early Narratives of the Northwest, 1634–1699,* ed. Louise Phelps Kellogg (New York: Scribner's, 1917), 183. For other examples of Native people feigning intoxication, see Craig MacAndrew and Robert B. Edgerton, *Drunken Comportment: A Social Explanation* (Chicago: Aldine, 1969), 152–55.

41. *JR,* 16:201.

42. Ibid., 10:81, 28:187.

43. Ibid., 17:177.

44. Ibid., 30:101.

45. Ibid., 9:211, 6:239.

46. Ibid., 24:137–39.

47. Kiliaen van Rensselaer to Wouter van Twiller, April 23, 1634, in *VRBM,* 283. See also Trelease, *Indian Affairs,* 51.

48. "Ordinance of the Director and Council of New Netherland further prohibiting the sale of Intoxicating Liquors to Indians. *Passed* 21 *November* 1645," in *Laws and Ordinances of New Netherland, 1638–1674,* comp. and trans. E. B. O'Callaghan (Albany: Weed, Parsons, 1868), 52 (hereafter cited as *LONN*).

49. See "Ordinance of the Director and Council of New Netherland further prohibiting the sale of Intoxicating Liquor to Indians. *Passed* 13 *May,* 1648," in *LONN,* 100.

50. See Trelease, *Indian Affairs,* 93–94.

51. A. J. F. Van Laer, *Minutes of the Court of Rensselaerwyck, 1648–1652* (Albany: State University of New York, 1922), 97.

52. Dennis Sullivan, *The Punishment of Crime in Colonial New York: The Dutch Experience in Albany during the Seventeenth Century* (New York: Peter Lang, 1997), 74–75.

53. *JR,* 22:241.

54. DeVries, "Korte Historiael," 216

55. *JR,* 24:143, 5:231.

56. Ibid., 35:237, 269.

57. Ibid., 29:65.

Chapter 6. The Changed Relationship with the Beaver and Other Nonhumans

1. See the introduction for a more complete account of the Iroquoian creation myth.

2. For "Other Than Human Person," see Richter, *Ordeal,* 24–25. For "Beings Other Than Human," see Tooker, *Native North American Spirituality,* 11–13. See also Sagard, *Long Journey,* 170–72.

3. Baron [Louis Armand de Lom d' Arce] Lahontan, *New Voyages to North America,* ed. Rueben Gold Thwaites, 2 vols. (Chicago: A. C. McClurg, 1905), 2:476.

4. As I write this, the example uppermost in my mind is the reaction of the general public to the Makah Indians killing of a gray whale off the coast of Washington State on May 17, 1999. In reading the letters and e-mail sent to the *Seattle Times* in the

days after hunt, some letter writers claimed that the whale was the equal of human beings. At the same time, the Makahs were castigated for their "savagery" and "barbarism." Indeed, one protestor displayed a sign reading, "save a whale, harpoon a Makah."

5. *JR,* 1:85, 281; 24:171–73; 9:173–75; 31:221; 13:3; 26:163; 4:207; 10:217; 6:179–83. See also De Laet, "New World," 57; Megapolensis, "Short Account" 173.

6. Paul Chrisler Phillips, *The Fur Trade,* 2 vols. (Norman: University of Oklahoma Press, 1961), 1:11–14, 546.

7. Van der Donck, *Description of the New Netherlands,* 110–11.

8. Apparently, some Jesuits considered 10 livres too high, but it was a stable price, not changing between 1612 and 1632. See *JR,* 2:127, 4:255n.19.

9. Lescarbot, *History,* 3:3. The biscuit Lescarbot referred to is a sea biscuit, a sailor's ration.

10. These comparisons are from 1689, when the Dutch no longer had colonies in North America. Given the differing rates of taxation of the fur trade by the French, English, and Dutch and their respective abilities (and sometimes inability) to transport goods to North America, this comparison should be valid for the purposes of this work. French goods cost more because the tax rate—25 percent—was far higher than the 5–10 percent that the English and Dutch governments levied on their goods. French traders, to make a profit, had to pass the difference on to their Native clientele. See *NYCD,* 9:408–9. See also "Differences des traittes, avec les Sauvages, entre Montreal, en Canada, et Orange, a la Nouvelle Angleterre," in *Collection de Documents Relatifs a l' Historie de la Nouvelle-France,* 4 vols. (Quebec: A. Cole, 1883–85), 1:476–77 (hereafter cited as *Nouvelle-France*). See also Perrot, "Memoir," 1:259n. For the tax rates, see Phillips, *Fur Trade,* 1:249; Harold A. Innis, *The Fur Trade in Canada: An Introduction to Canadian Economic History,* rev. ed. (Toronto: University of Toronto Press, 1956), 52n. See also Trelease, *Indian Affairs,* 246–47; Karl H. Schlesier, "Epidemics and Indian Middlemen: Rethinking the Wars of the Iroquois, 1609–1653," *Ethnohistory* 23, no. 2 (1976): 129–45; W. J. Eccles, *France in America* (East Lansing: Michigan State University Press, 1990), 88–89.

11. Lescarbot, *History,* 3:168.

12. Lahontan, *New Voyages,* 2:476. For other examples of beavers being regarded as having reason or "sense," see Calvin Martin, *Keepers of the Game: Indian-Animal Relationships and the Fur Trade* (Berkeley: University of California Press, 1978), 35.

13. *JR,* 20:199.

14. Genesis 1:28.

15. William W. Canfield, *The Legends of the Iroquois, Told by "The Cornplanter"* (New York: A. Wessels, 1902), 103–18.

16. Lahontan, *New Voyages,* 2:482.

17. *JR,* 3:79, 83.

18. Sagard, *Long Voyage,* 233. See also Perrot, "Memoir," 1:104–6.

19. Hunt, *Wars of the Iroquois,* 33–34.

20. See "The Representation of New Netherland, 1650," in *NNN,* 297.

21. Megapolensis, "Short Account," 173.

22. De Vries, "Korte Historiael," 221.

23. Van der Donck, *Description of the New Netherlands,* 47.

24. *JR,* 21:99.

25. Ibid., 5:161, 32:31–33. See Stephen Irwin, *The Providers* (Blaine, Wash.: Hancock House, 1984), 275–76. Steel traps did not come into common use until the late eighteenth century. See also Martin, *Keepers of the Game,* 16–17. Steel traps almost never are mentioned in seventeenth-century sources. Either they were uncommon or they were too heavy for easy transport by traders. Given the mass hunting methods—groups of hunters taking large amounts of animals—mentioned in most sources, Native peoples had the traps been available, would have probably deemed them unnecessary. Axes, used to penetrate beaver lodges, were a far more versatile and hence in Native peoples' eyes, a more desirable tool.

26. Champlain, *Works,* 3:83, 85. See also DeVries, "Korte Historiael," 220–21.

27. *JR,* 6:299; Lahontan, *New Voyages,* 2:482.

28. *JR,* 6:299–301.

29. See Perrot, "Memoir," 1:104–6; Lahontan, *New Voyages,* 2:482–83.

30. For a more complete description of Iroquoian burial practices and the Huron Feast of the Dead, see chapter 3.

31. Trigger, *Children of Aataentsic,* 1:85–88. For the notion that the village of the souls was in the west, see *JR,* 10:145. For the number of pelts that went into each burial robe, see *JR,* 4:203.

32. Paul Le Jeune, "Containing a Journal of things which could not be set forth in the preceding chapters," in *JR,* 8:57.

33. Despite the presence of the Mohawk and Hudson River valleys, most of Iroquoia consisted of wooded highlands. See Megapolensis, "Short Account," 168. See also Trigger, *Children of Aataentsic,* 1:91.

34. Lahontan, *New Voyages,* 2:481.

35. Sagard, *Long Journey,* 232.

36. *JR,* 8:57.

37. For Huron mass killings of beavers and reliance on western trade networks, see *JR,* 8:57. For Iroquois' killing beavers regardless of season, see Van der Donck, *Description of the New Netherlands,* 115–16. See also Martin, *Keepers of the Game,* 27.

38. *JR,* 9:165, 8:57 (emphasis mine).

39. Ibid., 10:283–301, 8:87–89.

40. Ibid., 10:299, 293, 301; Sagard, *Long Journey,* 211–214.

41. Ibid., 10:301.

42. Du Creux, *History of Canada,* 1:129.

Chapter 7. European Technology and the Separation of Iroquoian Peoples from the Earth

1. *JR,* 17:47–49.

2. The "technological imagination" concept can be applied to nearly every other Native American group during the period of European colonization.

3. Axtell, *Beyond 1492,* 138.

4. The technological imagination, at least in this context, is very much a concept that applies to preliterate and prescientific populations. It does not work in the same way for people living in the Western world during the nineteenth, twentieth, and twenty-first centuries. Persons living through those periods have seen an explosion of new technologies, in transportation, communication, medicine, and so forth. Often we have seen several advances within our lifetimes. In this context, technological advances move beyond the accepted and into the expected.

5. Van den Bogaert, "Journey," 3.

6. David Horowitz, *The First Frontier: The Indian Wars and America's Origins, 1607–1776* (New York: Simon and Schuster, 1978), 146.

7. Cronon, Changes in the Land, 49.

8. Rasieres, "Letter," 107.

9. For stone axes, see *JR,* 8:41, 11:199, "What has been done for the instruction of other savages." See De Laet, "New World," 57. For native people's preference for metal hatchets and kettles, see *JR,* 17:49. See also Calvin Martin, "The Four Lives of a Micmac Copper Pot," *Ethnohistory* 22, no. 2 (1975): 111–33.

10. Lescarbot, *History,* 3:201. See also Sagard, *Long Journey,* 108; Martin, "Four Lives," 124; George Irving Quimby, *Indian Culture and European Trade Goods* (Madison: University of Wisconsin Press, 1966), 72

11. Sagard, *Long Journey,* 108, 109. See also *JR,* 5:95.

12. *JR,* 6:297, 299.

13. Champlain, *Works,* 2:339–45.

14. Trigger, *Children of Aataentsic,* 1:286.

15. Nicolaes van Wassenaer, "Historisch Verhael," in *NNN,* 83. See also Hunt, *Wars of the Iroquois,* 33

16. *NYCD,* 13:27n. See also Edmund B. O'Callaghan, *History of New Netherland; or, New York under the Dutch,* 2 vols. (1848; reprint, Spartanburg, S.C.: Reprint Company, 1966), 310n; Trelease, *Indian Affairs,* 131.

17. Van den Bogaert, "Journey," 8.

18. James W. Bradley, *Evolution of the Onondaga Iroquois: Accommodating Change, 1500–1655* (Syracuse, N.Y.: Syracuse University Press, 1987), 116, 130.

19. Axtell, *Beyond 1492,* 136–39.

20. See the opening quote to this chapter.

21. Many remains of kettles recovered from Iroquois village sites do not show evidence of burning or charring. See Bradley, *Evolution,* 132.

22. Bradley, *Evolution,* 131. See also Richter, *Ordeal,* 79.

23. See Bradley, *Evolution,* 147 (axes into knives and scrapers); Champlain, *Works,* 4:250 (swords into fish spears); Trigger, *Children of Aataentsic,* 1:411 (knives into harpoon points).

24. Trigger, *Children of Aataentsic,* 1:409.

25. Axtell, *Beyond 1492,* 135–36.

26. Ibid., 138.

27. *JR,* 3:75.

28. DeVries, "Korte Historiael," 217.

29. *JR,* 38:241, 18:123.

30. Rasieres, "Letter," 107.

31. Megapolensis, "Short Account," 173. An ell is approximately 45 inches. See Quimby, *Indian Culture,* 65.

32. Axtell, *Beyond 1492,* 132–33.

33. "Letter of Issack de Rasieres to the Amsterdam Chamber of the West India Company," in *Documents Relating to New Netherland, 1624–1626 in the Henry E. Huntington Library,* trans. and ed. A. J. F. van Laer (San Marino, Calif.: Henry E. Huntington Library, 1924), 228–31 (hereafter cited as *NND*).

34. Ibid., 223–32.

35. *JR,* 15:21

36. Ibid., 10:293, 297. See also Kenneth E. Kidd, "The Excavation and Historical Identification of a Huron Ossuary," *American Antiquity* 18, no. 4 (1953): 370.

37. Kidd, "Excavation," 367, 369, 371; Quimby, *Indian Culture,* 83, 111.

38. Kidd, "Excavation," 369. See also Pfeiffer and Fairgrieve, "Evidence from Ossuaries," 48.

39. Sagard, *Long Journey,* 183.

40. Richter, *Ordeal,* 75; Harmen Meyndertsz van den Bogaert, *A Journey into Mohawk and Oneida Country: The Journal of Harmen Meyndertsz van den Bogaert,* trans. and ed. Charles T. Gehring and William A. Starna; word list and linguistic notes by Gunther Michelson (Syracuse, New York: Syracuse University Press, 1988), 62.

41. Megapolensis, "Short Account," 178.

42. *JR,* 3:69.

43. Ibid., 3:105.

44. Kidd, "Excavation," 369, 371.

45. *JR,* 10:301.

46. See Trigger, *Children of Aataentsic,* 1:220–21, 242.

47. Sagard, *Long Journey,* 98; Trigger, *Children of Aataentsic,* 1:409.

48. Trigger, *Children of Aataentsic,* 1:410.

49. See note 9 of this chapter.

50. Trigger, *Children of Aataentsic,* 1:413.

51. *JR,* 4:207.

52. Lahontan, *New Voyages,* 1:377–78.

53. *JR,* 17:223, 23:269, 24:271.

54. Ibid., 28:45.

55. Ibid., 28:57.

Chapter 8. Making War Lethal

1. Champlain, *Works,* 2:99–100

2. For works that cast this skirmish as the source of near perpetual Iroquois-French conflict, see Cadwallader Colden, *The History of the Five Indian Nations of Canada, Which are Dependant of the Province of New-York America, and Are the Barrier between the English and*

French in That Part of the World (London: Printed for T. Osborne, 1747), 24–25. See also nineteenth-century works such as Morgan, *League of the Iroquois,* 11, and Francis Parkman, *Pioneers of New France in the New World* (Boston: Little, Brown, 1865), 360. For twentieth-century historians who adhere to this view, see Robert A. Goldstein, *French-Iroquois Diplomatic and Military Relations 1609–1701* (The Hague: Mouton, 1969), 51. Josephy, in *The Patriot Chiefs,* 5, maintains the "Iroquois' anger mounted steadily against the French" in the years after this firefight. For the views of historians who believe that entirely too much has been made of this clash, see Eccles, *Canadian Frontier,* 25, and Francis Jennings, *The Ambiguous Iroquois Empire: The Covenant Chain Confederation of Indian Tribes with English Colonies from Its Beginnings to the Lancaster Treaty of 1744* (New York: Norton, 1984), 41–42. See also Axtell, *Beyond 1492,* 208; Richter, *Ordeal,* 54; Dennis, *Cultivating a Landscape,* 72–74; Snow, *Iroquois,* 79. For perhaps the most penetrating analysis of Iroquois-French hostilities, see Francis Jennings, "Iroquois Alliances in American History," in Jennings et al., eds., *History and Culture of Iroquois Diplomacy,* 37–66.

3. For a discussion of the impact of military technologies on non-European peoples, see George Raudzens, "War Winning Weapons: The Measurement of Technological Determinism in Military History," *Journal of Military History* 54, no. 4 (1990): 412–18. See also Michael Adas, *Machines as the Measure of Men: Science, Technology, and Ideologies of Western Dominance* (Ithaca, N.Y.: Cornell University Press, 1989), 160–61. For more of the effects of firearms on Native Americans, see Adam J. Hirsch, "The Collision of Military Cultures," *Journal of American History* 74, no. 4 (1988): 1194.

4. Champlain, *Works,* 2:100

5. Historically speaking, however, this sort of myopia is not uncommon among fighting men. It never seemed to occur to some World War I commanders that machine guns, used with such devastating effect on peoples in Africa and Asia, could be trained on their own troops as well. After the strike at Pearl Harbor, Japanese naval commanders were elated at the number of American battleships they destroyed or damaged. At the same time, they did not think that the American carriers they had missed were significant. They ignored, of course, that they had launched their own attack from carriers.

6. Sagard, *Long Journey,* 154.

7. For a discussion of the technological imagination, see chapter 7.

8. *JR,* 13:265, 22:279. The term "buckler" refers to a type of curved shield.

9. Ibid., 24:205.

10. Ibid., 24:207–9.

11. Ibid., 21:59, 61, 63; 32:19–21; 34:125–27.

12. Thomas S. Abler, "European Technology and the Art of War in Iroquoia," in *Cultures in Conflict: Proceedings of the Twentieth Annual Conference of the Archaeological Association of the University of Calgary,* ed. Diana Claire Tkaczuk and Brian C. Vivian (University of Calgary Archaeological Association, 1989), 276–77.

13. *JR,* 10:53. For the prohibition on bearing weapons, see Saint Ignatius of Loyola, *The Constitutions of the Society of Jesus,* ed. and trans. George E. Ganss (St. Louis: Institute of Jesuit Sources, 1970), 159. See also Axtell, *Beyond 1492,* 156.

14. Trigger, *Children of Aataentsic,* 2:513–15.

15. See chapter 9.

16. T. M. Hamilton, *Early Indian Trade Guns: 1625–1775* (Lawton, Okla.: Museum of the Great Plains, 1968), 21–27.

17. See the discussion of warfare in chapter 2.

18. Champlain, *Works,* 2:129–30. By "irresistible," Champlain meant that the Onondaga believed that harquebus shots could not miss. Perhaps the Onondaga had good reason to assume that each shot was accurate. Champlain claims that "we hardly missed a shot, and fired two or three bullets each time." Then again, Champlain, like many other marksmen, may have exaggerated his own abilities. Seventeenth-century harquebuses did not have a sighting mechanism. One prepared one's weapon and then pointed it in the general direction of the target. See Brian J. Given, *A Most Pernicious Thing: Gun Trading and Native Warfare in the Early Contact Period* (Ottawa: Carleton University Press, 1994), 15–19. See also Richter, "War and Culture," 539; Patrick M. Malone, *The Skulking Way of War: Technology and Tactics among the New England Indians* (Lanham, Md.: Madison Books, 1991), 57–58, 70.

19. Van Wassenaer, "Historisch Verhael," 73.

20. Ibid., 84–85.

21. Richter, *Ordeal,* 90; Dennis, *Cultivating a Landscape,* 131.

22. See "Ordinance of Director and Council of New Netherland, Prohibiting the Sale of Firearms to Indians and requiring vessels sailing to or from Fort Orange, the South River or Fort Hope, to obtain a permit" and "Ordinance of the colony of Rensselaerwyck prohibiting the sale of powder, lead, and firearms to the Indians," in *VRBM,* 426, 565–66.

23. "Journal of New Netherland, 1647," in *NNN,* 274.

24. See Given, *Most Pernicious Thing,* 15–19, and Malone, *Skulking Way of War,* 32–33, for illustrated explanations of the workings of both matchlocks and flintlocks.

25. Given, *Most Pernicious Thing,* 17; Malone, *Skulking Way of War,* 33.

26. Given, *Most Pernicious Thing,* 17–18.

27. Malone, *Skulking Way of War,* 35.

28. Abler, "European Technology," 275. See also Bradley, *Evolution,* 142–43; Joseph R. Mayer, *Flintlocks of the Iroquois, 1620–1687* (Rochester, N.Y.: Rochester Museum of Arts and Sciences, 1943), 18–31; Hamilton, *Early Indian Trade Guns.* Also, one should note the absence of matchlocks, or parts thereof, during Kidd's excavation of the 1636 Huron ossuary.

29. See Given, *Most Pernicious Thing,* 109–10; Abler "European Technology," 274.

30. Given, *Most Pernicious Thing,* 109.

31. Jennings, *Ambiguous Iroquois Empire,* 80–81.

32. "Journal of New Netherland," 274.

33. *JR,* 21:35–37.

34. Ibid., 21:37–61; 24:271, 295; 34:137.

35. See Richter, *Ordeal,* 62–64.

36. *JR,* 24:295.

37. "Representation of New Netherland," 303.

38. Lahontan, *New Voyages,* 2:497.

39. Malone, *Skulking Way of War,* 58.

40. Ibid., 52–54, 58.

41. See Eric R. Wolf, *Europe and the People without History* (Berkeley: University of California Press, 1982), 169. See also Trelease, *Indian Affairs,* 246.

42. *JR,* 25:27. For a Native person's view on the linkage of technology to conversion, see *JR,* 17:49.

43. *JR,* 1:269; 21:119, 269–71; 22:251, 269; 24:271; 25:59; 32:21; 34:123; 36:101; 38:67.

44. See *NYCD,* 9:408–9. See also Brandão, *"Your fyre shall burn no more,"* 56.

45. *JR,* 24:275–77.

46. Sagard, *Long Journey,* 262.

47. *JR,* 21:99.

48. Ibid., 22:307. The term "Flemings" refers to the Dutch.

49. Trigger, *Children of Aataentsic,* 1:408–9.

50. Van Wassenaer, "Historisch Verhael," 84–85.

51. Van den Bogaert, "Journey," 6, 8.

52. Richter, "War and Culture," 544.

53. Van den Bogaert, "Journey," 3.

54. *JR,* 30:229.

55. Champlain, *Works,* 2:97.

56. Keith Otterbein, "Huron vs. Iroquois: A Case Study in Inter-Tribal Warfare," *Ethnohistory* 26, no. 2 (1979): 141–53.

57. *JR,* 17:223. For the Five Nations' superiority in weaponry and tactics, see Keith F. Otterbein, "Why the Iroquois Won: An Analysis of Iroquois Military Tactics," *Ethnohistory* 11, no. 1 (1964): 56–63.

58. *JR,* 21:55–57.

59. Ibid., 23:35.

60. Ibid., 28:57. See also Nancy Bonvillain, "Missionary Role in French Colonial Expansion: An Examination of the Jesuit Relations," *Man in the Northeast* 29 (1985): 4.

Chapter 9. The Destruction of the Huron and Remaking of the Five Nations

1. Bruce G. Trigger, "The Mohawk-Mahican War (1624–1628): The Establishment of a Pattern," *Canadian Historical Review* 52, no. 3 (1971): 276–86.

2. Trigger, *Children of Aataentsic,* 1:209. See also Neal Salisbury, *Manitou and Providence: Indians, Europeans, and the Making of New England, 1500–1643* (New York: Oxford University Press, 1982), 79.

3. Trigger, "Mohawk-Mahican War," 278–79.

4. Van Wassenaer, "Historisch Verhael," 84, 89. The "Fresh River" is a reference to the Connecticut River.

5. Michaëlius, "Letter of Reverend Jonas Michaëlius, 1628" 131.

6. See Francis Jennings, *The Invasion of America: Indians, Colonialism, and the Cant of Conquest* (Chapel Hill: University of North Carolina Press, 1975), 220–25; Salisbury, *Manitou and Providence,* 221–22. See also Hirsch, "Military Cultures."

7. William Bradford, *Bradford's History of Plymouth Plantation, 1606–1646,* ed. William T. Davis (New York: Scribner's, 1920), 343

8. John Winthrop, *The Journal of John Winthrop, 1630–1649,* ed. Richard S. Dunn, James Savage, and Laetitia Yeandle (Cambridge, Mass.: Harvard University Press, 1996), 229

9. Otterbein, "Huron vs. Iroquois," 148–50.

10. Located in present-day Tiny Township, Ontario, Canada.

11. *JR,* 33:259, 39:239, 34:87. St. Joseph, of course, was the French appellation; the Huron called the village Teanaostaiaé. See Trigger, *Children of Aataentsic,* 2:753.

12. *JR,* 33:261; Trigger, *Children of Aataentsic,* 2:752.

13. *JR,* 33:261.

14. Trigger, *Children of Aataentsic,* 2:752.

15. *JR,* 33:261, 263; 34:89–91; 39:239–41.

16. Ibid., 33:265, 34:91, 39:241.

17. Trigger, *Children of Aataentsic,* 2:753. For Huron population estimates, see Heidenreich, *Huronia,* 91–103.

18. *JR,* 39:247, 34:125, 131. Ragueneau may have the timeline confused in his account. He claimed that the Iroquois entered St. Ignace "at daybreak," but later claims that they attacked St. Louys "before sunrise" on the same day. In all likelihood, it seems probable that the Iroquois seized control of St. Ignace sometime after midnight.

19. Ibid., 34:123.

20. See Hunt, *Wars of the Iroquois,* 92. Consult also Eccles, *Canadian Frontier,* 54. See also Snow, *Iroquois,* 115. Trigger, *Children of Aataentsic,* 2:763, argues that the Iroquois attacks of the previous year deterred the Huron from using their hunting territories east of Lake Simcoe, and this resulted in the Iroquois army remaining undetected.

21. *JR,* 39:247.

22. Ibid., 34:125, 39:247. Trigger, *Children of Aataentsic,* 2:763.

23. Ragueneau, in *JR,* 34:125–27, gives the figure of eighty warriors, and Bressani, in *JR,* 39:249, claims there were "about a hundred."

24. *JR,* 34:125. See also Otterbein, "Huron vs. Iroquois," 146.

25. *JR,* 34:127, 39:249.

26. Ibid., 34:27–37, 143–47; 39:253–55.

27. Ibid., 34:133, 135.

28. Ibid., 135.

29. Ibid., 34:135, 137.

30. Heidenreich, *Huronia,* 372. This is a straight-line distance; it is quite possible that there were natural obstacles that added distance to this Huron woman's trek.

31. *JR,* 34:137.

32. Brandão, *"Your fyre shall burn no more,"* 204.

33. See Otterbein, "Huron vs. Iroquois," 148; Brandão, *"Your fyre shall burn no more,"* 204.

34. *JR,* 34:197, 203, 223, 79; 35:79–81.

35. Ibid., 34:203–9; Trigger, *Children of Aataentsic,* 2:771; Yarnell, *Aboriginal Relationships,* 129.

36. *JR,* 34:203. The Jesuit sources often refer to this island as St. Joseph Island.

37. Ibid., 35:87, 85.

38. Ibid., 34:225; 35:85, 27.

39. Ibid., 35:99, 183.
40. Ibid., 35:89.
41. Ibid., 35:187, 191.
42. Ibid., 35:193; Trigger, *Children of Aataentsic,* 2:785.
43. *JR,* 35:193.
44. Ibid., 36:181. Trigger, *Children of Aataentsic,* 2:786–87.
45. *JR,* 36:185, 187.
46. Ibid., 44:21, 36:179.
47. Ibid., 41:47, 53–55.
48. Ibid., 43:187–89.
49. Ibid., 43:189. Ondesonk was the name by which both the Huron and the Iroquois knew Father Isaac Jouges. After his death at the hands of the Mohawk in 1644, they transferred the name to Father Simon Le Moyne
50. Ibid., 35:191, 41:59.
51. Ibid., 35:219.
52. See the introduction.

Epilogue

1. See, for example, Hunt, *Wars of the Iroquois*; Richter, *Ordeal.*
2. Richter, *Ordeal,* 65; Fenton, *Great Law,* 245–47.
3. Fenton, *Great Law,* 245–46
4. *JR,* 36:119, 121.
5. Richter, *Ordeal,* 65–66.
6. See Richter, *Ordeal*; Trigger, *Aataentsic.*
7. *JR,* 43:191.
8. Trigger, *Aataentsic,* 2:813.
9. *JR,* 43:69–77.
10. Perrot, "Memoir," 256–257. See also White, *Middle Ground,* 196; Michael N. McConnell, *A Country Between: The Upper Ohio Valley and Its Peoples, 1724–1774* (Lincoln: University of Nebraska Press, 1992), 62–63.
11. White, *Middle Ground,* 1–49.
12. Ibid., 200–201.
13. Gregory Evans Dowd, *A Spirited Resistance: The North American Indian Struggle for Unity, 1745–1815* (Baltimore: Johns Hopkins University Press, 1992), 34. See also White, *Middle Ground,* 279–81; McConnell, *Country Between,* 220–22.
14. See Dowd, *Spirited Resistance,* 55, 143–44, 185. See also R. David Edmunds, *The Shawnee Prophet* (Lincoln: University of Nebraska Press, 1983), 84–85, 128; Edmunds, *Tecumseh and the Quest for Indian Leadership* (New York: Harper-Collins, 1984), 161.
15. Daniel K. Richter, "Ordeals of the Longhouse," in *Beyond the Covenant Chain: The Iroquois and Their Neighbors in Indian North America, 1600–1800,* ed. Daniel K. Richter and James H. Merrell (Syracuse, N.Y.: Syracuse University Press, 1987), 21–24.
16. Richter, *Ordeal,* 115–19.

17. Ibid., 119–20.

18. See, for example, John Demos, *The Unredeemed Captive: A Family Story from Early America* (New York: Knopf, 1994).

19. Jennings, *Ambiguous Iroquois Empire,* 210–12.

20. Richard Aquila, *The Iroquois Restoration: Iroquois Diplomacy on the Colonial Frontier, 1701–1754* (1983; reprinted with an introduction by the author, Lincoln: University of Nebraska Press, 1997), 65–67.

21. See Wallace, *Death and Rebirth.*

BIBLIOGRAPHY

Primary Sources

Belmont, François Vachon de. "Belmont's History of Brandy." Edited by Joseph P. Donnelly. *Mid-America* 34, no. 1 (1952): 42–63.

Blair Emma Helen, ed. *The Indian Tribes of the Upper Mississippi Valley and the Region of the Great Lakes*. 2 vols. 1911. Reprint, with an introduction by Richard White, Lincoln: University of Nebraska Press, 1996.

Bradford, William. *Bradford's History of Plymouth Plantation 1606–1646*. Edited by William T. Davis. New York: Scribner's, 1908.

Bullock, William. *Virginia impartially examined, and left to publick view, to be considered by all judicious and honest men: under which title is comprehended the degrees from 34 to 39, wherein lyes the rich and healthful countries of Roanock, the new plantations of Virginia and Maryland*. London: John Hammond, 1649.

Campeau, Lucien. *Établissement à Québec*. Quebec: Les Presses de L' Universite Laval, 1979.

———. *La Bonne Nouvelle Reçue (1641–1643)*. Montreal: Les Editions Bellarmin, 1990.

———. *Fondation de la Mission Huronne (1635–1637)*. Quebec: Les Presses de L' Universite Laval, 1987.

Champlain, Samuel de. *The Works of Samuel de Champlain*. Edited by H. P. Biggar. 6 vols. Toronto: Champlain Society, 1922–36.

Colden, Cadwallader. *The History of the Five Indian Nations of Canada, Which are Dependant of the Province of New-York America, and Are the Barrier between the English and French in That Part of the World* (London: Printed for T. Osborne, 1747).

Collection de Manuscrits contenant lettres, mémoires, et documents historiques Relatifs a la Nouvelle-France. 4 vols. Quebec: A. Cote, 1883–85.

Denys, Nicolas. *The Description and Natural History of the Coasts of North America (Acadia).* Translated and edited by William F. Ganong. 1908. Reprint, New York: Greenwood Press, 1968.

Du Creux, François. *The History of Canada or New France.* 2 vols. Translated by Percy J. Robinson. Edited by James B. Conacher. 1952. Reprint, New York: Greenwood Press, 1969.

Hart, Simon. *The Prehistory of the New Netherland Company: Amsterdam Notarial Records of the first Dutch Voyages to the Hudson.* Amsterdam: City of Amsterdam Press, 1959.

Jameson, J. Franklin, ed. *Narratives of New Netherland 1609–1664.* New York: Scribner's, 1909.

Kellogg, Louise Phelps, ed. *Early Narratives of the Northwest, 1634–1699.* New York: Scribner's, 1917.

Lafitau, Joseph François. *Customs of the American Indians Compared with the Customs of Primitive Times.* Edited and translated by William N. Fenton and Elizabeth L. Moore. 2 vols. Toronto: Champlain Society, 1974–77.

Lahontan [Louis Armand de Lom d'Arce] Baron de. *New Voyages to North America.* Edited by Rueben Gold Thwaites. 2 vols. Chicago: A. C. McClurg, 1905.

Le Clercq, Chrestien. *New Relation of Gaspesia, With the Customs and Religions of the Gaspesian Indians.* Translated and edited by William F. Ganong. 1910. Reprint, New York: Greenwood Press, 1968.

Lescarbot, Marc. *History of New France.* Translated by W. L. Grant. 3 vols. 1907–14. Reprint, New York: Greenwood Press, 1968.

Loyola, Saint Ignatius of. *The Constitutions of the Society of Jesus.* Edited and translated by George E. Ganss. St. Louis: Institute of Jesuit Sources, 1970.

O'Callaghan. E. B., comp. and trans. *Laws and Ordinances of New Netherland, 1638–1674.* Albany: Weed, Parsons, 1868.

———, ed. *The Documentary History of the State of New York.* 4 vols. Albany: Weed, Parsons, 1849–51.

O'Callaghan, E. B., John Romeyn Broadhead, and Berthold Fernow, eds. *Documents Relative to the Colonial History of the State of New York.* 15 vols. Albany: Weed, Parsons, 1853–87.

Radisson, Pierre Esprit. *The Explorations of Pierre Esprit Radisson.* Edited by Arthur T. Adams. Minneapolis: Ross and Haines, 1961.

Sagard, Gabriel. *Histoire Du Canada.* 4 vols. Paris, 1865.

———. *The Long Journey to the Country of the Hurons.* Translated by H. H. Langton. Edited with introduction and notes by George M. Wrong and translated into English by H.H. Langton. 1939. Reprint, New York: Greenwood Press, 1968.

Snow, Dean R., Charles T. Gehring, and William A. Starna. *In Mohawk Country: Early Narratives about a Native People.* Syracuse, N.Y.: Syracuse University Press, 1996.

Thwaites, Rueben Gold, ed. *The Jesuit Relations and Allied Documents: Travels and Explorations of the Jesuit Missionaries in New France, 1610–1791.* 73 vols. Cleveland: Burrows Brothers, 1896–1901.

Van der Donck, Adriaen. *A Description of the New Netherlands*. Edited by Thomas F. O'Donnell. Syracuse, N.Y.: Syracuse University Press, 1968.

Van Laer, A. J. F., trans. and ed. *Documents Relating to New Netherland 1624–1626 in the Henry E. Huntington Library*. San Marino, Calif.: Henry E. Huntington Library, 1924.

———. *Minutes of the Court of Rensselaerwyck, 1648–1652*. Albany: State University of New York, 1922.

———. *New York Historical Manuscripts: Dutch*. 4 vols. Baltimore: Genealogical Publishing Company, 1974.

Van Rensselaer, Kiliaen. *Van Rensselaer Bowier Manuscripts*. Translated and edited by A. J. F. Van Laer. Albany: State University of New York, 1908.

Winthrop, John. *The Journal of John Winthrop 1630–1649*. Edited by Richard S. Dunn, James Savage, and Laetitia Yeandle. Cambridge, Mass.: Harvard University Press, 1996.

Secondary Sources

Abler, Thomas S. "Iroquois Cannibalism: Fact Not Fiction." *Ethnohistory* 27, no. 4 (1980): 309–16.

Adas, Michael. *Machines as the Measure of Men: Science, Technology, and Ideologies of Western Dominance*. Ithaca, N.Y.: Cornell University Press, 1989.

Aquila, Richard. *The Iroquois Restoration: Iroquois Diplomacy on the Colonial Frontier, 1701–1754*. Reprint, with an introduction by the author. Lincoln: University of Nebraska Press, 1997.

Axtell, James. *After Columbus: Essays in the Ethnohistory of Colonial North America*. New York: Oxford University Press, 1988.

———. *Beyond 1492: Encounters in Colonial North America*. New York: Oxford University Press, 1992.

———, ed. *The Indian Peoples of North America: A Documentary History of the Sexes*. New York: Oxford University Press, 1981.

———. *The Invasion Within: The Contest of Cultures in Colonial North America*. New York: Oxford University Press, 1985.

Bamann, Susan, Robert Kuhn, James Molnar, and Dean Snow. "Iroquoian Archaeology." *Annual Review of Anthropology* 21 (1992): 435–60.

Barbeau, C. M. "Supernatural Beings of the Huron and Wyandot." *American Anthropologist* 16 (1914): 288–313.

Beauchamp, W. M. "Onondaga Tale of the Pleiades." *Journal of American Folklore* 13 (1900): 281–82.

Becker, Carl. *The Heavenly City of the Eighteenth Century Philosophers*. New Haven, Conn.: Yale University Press, 1932.

Berkhofer, Robert F. *The White Man's Indian: Images of the American Indian from Columbus to the Present*. New York: Knopf, 1978.

Bonvillain, Nancy. "Missionary Role in French Colonial Expansion: An Examination of the Jesuit Relations." *Man in the Northeast* 29 (1985): 1–14.

———, ed. *Studies on Iroquois Culture.* Rindge, N.H.: Occasional Publications in Northeastern Anthropology, no. 6, 1980.

Bradley, John W. *Evolution of the Onondaga Iroquois: Accommodating Change, 1500–1665.* Syracuse, N.Y.: Syracuse University Press, 1987.

Brandão, José António. *"Your fyre shall burn no more": Iroquois Policy toward New France and Its Native Allies to 1701.* Lincoln: University of Nebraska Press, 1997.

Breen, Timothy. *Tobacco Culture: The Mentality of the Great Tidewater Planters on the Eve of Revolution.* Princeton, N.J.: Princeton University Press, 1985.

Canfield, William W. *The Legends of the Iroquois Told by "The Cornplanter."* New York: A. Wessels, 1902.

Carpenter, Edmund S. "Alcohol in the Iroquois Dream Quest." *American Journal of Psychiatry* 116, no. 2 (1959): 148–51.

Ceci, Lynn. *The Effect of European Contact and Trade on the Settlement Pattern of Indians in Coastal New York, 1524–1665.* New York: Garland Publishing, 1990.

———. "Watchers of the Pleiades: Ethnoastronomy among Native Cultivators in Northeastern North America" *Ethnohistory* 25, no. 4 (1978): 301–17.

Dailey, R. C. "The Role of Alcohol among North American Indian Tribes as Reported in the *Jesuit Relations*." *Anthropologica* 10, no. 1 (1968): 45–59.

Demos, John. *The Unredeemed Captive: A Family Story from Early America.* New York: Knopf, 1994.

Dennis, Matthew. *Cultivating a Landscape of Peace: Iroquois-European Encounters in Seventeenth Century America.* Ithaca, N.Y.: Cornell University Press, 1993.

Dorsey, Peter A. "Going to School with Savages: Authority and Authorship among the Jesuits of New France." *William and Mary Quarterly,* 3rd ser., 55, no. 3 (1998): 399–420.

Dowd, Gregory Evans. *A Spirited Resistance: The North American Indian Struggle for Unity, 1745–1815.* Baltimore: Johns Hopkins University Press, 1992.

Eccles, W. J. *The Canadian Frontier 1534–1760.* New York: Holt, Rinehart and Winston, 1969.

———. *France in America.* Rev. ed. East Lansing: Michigan State University Press, 1990.

Edmunds, R. David. *The Shawnee Prophet.* Lincoln: University of Nebraska Press, 1983.

———. *Tecumseh and the Quest for Indian Leadership.* New York: Harper-Collins, 1984.

Eekhof, A. *Jonas Michaëlius, Founder of the Church in New Netherland.* Leyden: A. W. Sijthoff's Publishing Company, 1926.

Feister, Lois M. "Linguistic Communication between the Dutch and Indians in New Netherland 1609–1664." *Ethnohistory* 20, no. 1 (1973): 25–38.

Fenton, William N. *The Great Law and the Longhouse: A Political History of the Iroquois Confederacy.* Norman: University of Oklahoma Press, 1998.

Fitting, James E. "The Huron as an Ecotype: The Limits of Maximization in a Western Great Lakes Society." *Anthropologica* 14, no. 1 (1972): 3–18.

Foster, Michael K., Jack Campisi, and Mariann Mithun, eds. *Extending the Rafters: Interdisciplinary Approaches to Iroquoian Studies.* Albany: State University of New York Press, 1984.

Given, Brian J. *A Most Pernicious Thing: Gun Trading and Native Warfare in the Early Contact Period.* Ottawa: Carleton University Press, 1994.

Goldmann, Lucien. *The Philosophy of the Enlightenment; The Christian Burgess and the Enlightenment.* Translated by Henry Maas. London: Routledge, 1973.

Goldstein, Robert A. *French-Iroquois Diplomatic and Military Relations, 1609–1701.* The Hague: Mouton, 1969.

Goody, Jack, ed. *Literacy in Traditional Societies.* New York: Cambridge University Press, 1968.

Graff, Harvey J. *The Legacies of Literacy: Continuities and Contradictions in Western Culture and Society.* Bloomington: Indiana University Press, 1987.

Hale, Horatio. *The Iroquois Book of Rites.* 1883. Reprint, with an introduction by William N. Fenton. Toronto: University of Toronto Press, 1963.

Hamilton, T. M. *Early Indian Trade Guns: 1625–1775.* Lawton, Okla.: Museum of the Great Plains, 1968

———. "Indian Trade Guns." *Missouri Archaeologist* 22 (December 1960).

Heckewelder, John. *History, Manners, and Customs of the Indian Nations Who Once Inhabited Pennsylvania and the Neighboring States.* 1876. Reprint, New York: Arno Press, 1971.

Heidenreich, Conrad. *The Huron: A Brief Ethnography.* York: York University Department of Geography, 1972.

———. *Huronia: A History and Geography of the Huron Indians, 1600–1650.* Ontario: McClelland and Stewart, 1971.

Henshaw, H.W. "Indian Origin of Maple Sugar." *American Anthropologist* 3, no. 1 (1890): 341–51.

Hewitt, J. N. B. "The Iroquoian Concept of the Soul." *Journal of American Folklore* 8 (1895): 107–16.

———. *Iroquoian Cosmology.* 1903 and 1928. Reprint, New York: AMS Press, 1974.

Hirsch, Adam J. "The Collision of Military Cultures in Seventeenth-Century New England." *Journal of American History* 74, no. 4 (1988): 1187–1212.

Horowitz, David. *The First Frontier: The Indian Wars and America's Origins 1607–1776.* New York: Simon and Schuster, 1978.

Houghton, Frederick. "The Characteristics of Iroquoian Village Sites of Western New York." *American Anthropologist* 18 (1916): 508–20.

Hultkrantz, Åke. *Native Religions of North America: The Power of Visions and Fertility.* New York: HarperCollins, 1987.

———. *Soul and Native Americans.* Originally published as *Conceptions of the Soul among North American Indians.* Edited by Robert Holland. 1952. Reprint, Woodstock, Conn.: Spring Publications, 1997.

Hunt, George T. *The Wars of the Iroquois: A Study in Intertribal Trade Relations.* Madison: University of Wisconsin Press, 1940.

Innis, Harold A. *The Fur Trade in Canada: An Introduction to Canadian Economic History.* Rev. ed. Toronto: University of Toronto Press, 1956.

Irwin, Stephen, *The Providers.* Blaine, Wash.: Hancock House, 1984.

Isaac, Rhys. *The Transformation of Virginia, 1740–1790.* Chapel Hill: University of North Carolina Press, 1982.

Jaenen, Cornelius J. *Friend and Foe: Aspects of French-Amerindian Contact in the Sixteenth and Seventeenth Centuries.* New York: Columbia University Press, 1976.

Jennings, Francis. *The Ambiguous Iroquois Empire: The Covenant Chain Confederation of Indian Tribes with English Colonies from Its Beginnings to the Lancaster Treaty of 1744.* New York: Norton, 1984.

———. *The Invasion of America: Indians, Colonialism, and the Cant of Conquest.* Chapel Hill: University of North Carolina Press, 1975.

Jennings, Francis, William N. Fenton, Mary A. Druke, and David R. Miller, eds. *The History and Culture of Iroquois Diplomacy: An Interdisciplinary Guide to the Treaties of the Six Nations and Their League.* Syracuse, N.Y.: Syracuse University Press, 1985.

Josephy, Alvin M. *The Patriot Chiefs: A Chronicle of American Indian Resistance.* New York: Viking, 1961.

Kidd, Kenneth E. "The Excavation and Historical Identification of a Huron Ossuary." *American Antiquity* 18, no. 4 (1953): 359–79.

Knowles, Nathaniel. "The Torture of Captives by the Indians of Eastern North America." *Proceedings of the American Philosophical Society* 82, no. 2 (1940): 151–225.

Kupperman, Karen Ordahl. "The Puzzle of the American Climate in the Early Colonial Period." *American Historical Review* 87, no. 5 (1982): 1262–89.

Larsen, Clark Spencer, and George R. Milner, eds. *In the Wake of Contact: Biological Responses to Conquest.* New York: Wiley-Liss, 1994.

Larsen, Esther Louise. "Pehr Kalm's Description of Maize, How It Is Planted and Cultivated in North America, Together with the Many Uses of This Crop Plant." *Agricultural History* 9, no. 2 (1935): 107.

Leacock, Eleanor Burke, and Nancy Oestreich Lurie, eds. *North American Indians in Historical Perspective.* New York: Random House, 1971.

MacAndrew, Craig, and Robert B. Edgerton. *Drunken Comportment: A Social Explanation.* Chicago: Aldine, 1969.

Malone, Patrick M. *The Skulking Way of War: Technology and Tactics among the New England Indians.* Lanham, Md.: Madison Books, 1991.

Mancall, Peter C. *Deadly Medicine: Indians and Alcohol in Early America.* Ithaca, N.Y.: Cornell University Press, 1995.

Mann, Barbara A., and Jerry L. Fields, "A Sign in the Sky: Dating the League of the Haudenosaunee." *American Indian Culture and Research Journal* 21, no. 2 (1997): 105–63.

Martin, Calvin. "The European Impact on the Culture of a Northeastern Algonquian Tribe: An Ecological Interpretation." *William and Mary Quarterly,* 3rd ser., 31, no. 1 (1974): 3–26.

———. "The Four Lives of a Micmac Copper Pot." *Ethnohistory* 22, no. 2 (1975): 111–33.

———. *Keepers of the Game: Indian-Animal Relationships and the Fur Trade.* Berkeley: University of California Press, 1978.

Mayer, Joseph R. *Flintlocks of the Iroquois, 1620–1687*. Rochester, N.Y.: Rochester Museum of Arts and Sciences, 1943.

Maxwell, Hu. "The Use and Abuse of Forests by the Virginia Indians." *William and Mary Quarterly*, 2nd ser., 19, no. 2 (1910): 73–103.

McConnell, Michael N. *A Country Between: The Upper Ohio Valley and Its Peoples, 1724–1744*. Lincoln: University of Nebraska Press, 1992.

McLuhan, Marshall. *The Gutenberg Galaxy: The Making of Typographic Man*. Toronto: University of Toronto Press, 1962.

Merrell, James H. *The Indians' New World: Catawbas and Their Neighbors from European Contact through the Era of Removal*. Chapel Hill: University of North Carolina Press, 1989.

Miller, Christopher L., and George R. Hamell. "A New Perspective on Indian-White Contact: Cultural Symbols and Colonial Trade. *Journal of American History* 73, no. 2 (1986): 311–28.

Miller, Perry. *The New England Mind: From Colony to Province*. Cambridge, Mass.: Harvard University Press, 1953.

———. *The New England Mind: The Seventeenth Century*. New York: Macmillan, 1939.

Morgan, Lewis Henry. *League of the Iroquois*. 1851. Reprint, with an introduction by William N. Fenton. Secaucus, N.J.: Citadel Press, 1962.

O'Callaghan, E. B. *History of New Netherland; or, New York under the Dutch*. 2 vols. 1845. Reprint, Spartanburg, S.C.: Reprint Company, 1966.

Ong, Walter J. *Orality and Literacy: The Technologizing of the Word*. New York: Methuen, 1982.

———. *The Presence of the Word: Some Prolegomena for Cultural and Religious History*. New Haven, Conn.: Yale University Press, 1967.

Otterbein, Keith F. "Huron vs. Iroquois: A Case Study in Inter-Tribal Warfare." *Ethnohistory* 26, no. 2 (1979): 141–53.

———. "Why the Iroquois Won: An Analysis of Iroquois Military Tactics." *Ethnohistory* 11, no. 1 (1964): 56–63.

Parker, Arthur Caswell. *Parker on the Iroquois*. Edited and introduction by William N. Fenton. Syracuse, N.Y.: Syracuse University Press, 1968.

Parkman, Francis. *Pioneers of New France in the New World*. Boston: Little, Brown, 1865.

Phillips, Paul Chrisler. *The Fur Trade*. 2 vols. Norman: University of Oklahoma Press, 1961.

Pyne, Stephen J. *Fire in America: A Cultural History of Wildland and Rural Fire*. Princeton, N.J.: Princeton University Press, 1982.

Quimby, George I. *Indian Culture and European Trade Goods: The Archaeology of the Historic Period in the Western Great lakes Region*. Madison: University of Wisconsin Press, 1966.

Radudzens, George. "War Winning Weapons: The Measurement of Technological Determinism in Military History." *Journal of Military History* 54, no. 4 (1990): 403–33.

Richter, Daniel K. "Iroquois versus Iroquois: Jesuit Missions and Christianity in Village Politics, 1642–1686." *Ethnohistory* 32, no. 1 (1985): 1–16

———. *The Ordeal of the Longhouse: The Peoples of the Iroquois League in the Era of European Colonization*. Chapel Hill: University of North Carolina Press, 1992.

———. "War, Peace, and Politics in Seventeenth Century Huronia." In *Cultures in Conflict: Current Archaeological Perspectives: Proceedings of the Twentieth Annual Conference of the Archaeological Association of the University of Calgary,* edited by Diana Claire Tkaczuk and Brian C.Vivian. Calgary: University of Calgary Archaeological Association, 1989.

———. "War and Culture: The Iroquois Experience." *William and Mary Quarterly,* 3rd ser., 40, no. 4 (1983): 528–59.

Richter, Daniel K., and James H. Merrell, eds. *Beyond the Covenant Chain: The Iroquois and Their Neighbors in Indian North America, 1600–1800.* Syracuse, N.Y.: Syracuse University Press, 1987.

Ritchie, William A. *The Archaeology of New York State.* 2nd ed. Garden City: N.Y.: Natural History Press, 1969.

Sale, Kirkpatrick. *The Conquest of Paradise: Christopher Columbus and the Columbian Legacy.* New York: Knopf, 1990.

Salisbury, Neal. *Manitou and Providence: Indians, Europeans, and the Making of New England, 1500–1643.* New York: Oxford University Press, 1982.

Schlesier, Karl H. "Epidemics and Indian Middlemen: Rethinking the Wars of the Iroquois 1609–1653." *Ethnohistory* 23, no. 2 (1976): 129–45.

Schult, Robert C., and Donald J. Hughes, eds. *Ecological Consciousness: Essays from the Earthday X Colloquium.* Washington, D.C.: University Press of America, 1981.

Schwartz, Stuart B., ed. *Implicit Understandings: Observing, Reporting, and Reflecting on the Encounters between Europeans and Other Peoples in the Early Modern Era.* New York: Cambridge University Press, 1994.

Snow, Dean. *The Iroquois.* Cambridge, Mass.: Blackwell, 1994.

Speck, Frank G. *Midwinter Rites of the Cayuga Longhouse.* 1949. Reprint, with an introduction by William N. Fenton, Lincoln: University of Nebraska Press, 1995.

Starna, William A., George R. Hamell, and William L. Butts. "Northern Iroquoian Horticulture and Insect Infestation: A Cause for Village Removal." *Ethnohistory* 31, no. 3 (1984): 197–207.

Steele, Ian K. *Warpaths: Invasions of North America.* New York: Oxford University Press, 1994

Sullivan, Dennis. *The Punishment of Crime in Colonial New York: The Dutch Experience in Albany during the Seventeenth Century.* New York: Peter Lang, 1997.

Timmins, Peter A. *The Calvert Site: An Interpretive Framework for the Early Iroquoian Village.* Hull, Quebec: Canadian Museum of Civilization, 1997.

Tkaczuk, Diana Claire, and Brian C.Vivian. *Cultures in Conflict: Proceedings of the Twentieth Annual Conference of the Archaeological Association of the University of Calgary.* University of Calgary Archaeological Association, 1989.

Tooker, Elisabeth. *An Ethnography of the Huron Indians, 1615–1649.* Washington, D.C.: Bureau of American Ethnology, 1964. Reprint, Syracuse, N.Y.: Syracuse University Press, 1991.

———. *The Iroquois Ceremonial of Midwinter*. Syracuse, N.Y.: Syracuse University Press, 1970.

———, ed. *Iroquois Culture, History, and Prehistory: Proceedings of the 1965 Conference on Iroquois Research*. Albany: University of the State of New York, 1967.

———. *Native North American Spirituality of the Eastern Woodlands: Sacred Myths, Dreams, Visions, Speeches, Healing Formulas, Rituals and Ceremonials*. New York: Paulist Press, 1979.

Trelease, Allen W. *Indian Affairs in Colonial New York: The Seventeenth Century*. 1960. Reprint, with an introduction by William A. Starna. Lincoln: University of Nebraska Press, 1997.

———. "The Iroquois and the Western Fur Trade." *Mississippi Valley Historical Review* 49, no. 1 (1962): 32–51.

Trigger, Bruce G. *The Children of Aataentsic: A History of the Huron People to 1660*. 2 vols. Montreal: McGill-Queen's University Press, 1976.

———. "The Destruction of Huronia: A Study in Economic and Cultural Change, 1609–1650." *Royal Canadian Institute Transactions* 33, no. 68 (1960): 14–45.

———. "Early Native North American Responses to European Contact: Romantic versus Rationalistic Interpretations." *Journal of American History* 77, no. 4 (1991): 1195–1215.

———. "The French Presence in Huronia: The Structure of Franco-Huron Relations in the First Half of the Seventeenth Century." *Canadian Historical Review* 49, no. 2 (1968): 107–41.

———. *The Huron: Farmers of the North*. New York: Holt, Rinehart and Winston, 1969.

———. "The Mohawk-Mahican War (1624–1628): The Establishment of a Pattern." *Canadian Historical Review* 52, no. 3 (1971): 276–86.

———. *Natives and Newcomers: Canada's "Heroic Age" Reconsidered*. Montreal: McGill-Queen's University Press, 1985.

———. "Settlement as an Aspect of Iroquoian Adaptation at the Time of Contact." *American Anthropologist* 65, no. 1 (1963): 86–101.

———, ed. *The Handbook of North American Indians: Northeast*. Vol. 15 of *Handbook of North American Indians,* William C. Sturtevant, general editor. Washington, D.C.: Smithsonian Institution, 1978.

Tuck, James A. *Onondaga Iroquois Prehistory: A Study in Settlement Archaeology*. Syracuse, N.Y.: Syracuse University Press, 1971.

Wallace, Anthony F. C. *The Death and Rebirth of the Seneca*. New York: Knopf, 1970.

———. "The Dekanawideh Myth as the Record of a Revitalization Movement." *Ethnohistory* 5 (1958): 118–30.

———. "Dreams and Wishes of the Soul: A Type of Psychoanalytic Theory among the Seventeenth Century Iroquois." *American Anthropologist* 60, no. 2 (1958): 234–48.

Wallace, Paul A. W. "The Iroquois: A Brief Outline of Their History." *Pennsylvania History* 23, no. 1 (1956): 15–28.

———. *The White Roots of Peace*. Philadelphia: University of Pennsylvania Press, 1946.

White, Richard. "Discovering Nature in North America." *Journal of American History* 79, no. 3 (1992): 874–91.

———. *The Middle Ground: Indians, Empires, and Republics in the Great Lakes Region, 1650–1815.* New York: Cambridge University Press, 1991.

Willits, C. O., and Claude H. Hills. *Maple Sirup Producers Manual.* Rev. ed. Washington, D.C.: U.S. Government Printing Office, 1976.

Wolf, Eric R. *Europe and the People without History.* Berkeley: University of California Press, 1982.

Yarnell, Richard Asa. *Aboriginal Relationships between Culture and Plant Life in the Upper Great Lakes Region.* Ann Arbor: University of Michigan, 1964.

INDEX

THE RENEWED, THE DESTROYED, AND THE REMADE